Statistics for Linguists

Statistics for Linguists:

A Step-by-Step Guide for Novices

By

David Eddington

Cambridge
Scholars
Publishing

Statistics for Linguists: A Step-by-Step Guide for Novices

By David Eddington

This book first published 2015

Cambridge Scholars Publishing

Lady Stephenson Library, Newcastle upon Tyne, NE6 2PA, UK

British Library Cataloguing in Publication Data
A catalogue record for this book is available from the British Library

ISBN (10): 1-4438-7638-0
ISBN (13): 978-1-4438-7638-4

FOR SILVIA

CONTENTS

ACKNOWLEDGEMENTS

So many people have had a hand in the production of this book. I am indebted to the College of Humanities and the Department of Linguistics and English Language at Brigham Young University for their financial support. Mel Thorne, Jennifer McDaniel, and the staff at the Faculty Editing Service are responsible for the production of a much more polished manuscript than I could have managed on my own. Karen Grace-Martin of the Analysis Factor also deserves a great deal of credit for the numerous hours she spent consulting me on statistical matters. The following researchers were gracious enough to make their data available: Benjamin Bergen, Travis Bradley, Ann Marie Delforge, Vineeta Chand, Ewa Dąbrowska, Jean-Marc Dewaele, Dan Dewey, Jennifer Bown, Wendy Baker, Rob Martinsen, Carrie Gold, Dennis Eggett, Martin Hilpert, Mary Johnson, John Grinstead, Frank Keller, Mirella Lapata, Azadeh Nemati, Steve Parker, Daniel Tight, Michael Taylor, Bodo Winter, and Sven Grawunder. I thank my wife, Silvia Gray, for putting up with my obsession with all things statistical while preparing this text.

INTRODUCTION

Over the course of the last few decades, linguistics has seen a gradual shift away from armchair theorizing toward more data-oriented analysis. Subfields such as corpus linguistics, psycholinguistics, language acquisition, and sociolinguistics—all of which rely on quantitative data—have experienced a great deal of growth. Acoustic phonetic research, which used to require equipment costing the equivalent of the entire yearly salary of four assistant professors, can now be carried out on any personal computer thanks to programs such as PRAAT. Corpora designed for linguistic data-mining, such as the British National Corpus and Corpus of Contemporary American English contain hundreds of millions of words, while the Google Book corpus contains a number of corpora containing billions of words. With this proliferation of data, language researchers are obliged to find means to describe and summarize them, as well as to use them to test linguistic hypotheses.

While quantitative analyses are ever more frequent in the linguistic literature, many linguistics programs have not kept pace. Far too many linguists lack familiarity and training in statistics simply because it was not offered by or required in their programs. Of course, a plethora of introductory texts on statistics exist, and colleges and universities offer courses on the topic. Nevertheless, linguists often find that existing materials focus on solving problems in social and physical sciences. Many texts use topics such as birthrate trends in Asia or moisture content in soil samples to illustrate statistical principles, which often leaves linguists scratching their heads trying to understand how those procedures could apply to formant frequencies, reaction times, or pronoun deletion. What's more, language data lend themselves to statistical methods that are often not dealt with in introductory texts. My experience with statistics labs in a number of different universities is that those who staff the labs find it hard to wrap statistics around the kinds of data linguists use. For this reason, it is heartening to see a number of recent books on statistics written specifically for the field of linguistics (Baayen 2008, Cantos Gómez 2013, Gries 2013, Johnson 2008, Larson-Hall 2010, Rasinger 2008).

At this point, I would like the reader to imagine a person named Kim who has grown tired of fast food and wants to learn to cook. Kim shows up for class at a prestigious school of culinary arts. The first day is spent discussing the inner workings of industrial mixers and ovens. The next day Kim learns about different kinds of yeasts and their reproduction rates in environments that vary in their sugar content and temperature. The third day the class revolves around the chemical process of fermentation.

After a few weeks of this, Kim finally gets up the courage to admit to the instructor, "I just want to learn the steps to take to prepare a nice meal. Why do I need to know about how the ingredients are fabricated and what kitchen tools look like on the inside?" "Ah," replies the instructor, "this information makes you more knowledgeable and better able to appreciate the complexities behind the ingredients you will use in preparing *haute cuisine* and the machinery used in their preparation. You will be more empowered to understand their chemistry and mechanics." "But I just want to learn how to make a quiche," protests Kim, "I don't want to repair kitchen appliances or produce raw ingredients."

Ultimately, Kim leaves the class in despair and picks up a pizza on the way home In too many cases, I have observed statisticians getting so wrapped up in the mechanics of the math that goes on under the hood, so overzealous about teaching every intricacy and nuance of statistical theory, they overlook the fact that many researchers just want to learn to correctly apply statistical analysis to their data—not learn the math behind it. For many, an introductory book on statistics that contains pages and pages of formulas like this,[1]

$$l = 2c \cdot \ln\left[\left(\frac{S^2 - h^2}{4c^2}\right)^{\frac{1}{2}} + \left(\frac{S^2 - h^2}{4c^2} + 1\right)^{\frac{1}{2}}\right] \quad (4)$$

or instructions that look like this,

```
twosam <- function(y1, y2) {
    n1 <- length(y1); n2 <- length(y2)
    yb1 <- mean(y1); yb2 <- mean(y2)
    s1 <- var(y1); s2 <- var(y2)
    s <- ((n1-1)*s1 + (n2-1)*s2)/(n1+n2-2)
    tst <- (yb1 - yb2)/sqrt(s*(1/n1 + 1/n2))
    tst
}
```

feels the same as most people do when they see this,[2]

---

[1] Image retrieved from http://commons.wikimedia.org/wiki/File:Formula10.png.
[2] Image retrieved from http://commons.wikimedia.org/wiki/File:Servers_in_a_Rack.jpg.

All of this can be overwhelming, especially when housed in a hefty 600-page book. Many of the statistically uninitiated will not get past the initial flip through and will simply toss the book aside in despair.

The present book is designed to address this problem. It is written for linguists who would like to have a practical, hands-on understanding of statistics so they can carry out quantitative studies of their own and so they can better understand the linguistic literature that includes such analysis. It is meant to be a truly basic introduction—not just in title, but in essence. The focus is on applying statistical recipes without cracking the machinery open to explore the mechanisms that underlie the mathematical engine. By adopting this approach, I hope to draw researchers into the quantitative world by avoiding what often prove to be stumbling blocks to the statistically uninitiated: mathematical formulas and total reliance on line command interfaces.

By using the previous cookbook analogy, by no means do I imply that I condone sloppy methodology. Too many basic introductory texts let crucial concepts, such as statistical assumptions, slide by with only a mention of how most statistics are robust in the face of violations (meaning that they still give valid results when the assumptions aren't met). Others merely intimate that there are other non-parametric tests readers can use, rather than showing readers how to actually use them. Therefore, the goal of this book is to provide recipes that are complete enough that, when followed, will result in sound results.

In order to achieve the aims of this book, I have designed it with a number of things in mind. First, the examples and data sets are mostly linguistic in nature, which should not only make them more accessible to the reader, but suggest ways in which other linguistic questions may be answered using the same statistical method. Second, the sheer number of different statistical analyses is somewhat overwhelming; for this reason, I have included the analyses that, in my opinion, are the most often used or the most appropriate to use with linguistic data. When there is more than one way to analyze a particular kind of data, I've mostly limited myself to explaining only one of them. Third, I have intentionally chosen a very informal writing style where I refer to the reader in the second person *you* and do not hide the identity of the author behind the passive voice, so I use the pronouns *I, we,* and *me* liberally. Fourth, for simplicity's sake, I have chosen to demonstrate how to carry out the different statistical analyses using software that has a graphical user interface (GUI), principally SPSS® version 20.[3] The differences between this version of SPSS and other newer versions (16 and higher, 2007 and later) are not large enough that the instructions and graphics in this book differ much from other recent versions. I understand that this excludes the program R (R Development Core Team 2011). I am well aware that in comparison to SPSS, R is more powerful, produces better graphics, and is free. However, its command line interface makes the learning curve much steeper in comparison to programs with graphical user interfaces,[4] and it is also quite intimidating for many computer users who are accustomed to point and click programs. Given the introductory nature of the present book, SPSS is a much gentler way of introducing people to statistics.

Of course, a primer of this sort is not meant to be a comprehensive answer-all; many topics are left uncovered. Instead, this primer serves as a gateway to the field. I trust that once a person grasps the basics of statistical analysis contained in this book, they will then be in an ideal position to perform more complex analyses, and begin to dig deeper, if so inclined.

---

[3] SPSS Inc. was acquired by IBM in October, 2009.

[4] There are a number of graphical interfaces for R (e.g., Deducer, R Commander, JGR, RKWard, Rattle) and choosing among them is problematic in and of itself. In contrast, SPSS has one well-documented GUI. In any event, R enthusiasts generally avoid using GUIs when writing texts.

CHAPTER ONE

GETTING TO KNOW SPSS

The best way to work through this book is with SPSS opened to the data that we are discussing on the screen. This allows you to replicate what you see on the pages in SPSS. Don't get freaked out if the windows on your computer look just a bit different from the screen shots in the book, or if they give a slightly different numeric output. These differences may be due to the fact that you have a different version of SPSS or run a different operating system on your computer.

To follow along, you will also need the data sets we'll use. They can be downloaded from http://linguistics. byu.edu/faculty/eddingtond/Data_sets. Once you have the data sets saved in a handy place on your computer, you are ready to begin.

1.1 Opening an Existing File in SPSS Software

Open the SPSS program by clicking on the icon (or doing whatever you do to start a new program). When you first run SPSS, it either opens two windows (Figure 1-1) or just the spreadsheet window (depending on the version). At this point, you can begin to enter data manually by checking *Type in data* on the right-hand side of the screen, which allows you to enter your data like a spreadsheet. However, hopefully you will already have your data in a file of some sort and won't need to do this.

Figure 1-1. Opening an existing file in SPSS software.

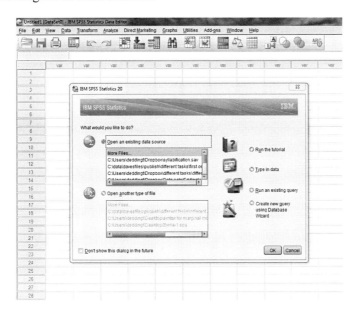

Let's start by opening one of the data files that you have downloaded. (You have downloaded the data sets, right?) Do this by checking *Open an existing data source* (again, see Figure 1-1). Any files you have already opened in SPSS will appear in the box directly underneath this option (and you could click on the file name then *OK,* if that were the case). However, your file is probably not named in the box, so click on *More Files*, which brings up the *Open Data* dialog box (Figure 1-2). Use this window and the *Look in* drop-down menu to navigate to where you stored the files that accompany this text.

SPSS has a very narcissistic habit of only highlighting SPSS files that have the *.sav* extension. If the file you are looking for is of a different type, it won't show up until you pull down the *Files of type* drop-down menu (Figure 2). At the very bottom of that menu, you can choose to display *All Files.* As you can see in the drop-down menu, SPSS can import data from many different file formats.

Figure 1-2. *Files of Type* drop-down menu in the *Open Data* dialog box.

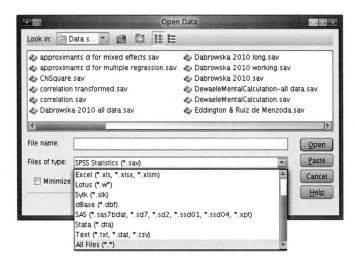

If you are already in SPSS and need to open a file, or if your version doesn't automatically open up the dialog box in Figure 1-1, you can access the *Open Data* dialog box by clicking on *File* in the top left-hand corner of the screen, choosing *Open*, and then choosing *Data* (Figure 1-3).

Figure 1-3. Opening a file from within SPSS.

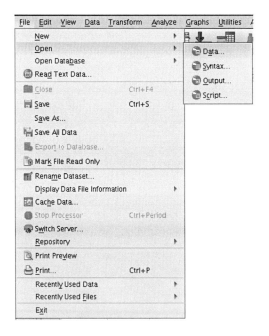

To shorten things a bit, and to avoid saying "then choosing" ad nauseam, from now on I'll describe series of commands like this:

Click on *File > Open > Data*

1.2 The *Statistics Viewer* and *Data Editor* Windows

When you open the data file both of SPSS's windows will open: the *IBM SPSS* window and the *IBM SPSS* window (see Figure 1-4; both windows will be open, although one may be on top of the other).

The *Statistics Viewer* window keeps track of all the commands you have given SPSS, and it is where you can see the results of your analyses. The *Data Editor* window works like a spreadsheet. This is where you put your data.

In the file, there are 17 scores. Notice that things like scores, age, gender, time, participant number, and other things like that go in columns. Rows are for cases, which in linguistics are usually participants or test items or responses in a study. So in this case, the 17 rows represent the test scores of 17 imaginary people (or "ideal speaker-hearers," if you prefer).

Figure 1-4. *Data Editor* and *Statistics Viewer* windows.

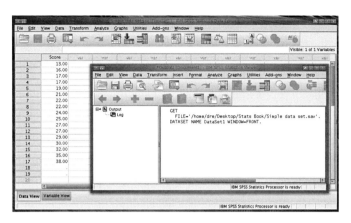

1.3 Specifying Information about the Data in the Window

The raw data are the heart of any analysis, but SPSS is not very bright on its own—it needs you to tell it more about what those numbers and letters mean before it can correctly deal with them. You can specify this information in the window. On the bottom left-hand corner there are two tabs: *Data View* and *Variable View*.

Click on the *Variable View* tab to see that window (Figure 1-5). The switch between windows can be confusing since the information that appears in columns in the *Data View* window appears in rows in the *Variable View* window.

Figure 1-5. The *Variable View* window.

The name I gave the numbers is the bland-sounding *score*, which appears in the column. You can give your variables any name you want, except that you can't use spaces or characters like /, +, =, , &, or you'll get an error message. The name you put here is the name that shows up in the column header in the *Data View* window.

HINT
The columns in the *Data View* window appear as rows in the *Variable View* window and vice versa.

In the column, you need to specify what kind of data appear in that column. When you click in this column, a drop-down button appears that, when clicked, brings up the *Variable Type* dialog box in Figure 1-6. Of all the possibilities in that box, we linguists generally only need to use two. If the data are numeric, choose *Numeric*; if they are letters or words, choose *String*. Here's a heads up: in a lot of cases (but not all), anything that you are going to use in an analysis, whether it is numeric or not, needs to be made numeric here. (Sorry—I didn't invent the program, I just work around it.) So, if you have three different languages, under the heading *Languages* you can call them 1, 2, 3 here. If you have Male, Female, call them 1, 2. You can sort out what the numbers mean in the column. Save for things like participant name, test word, test condition, or test sentence.

Figure 1-6. The *Variable Type* dialog box.

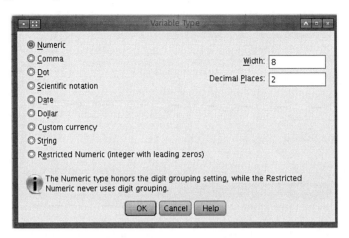

Sometimes when you have missing data you want to give it a special value, which is what the column is for. Remember that in the column, you specify how many characters are allowable. In the *Columns* column, you say how many of those characters will actually show up in the spreadsheet. *Align* lets you change whether the values in a column are left-aligned, right-aligned, or centered.

The *Measure* and columns aren't crucial to performing an analysis. They are places to help you keep track of what kind of data you have in each column and what they are used for. In *Measure* you can specify what kinds of data are in the column, which we'll discuss this in greater detail in Chapter 2. For now, just remember that is what I'll refer to as "continuous." Older versions of SPSS don't have a *Role* column at all. In newer versions, you can keep track of what role the variable you are defining plays in the analysis. For example, *Input* is an independent variable and *Target* is a dependent variable. We'll get to this later.

> **HINT**
> Sometimes it's helpful to have the same variables coded twice, once by name (e.g., *Gender* = male, female) and once by numbers (e.g., *GenderNumeric* = 0, 1). Some analyses allow string variables and others require only numerically coded data.

Also, in this dialog box, you can choose how many decimal places to display (*Decimal Places*) as well as the maximum number of characters that can fit in the column (*Width*). If you forget to specify this information here, notice that this same information can be entered in the *Width* and *Decimal* columns in the *Variable View* window.

The column is a place where you can describe in detail what the name you put in the *Name* column means. For example, if the value in the column is *NumYears,* which means "number of years living in target language country," put that long descriptor here since it is way too big for the *Name* column and has a bunch of spaces in it anyway that make it illegal in the *Name* column.

Figure 1-7. The *Value Labels* dialog box.

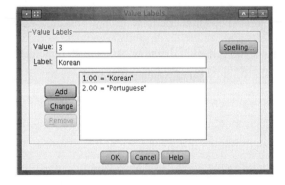

The *Values* column is where you tell SPSS exactly what the numbers in a variable like *Languages* actually mean. Clicking on a cell in the column opens the *Value Labels* dialog box (Figure 1-7), which is already partially filled out. Specify the number you want to define in the *Value* box, give it a name in the *Label* box, and press *Add.* SPSS has even provided a handy spelling check button here for your continuing statistical enjoyment.

1.4 Saving a File in SPSS

Click on *File > Save as* to open the *Save Data As* dialog box (Figure 1-8). Write the name you want to give the file in the *File name* box and select the format in the *Save as type* drop-down menu. There are many different formats that can be chosen. SPSS uses its own *.sav* format.

Figure 1-8. *Save Data As* dialog box.

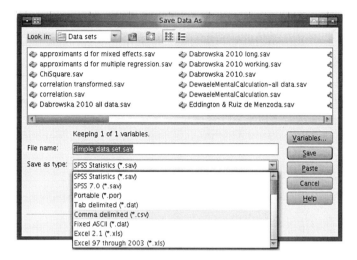

1.5 Sorting the Data

Click on *Data > Sort Cases* and click on *Scores* in the box on the left. Move the term into the *Sort by* box by clicking on the arrow button between the boxes (Figure 1-9). Now choose whether you want to sort it in ascending or descending order, then click *OK*.

Figure 1-9. *Sort Cases* dialog box.

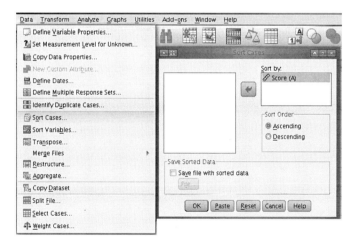

This is a fairly simple sort with only one column involved. It is possible to do more complex sorts. Remember that the first column of data that you specify takes priority over subsequent ones. So if you had *test score* and *gender* as columns and you put *gender* first in the *Sort by* field, you would get the first two columns in Table 1-1. If you put *test score* in before *gender*, the result would be the last two columns.

Table 1-1. Sorting gender and test score by different priorities.

Gender First		Score First	
Gender	*Score*	*Gender*	*Score*
F	89	M	90
F	79	F	89
F	76	M	87
F	61	M	87
M	90	F	79
M	87	F	76
M	87	F	61
M	42	M	42

1.6 Adding, Deleting, Copying, Pasting, and Cutting Rows and Columns

Go to the *Data View* tab. If you needed to add a column to the left of the *Score* column, you right-click on the title of the column (*Score*) and choose *Insert Variable* from the dialog box that appears (Figure 1-9). From this handy dialog box, you can also clear, cut, paste, or sort the contents of the column. To add a row, right-click on the row number on the left-hand side of the screen and choose *Insert cases*. The option to cut, clear, or copy the row also appears.

Figure 1-9. Insert, cut, copy, paste, clear, sort variable dialog box.

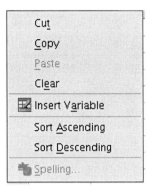

Of course, what I've shown you here is far from an exhaustive list of commands, but it should get you started. I certainly don't want to bore you only a few pages into the book, so I'll introduce other commands as they relate to the concepts in each chapter.

CHAPTER TWO

DESCRIPTIVE AND INFERENTIAL STATISTICS

2.1 Types of Data

The purpose of statistics is to organize, describe, summarize, and interpret data. It allows us to find trends, discover relationships between variables, and determine whether there are any causal relationships between them. Most importantly, statistics help us explore whether results can be extrapolated beyond the cases we consider, which allows us to test hypotheses about linguistic issues. However, to correctly order the data to be used in a statistical procedure as well as to choose which procedure to carry out, it is crucial to correctly classify the data, since not all data are of the same type.

2.1.1 Categorical data

In linguistics, much of the data we are interested in is CATEGORICAL.[1] This means that it can fit into named, unordered categories. Some examples of categorical data are

- Gender: male or female
- Country of origin: Korea, Canada, Brazil, or France
- Education: high school graduate or not
- Ethnicity: Hispanic, Caucasian, Asian, or Polynesian
- Childhood language background: monolingual, bilingual, or multilingual
- Prodrop: subject pronoun used with verb or subject pronoun not used with verb
- Language abilities of participant: native or nonnative
- Teaching method: total physical response, audiolingual, or grammar translation
- Word used for "large sandwich": *hoagie, subway, grinder,* or *po' boy*
- Pronunciation of /t/: $[t^h]$, $[ʔ]$, or $[ɾ]$

Notice that the number of things that are categorical may be counted, but you may not treat the category as if it were a number. For example, if you imposed a number system on the words people use for "large sandwich," such that 1 = *hoagie*, 2 = *subway*, 3 = *grinder*, and 4 = *po' boy*, the numbers make it seem like *subway* is somehow closer to *grinder* and further from *po' boy*. This, of course, makes no sense. It is impossible to plug categorical categories into mathematical formulas. These variables are merely named, not numbered. There are times, however, when you will need to identify categorical items with numerals, then specify what those numbers mean (see Chapter 1). However, the variables are always marked as categorical when they are used in an analysis.

2.1.2 Ordinal data

ORDINAL DATA are best exemplified by the order in which runners cross the finish line. The first-place runner may finish only a fraction of a second before of the second-place runner, yet the time between the second- and third-place runners could be several seconds. For ordinal data, the distance between each number is not relevant—only the order in which the numbers occur. Some examples of ordinal data in linguistics are

- The order in which children acquire certain morphemes.
- The way a test participant orders a series of five recordings of nonnatives from *most fluent* to *least fluent*.

Notice that you cannot subdivide ordinal data. It makes no sense to say that the runner from Ghana came in third and a half in the race.

Some measures involve choosing a point along a labeled scale. For example, in response to the statement, "The person in this recording has a strong foreign accent," you can choose one of the following: *strongly agree, agree, neither agree nor disagree, disagree, strongly disagree.* It is clear that *strongly agree* indicates a judgment of more foreign accent than *agree*, but does choosing *strongly agree* really mean twice as much accent as *agree*? In this case, the intervals between each label are very subjective and hard to quantify numerically, so it may be better to treat them

---

[1] Some other names for categorical variables are NOMINAL or FACTOR variables.

as ordinal rather than continuous (see next section), although some claim that it's okay to treat them as continuous (Carifio & Perla 2007), so I'll leave it up to your discretion. Because ordinal data have unequal (or unclear) intervals between each point, they are treated differently in statistical analyses from other numeric data that do have equal intervals.

2.1.3 Continuous data

CONTINUOUS DATA[2] are numeric data in which the distances between numbers are equal. For instance, a person who has lived in a foreign country for two years has lived twice as long there as a person who has only lived there one year. Examples of continuous data are

- Age
- Number of years of formal schooling
- Months spent living in a foreign country
- Time required to recognize a word during an experiment
- Frequency of a formant
- Duration of consonant closure
- Hours spent sending text messages

In contrast to ordinal data, subdividing continuous data results in interpretable outcomes: it is possible for a person to be 21.3 years old and to spend 5.4 hours a day writing text messages. Believe me; I know such a person.

2.2 Variables

Variables are simply characteristics that change from situation to situation, object to object, or person to person. A person's biographic information is a series of variables. Some variables are continuous: age, number of years of schooling past high school, number of years living at the present address, number of children. Others are categorical: gender, ethnicity, county of residence, marital status. Some variables are ordinal: ranking among high school class, birth order among siblings, order of preference among potential dates in your little black book.

2.2.1 Independent and dependent variables

In quantitative research, we are interested in the relationship between certain variables. Perhaps the best way to frame a research question is this: What is the influence of X on Y? X is called the INDEPENDENT VARIABLE.[3] It is what we think makes a difference in Y, or causes Y, or is related to Y, or changes Y somehow. The relationship of the independent variable to the DEPENDENT VARIABLE is what you really want to research. Y is the dependent variable. It is the thing that may be changed, related to, or influenced by X. This is what you measure to determine if the independent variable has any effect on it.

If a research project cannot be stated in terms of how X affects Y, it is difficult to determine how to apply a quantitative analysis to it. For some, the most difficult step in doing research is framing one's ideas in terms of variables. Below are a few examples of research questions and the variables they entail.

Idea 1: People seem to use *myself* as the nonreflexive object of a preposition rather than as a reflexive a lot more nowadays (e.g., *as for myself*).
Quantified question 1: What is the effect of time (1950s, 1960s, etc.) on the use of *myself* as the nonreflexive object of a preposition?
Variables in 1: Time is a continuous independent variable, and number of uses of *myself* as the object of a preposition is a continuous dependent variable.

Idea 2: It seems that women always outnumber men in foreign language classes.
Quantified question 2: What is the effect of gender on enrollment in foreign language classes?
Variables in 2: Gender is the categorical independent variable, and number of students enrolled is the continuous dependent variable.

Idea 3: I wonder if daily consumption of greasy American-style fast food is likely to shorten my life—yes.

---

[2] For those who know that there are actually two kinds of continuous data, I have collapsed ratio and interval data into this category, since it is not relevant to what kind of statistical analysis is used. Continuous variables are also sometimes called COVARIATES.
[3] It is also known as the PREDICTOR VARIABLE, although some people make subtle differences between the two.

2.2.2 Control variables

One difficulty in carrying out research is that linguistic behavior is human behavior, which is always influenced by a myriad of variables, some of which we may be aware of and others that lurk silently in the dark, waiting to pounce on us and undermine our—mostly—carefully constructed experiment. If we know of a variable that may affect the results, we would want to control for its influence. Such variables are called CONTROL VARIABLES. Suppose you are interested in how textual genre influences the use of the alternative past tenses of *sneak* (*snuck* and *sneaked*). You also know or suspect that there may be differences between British and American uses, but that is not the focus of your study. You could control for the influence of variety of English simply by limiting your search to only British or American corpora. Another way to control for the effect of any such variables that you are aware of is by including them in the statistical analysis.

2.2.3 Confounding variables

Confounding variables are the most pesky, because we often do not know they exist, or we only find out about their existence after the data have been gathered and analyzed. Although a good study tries to control for as many variables as possible so that the only one that affects the results of the study is the independent variable, sometimes confounding variables creep in and sabotage the study. Imagine a study designed to determine whether words with many morphemes, such as *industrialize* and *postmodernist*, take longer to recognize than monomorphemic words, such as *cabbage* and *alligator*. The results suggest this is true because polymorphemic words take longer to recognize. However, as psycholinguists know, this study contains a number of confounding variables. Word length and word frequency are also at work. Shorter words and more frequent words are recognized more quickly. Since these variables are not controlled for, they confound the results of this study and make it impossible to determine the exact effect the number of morphemes has on response time.

2.3 Descriptive Statistics

If you were handed a list of numbers, merely looking them over wouldn't give you much of a sense of the story they tell. This is where descriptive statistics come in. They provide concise summaries of the numbers taken as a whole, rather than individually. We'll use the data in Table 2-1 to illustrate descriptive statistics. Later on I'll describe how to use SPSS to obtain these statistics. If you really want to see where they come from, skip forward to Table 2-3.

2.3.1 Central tendency: Mean

A spreadsheet containing raw data is something that only true geeks can easily wrap their heads around. Descriptive statistics were invented to help the rest of us, since they summarize the data into easily digestible numbers. For example, the first thing a student generally wants to know upon receiving his or her test score is what the average of the class is. This is because a test score by itself is not very meaningful. It needs to be considered in the context of the population it comes from, that is, the scores everyone else received. The average test score, more precisely referred to as the MEAN rather than the average, is a measure of central tendency. It lets you know what middle number the scores cluster around. Consider the scores in Table 2-1. If your score is one of the two 27s, and the mean on the test is 24.35, then you did better than the average student. However, if your score is 5, then look for another major. The mean is calculated by summing up all of the scores and dividing by the total number of scores.

Table 2-1. Distribution of 17 scores.

Test Scores	
13	
16	
17	
17	
19	
21	
22	
22	
24	← median (24)
25	← mean (24.35)
27	
27	
29	
30	
32	
35	
38	

2.3.2 Central tendency: Median

Now, consider the test scores again. Another measure of central tendency is the MEDIAN, which is the middle score (or the grassy area between traffic lanes for some people). If you order all of the scores from lowest to highest, the median is the middle one.

In this case the median is 24, which is not far from the mean of 24.35. If the mean and median are about the same, why are they both needed? To answer this, look back at the list of scores and assume that there are two additional scores: 62 and 69. It should be obvious that these scores fall extremely far from the rest of the scores. They are outliers. When you include these two scores and recalculate the mean, it moves from 24.35 to 28.65, which is now quite a bit off-center. The median, on the other hand, only increases from 24 to 25. In other words, when there are outliers in the data, they affect the mean and make it a less accurate measure of central tendency. That is why the median is better when there are extreme scores. Medians are also used to report ordinal data. For example, imagine that you graduated tenth in your class—is that good? Well, if it was a small graduating class with a median of 10, not really. You are right in the middle of the class. However, if the median is 40, you are starting to look stellar.

2.3.3 Central tendency: Mode

Another measure of central tendency, that is much less often used, is the MODE, which is simply the most often occurring score. The above data actually has three modes, 17, 22, and 27, which are bolded in the data set in Table 2-1. Means and medians make sense for continuous data, but what gives us a sense of the middle if the data are categorical? In this case the mode is the measure of central tendency to use. Table 2-2 shows the number of students from different countries in an ESL class.

Table 2-2. Number of students in a class by country of origin.

Country	Number of students
Korea	6
Spain	3
Jordan	1
Mexico	4
China	4
Japan	2
Uruguay	1

For categorical data, the mode as a number makes little sense; you couldn't say that the mode country is 3.75. Instead it is reported as a category, so the mode for these data is Korea because that is the country that more students come from.

2.3.4 Dispersion

Knowing where the middle of the data falls is important but by itself is actually not very useful. Another crucial piece of data is how spread out the scores are, known as the score's DISPERSION. If you received a score of 27 on a test whose mean was 24.35, you may feel smug because you scored above average, but what if the highest score on the test were 50 and the lowest, 5? That look on your face melts away as you realize that the scores are more spread out or disperse. On the other hand, if the highest score were 30 and the lowest 17, your 27 is a phenomenal score because the scores are less disperse and cluster closer to the mean, which allows you to retain your air of self-importance. A simple measure of dispersion is the RANGE, which is simply the highest minus the lowest score. In the first case, the range is 45 (50 − 5), whereas the range is only 13 (30 − 17) in the second.

2.4 Using SPSS to Calculate Descriptive Statistics

We've been talking about the data in Table 2-1 and the statistics that describe them. Let's go over the steps of how to get SPSS to calculate them. I warn you that this produces a boatload of tables and graphs. I'll explain each one in time. As far as the tables are concerned, they contain an overwhelming amount of data. Be patient, and I will get to them and point out what to focus on. I include them all here so that you can see all of the output of the descriptive statistics that SPSS produces when you follow these instructions. I'll refer you back to some of these tables in later chapters.

1. Download the file *Simple data set.sav* from the text website. Open SPSS > Check *Open existing data source* > *More files* > *OK* and navigate to where you downloaded the file > *OK*.

Remember that SPSS will automatically highlight only the *.sav*-type files unless you pull down the *Files of type* drop-down menu. At the very bottom of that menu you can choose to display *All Files*.

At this point, complete the following steps to generate the descriptive statistics and graphs used in this chapter.
2. Click on *Analyze > Descriptive Statistics > Explore* (Figure 2-1).

Figure 2-1. Descriptive statistics using *Explore*.

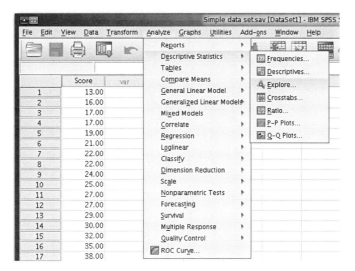

3. Click on the variable name > *Score*, and move it to the *Dependent List* by clicking on the arrow between the boxes. Click on *Statistics* > check the box next to *Descriptives* > *Continue* (Figure 2-2).

Figure 2-2. *Explore* dialog box.

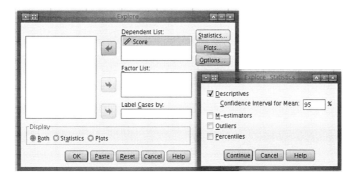

4. Click on *Plots* > check the boxes next to *Histogram* and *Normality plots with tests* > *Continue* > *OK* (Figure 2-3).

All of these tables and figures will appear in your *Statistics Viewer* window, and you may need to scroll down to see them. This generates the histogram in Figure 2-6, the boxplot in Figure 2-7, and the Q-Q plot in Figure 2-12. The descriptive statistics that are produced are given in Tables 2-3 and 2-4. These tables and figures are referred to later on in this chapter.

Figure 2-3. *Explore Plots* dialog box.

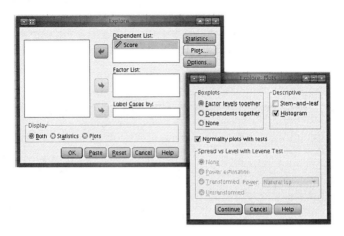

Table 2-3. Descriptive statistics for data in Table 2-1.

Descriptives			Statistic	Std. Error
Score	Mean		24.3529	1.69762
	95% Confidence Interval for Mean	**Lower Bound**	20.7541	
		Upper Bound	27.9517	
	5% Trimmed Mean		24.2255	
	Median		24.0000	
	Variance		48.993	
	Std. Deviation		6.99947	
	Minimum		13.00	
	Maximum		38.00	
	Range		25.00	
	Interquartile Range		11.50	
	Skew		.301	.550
	Kurtosis		−.589	1.063

Table 2-4. Tests of Normality for data in Table 2-1.

Tests of Normality	Kolmogorov-Smirnov[a]			Shapiro-Wilk		
	Statistic	df	Sig.	Statistic	df	Sig.
Score	.102	17	.200[*]	.978	17	.939

*. This is a lower bound of the true significance.
a. Lilliefors Significance Correction

To get the mode, which is not included in Table 2-3 click on *Analyze > Descriptive Statistics > Frequencies.* Move *Score* into the *Variables* box > click on the *Statistics* button > check *Mode* box > *Continue > OK* (Figure 2-4).

Figure 2-4. Obtaining the mode.

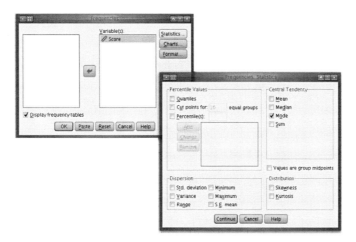

In order to superimpose the normal distribution curve on the histogram in Figure 2-6, double-click on the histogram itself, which appears in the *Statistics Viewer* window. (The histogram looks pretty much like what you see in Figure 2-5. You will have to scroll down to see it.) Then in the *Chart Editor* choose *Elements > Show Distribution Curve*. Close the *Properties* and *Chart Editor* windows.

Figure 2-5. Superimposing the distribution curve.

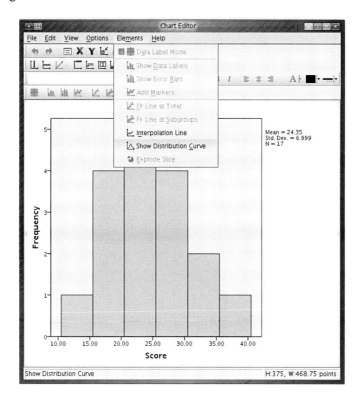

2.5 Visualizing the Data

2.5.1 Histogram

One way to visualize dispersion is with a HISTOGRAM. Figure 2-6 is a histogram of the scores we've been discussing. The bars indicate how many scores there are with a particular value or set of close values. For example, the leftmost bar contains the single score of 13. The second bar includes the four scores 16, 17, 17, and 19, and so on. The range for these data is $38 - 13 = 25$. It should be clear that the central part of the distribution of these scores is about 24, where the mean and median indicate that it is. I will explain the curve in the histogram later.

Figure 2-6. Histogram of data in Table 1-1.

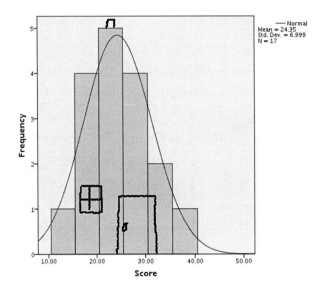

2.5.2 Boxplot

Another way to visualize the data is with a BOXPLOT, as in Figure 2-7. One way of conceptualizing the relationship between the histogram in Figure 2-6 and the boxplot in Figure 2-7 is to imagine the histogram as a new age–type building seen from street level. The door and window should give you the idea. The boxplot is more analogous to viewing the same building from a helicopter hovering directly above the building. The dark line in the middle of the box represents the median, which is usually the tallest bar on the histogram. In the histogram, the median is where the chimney is. The box itself incorporates the data that are in the twenty-fifth to seventy-fifth percentiles. This means that only about 25% of the data fall above the box and about 25% below, so the box shows the middle 50% of the scores. The whiskers are the lines that extend above and below the box. On the histogram the ends of the whiskers indicate more or less where the curve comes closest to touching the street. They extend to lines that mark the largest and smallest scores as long as those are not farther away than one and a half times the length of the box. Scores beyond the ends of the whiskers are outliers because of their extreme values. There are no possible outliers in Figure 2-7, but if there were, they would appear as dots.

Figure 2-7. Boxplot of data in Table 2-1.

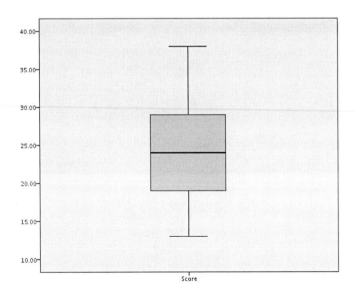

2.6 Normal Distribution

The curve that is superimposed on the histogram in Figure 2-6 shows what the data would look like if they followed a NORMAL DISTRIBUTION, which is often referred to as a bell curve. The much dreaded but often loved practice of grading on the curve entails forcing the test scores into a bell curve regardless of what their actual distribution is. In a normal distribution, the mean, median, and mode are identical. They all appear in the center of the bell curve on top of the highest bar. What's so special about the bell curve? Well, mathematicians noticed that when you measure a lot of different things (but not everything), they tend to have the distribution shown by the bell curve. What this means is that most people and things tend to fall in the middle, that is, they are average. If you measured how many words people say each day, how many different people they interact with, how many eggs a sea turtle lays, or the temperature in Kathmandu at noon every day for a year, most of these measurements would fall in the middle of the curve. Only a few people speak way too much (or way too little), and only a few turtles lay lots of (or few) eggs. These more extreme measurements are found in the tails of the curve, and there usually aren't many of them. Of course, if you only make a handful of measurements, they will not fit into the normal distribution, but for a lot of things that you may measure, the more measurements you add, the closer the distribution starts to approximate a bell curve.

2.6.1 Standard deviation and variance

Whereas the range is one measurement of how spread out from the middle the scores are, an even more precise way of looking at their dispersion is the ominous-sounding standard deviation. Every score falls at a particular distance from the mean. The standard deviation represents the average distance the scores are from the mean score. The curve in Figure 2-8 illustrates the idea of standard deviation. It is just a way of dividing up the bell curve. So, about 34% of the scores fall within what is called the first standard deviation above the mean and 34% within the first standard deviation below the mean. In other words, about 68% of the scores fall within the first standard deviation. This division of the curve is found regardless of what the values of the scores are or the unit used to measure them (e.g., TOEFL scores in points, beer consumption in pints, reaction times in milliseconds, weight in kilos). That's what they mean by *standard* deviation.

When you move to the second standard deviation, about 95% of the scores are included. The best way to make this abstract idea concrete is to refer back to Table 2-1, in which the mean is 24.35 and the standard deviation is 6.9. Let's use round numbers for simplicity's sake. Simpler is always better, so the mean is 24 and standard deviation is 7. The first standard deviation is 7 points above and 7 points below the mean, so about 68% of the scores should fall between 17 and 31. Actually, 12 of the 17 scores (70.5%) do. (This is a small data set, so it's not going to fit exactly.) We expect about 95% of the scores to be within two standard deviations—that is, scores that are between 14 points higher and 14 points lower than the mean (i.e., 38 and 10). In our sample, 100% of the scores fall within two standard deviations from the mean. Another measure of average spread that we will talk about in subsequent chapters is VARIANCE. For now, know that it is simply the standard deviation squared.

Figure 2-8. Normal distribution (bell curve) with standard deviations.[4]

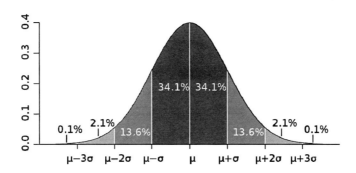

So, what does a small or large standard deviation tell you? It tells you how disperse the scores are. Figure 2-9 contains two different distributions that each have the same mean of 100. However, they differ greatly in their standard deviation. The tall, skinny distribution has a standard deviation of 10 whereas the short, squat one has a much larger dispersion with a standard deviation of 50. This illustrates how important it is to describe the data not with a mean alone but also with its sidekick—standard deviation.

---

[4] Image retrieved from http://upload.wikimedia.org/wikipedia/commons/3/37/Standard_deviation_diagram_%28decimal_comma%29.svg.

Figure 2-9. Two distributions with same mean, different standard deviations.[5]

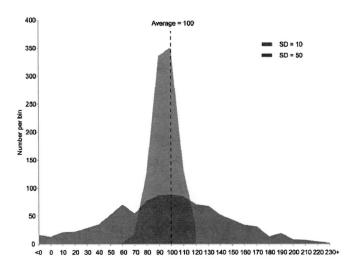

2.6.2 Skew

The concept of normal distribution is crucial in statistics. It is extremely important to determine whether the data you are working with come close to a normal distribution or not. Many statistical tests described below require the data to stick close to a normal distribution. If they don't, the results of the statistical analysis may be incorrect or the results can't be extended to other populations. Looking at a histogram or boxplot is the first step toward identifying a non-normal distribution. Note that we say non-normal, not weird, strange, irregular, odd, bizarre, or abnormal. The solid curves in Figure 2-10 indicate skewed distributions. These appear in a histogram as uncentered curves with a disproportionately long tail on one side. The dotted lines in the figure outline the normal distribution. Figure 2-11 shows how a boxplot appears with a skewed distribution. The line representing the median is not centered in the box, and there are some outliers. By the way, the numbers on the outliers are not their values but the line number on the *Data Editor* spreadsheet where those scores appear. That makes it easy to find them if needed.

Figure 2-10. Examples of skewed distributions.[6]

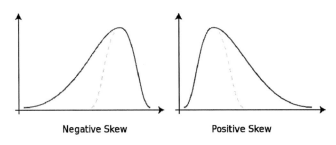

[5] Image retrieved from: http://upload.wikimedia.org/wikipedia/commons/f/f9/Comparison_standard_deviations.svg.
[6] Image retrieved from: http://commons.wikimedia.org/wiki/File%3ANegative_and_positive_skew_diagrams_(English).svg.

Figure 2-11. Boxplot of a skewed distribution.

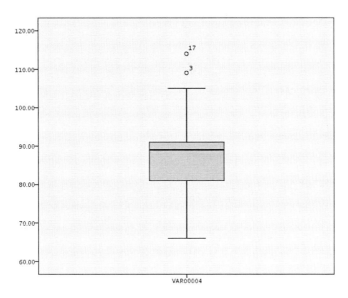

2.6.3 Q-Q plot

Another graphical representation of a normal distribution is a Q-Q PLOT (Figure 2-12). The diagonal line indicates where the data would fall if they followed a completely normal distribution. The dots represent the actual data, which in this case are quite close to the line. Large deviations from the line would be indicative of a non-normal distribution, but these look quite close.

Figure 2-12. Q-Q plot of data in Table 2-1.

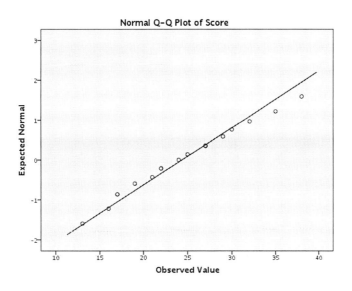

2.6.4 Kurtosis

Whereas skewed distributions are off-center, a distribution may be unskewed, because it is symmetric, but be irregular as far as its shape or KURTOSIS is concerned. A distribution that is centered but is fatter than a normal distribution, with thick tails, has kurtosis problems and is known as PLATYKURTIC. A thinner-than-normal distribution that is symmetric is referred to as LEPTOKURTIC. The two distributions in Figure 2-9 illustrate distributions that have kurtosis issues. One curve is much thinner and taller than normal, and the other is too short and wide to be normal.

2.6.5 Tests of normal distribution: Shapiro-Wilk, Kolmogorov-Smirnov, skew, kurtosis

Besides boxplots and histograms of the data, we can look at numeric measures of skew and kurtosis as well as statistical tests of normal distribution. For example, Shapiro-Wilk and Kolmogorov-Smirnov tests compare the distribution of the data with a normal distribution and determine whether there is a significant difference between them. Like most statistical tests, they often have weird, odd, or bizarre, (but not non-normal) names because they are named after the statisticians who invented them. Let's look at these measures as they relate to the distribution of the scores in Table 2-1. The SPSS output that they were extracted from is back on Table 2-4.

Table 2-5. Tests of normal distribution of scores from Table 1-1.

	Test Statistic	Significance	Standard Error	Test Statistic / Std. Err.
Shap.-Wilk	.978	.939		
Kol.-Sm.	.102	.200		
Skew	.301		.550	.542
Kurtosis	−.589		1.063	.554

The fact that the significance levels of the two tests are larger than .05 tells us that the distribution of the scores is not significantly different from a normal distribution. In other words, it is normal. (More about this .05 thing later.) There are two things to note about these two tests. The first is that neither should be taken as the ultimate truth. Think of them as estimates. If you choose to use them, always consider them along with your eyeballing of the graphical representations of the data. The second thing is that Shapiro-Wilk is often considered more accurate than Kolmogorov-Smirnov, especially with small data sets, like this one (Razali & Wah 2011). In addition, Kolmogorov-Smirnov is more prone to indicate that the distribution tested does not differ from normal when it really does. So, when in doubt, throw vodka out.

As far as the other measures are concerned, a completely symmetric distribution would have a skew number of 0. Positive skew numbers indicate a positively skewed distribution that has a tail pointing to the larger numbers. A negative number is telling of a distribution that is negatively skewed, and it has a tail pointing toward the smaller numbers. See? Some things are straightforward in statistics. For kurtosis, fat distributions result in positive numbers, and thin ones in negative kurtosis numbers, which is also intuitive. A good measure is obtained by dividing the skew and kurtosis numbers by their standard error. For real rule followers, the distribution is close to normal when the resulting number for skew or kurtosis is between +1 and −1, although some more permissive researchers suggest that anything between +2 and −2 is okay. The flaming liberals allow anything between +3 and −3. In this case, skew (.542) and kurtosis (.554) fall well within any of those ranges. What do you do if the data fall into a non-normal distribution? Well, that depends on what sort of statistical analysis you want to do, which is why I will give different options to deal with that below.

2.7 Reporting Descriptive Statistics

In this section, we've discussed the most common descriptive statistics that are used to describe a set of continuous data, which are the mean, median, mode, and standard deviation. Using these measures, the data in Table 2-1 could be described in prose: "The mean score was 24.35 with a standard deviation of 6.99." Or, these same data could be summarized as ($M = 24.35$, $SD = 6.99$), in which M is the mean and SD is the standard deviation. Notice the use of italics in those descriptions, and the fact that numbers are usually only reported to two or three decimal places. Only the truly masochistic enjoy seven digits after the decimal point. If the median or range are included, they would be given in this format, if not described in prose: range: 13−38, $Mdn = 24$.

2.8 Inferential Statistics

Descriptive statistics are good at helping us visualize and summarize the data. INFERENTIAL STATISTICS, on the other hand, serve a different purpose. They help us determine the extent to which the results of a study based on a small sample of the population can be assumed to be true for the entire population. For example, linguists are interested in the properties of a particular language, or how speakers process that language, or how they vary their speech according to the situation. We can't observe every word or sentence in a language, or test every speaker of the language, or follow all of them around with a microphone all day, as much as we would sometimes like to. For this reason, we must rely on samples of words, sentences, or people, then infer that what we found in the sample is representative of the language, or speakers of the language, in general. Inferential statistics allow us to do this and are the mechanism used to test the NULL HYPOTHESIS.

2.8.1 Null hypothesis testing

Traditional experimental practice is attributed principally to Sir Ronald A. Fisher (1890–1962). It works by setting up two hypotheses. The first is the NULL HYPOTHESIS. This is basically a statement to the effect that there is no relationship or no effect between X and Y. For example, if we are looking at whether men interrupt other people during conversations more than women, the null hypothesis is that gender is not related to interruption rates, or, in other words, neither men nor women interrupt more than the other. Generally, we're not as interested in the null hypothesis as we are in the alternative hypothesis, which in this case is that gender does influence interruption rates.

Once you've laid out the two hypotheses, the next step in null hypothesis testing is to devise a way of observing differences or setting up an experiment to test the null hypothesis. Go out and count some interruptions. Once you've got your count data, you can use them to determine the extent to which the data support the null hypothesis. You do that by applying inferential statistics to the data. If those statistics *fail* to reach a certain cutoff point that you have predetermined, then you confidently declare that the null hypothesis is correct and that men really don't interrupt more than women. But, what happens if your data do reach that cutoff point? In that case, you claim that given the null hypothesis, the chances of getting the results you got are so slim that the null hypothesis must be wrong, and if the null hypothesis is wrong, then the only other possibility is that the alternative hypothesis must hold.

2.8.2 Statistical significance

So what is that cutoff point? To answer that, you've got to consider probability. If you looked at a dozen statistics books, most of them introduce probability via coin flipping and go into tedious explanations about the relationship between coin flipping and randomness. I will spare you the torture and simply point out that getting tails three times in a row is very probable and may easily be due to chance. In contrast, getting tails 50 times in a row is so unlikely that you would highly suspect that something other than chance was at play, such as a two-tailed or weighted coin— especially if you had wagered your lunch money on it. Statistics provide researchers with tools for measuring whether the results of their study are about as likely as getting three heads in a row (very likely by chance), or more like getting 50 heads in a row (highly unlikely), with a small caveat that I'll explain below.

One day, Fisher decided that a chance of 1 in 20 is pretty slim. Since 1/20 is 5%, or .05, this minimal cutoff is referred to as the .05 LEVEL OF SIGNIFICANCE, or an ALPHA LEVEL of .05, or a p value of .05. (Often people will choose an alpha of .01 or even .001 before carrying out their analysis, but .05 is the minimum.) But what exactly does it mean if the results are significant? Here is the caveat. If the statistical results of our study of interruption rates yield a p value of .05 or smaller, then based on the assumption that the null hypothesis is true (there's no difference between men and women), the chances of getting those results (men interrupt more than women) are very slim—only 5%. Now, be careful, because there are some misconceptions about what p represents. First of all, it is not the probability of the null hypothesis being true or false given the results. In the same vein, it is not the probability that the alternative hypothesis is true or false either.

I know that's kind of an odd way to look at it because what you'd really like to know is whether the results themselves are significant, not how unlikely you are to get those results if the null hypothesis is right. In any case, once you've got significant results, the idea is that you can declare the null hypothesis to be false. Now if the null hypothesis is false, then something other than chance must be causing the outcome, and the general procedure is to affirm that that special something is the effect of the independent variable that you are considering in the alternative hypothesis, in this case, gender.

2.8.3 Limitations of p values and null hypothesis testing

Null hypothesis testing sounds pretty straightforward, right? It's actually not. What do scientists make of this method? I'm going to contrast two opposing views. The first is that .05 is the magic point at which the ultimate truth is established. If your results get you a .0501, they are not significant, and if you claim there may still be something there, good luck getting your research published in a journal of any reputation. On the other side of the fence, Rozeboom (1997:335) doesn't mince words when he condemns this business of testing the null hypothesis as "the most bone-headedly misguided procedure ever institutionalized in the rote training of science students." Meehl (1978:817) is equally scathing:

> The almost universal reliance on merely refuting the null hypothesis is a terrible mistake, is basically unsound, poor scientific strategy, and one of the worst things that ever happened in the history of psychology.

These are not lone voices in the wilderness either (see Cohen 1994, and Nickerson 2000 for reviews). There are some good reasons for skepticism. Consider the choice of .05. There is no real reason it is better than any other cutoff point. It was a completely arbitrary point set by Fisher. In fact, there are some reasons why it would make more sense if it were .1 in the behavioral sciences instead of .05 (Kline 2004). Another difficulty with p values is that they change depending on how much data they are based on. Statistics done on lots of data are more likely to have a small p compared to statistics done on small data sets.

Consider a corpus study that looks at how different placements of prepositions are related to different genres. The alternation is between expressions such as *turn the light on* and *turn on the light* (*turn on the Noun* and *turn the Noun on*). You find that *turn the Noun on* is 15% more common in fiction than in spoken discourse at $p = .002$. Meanwhile, another study that used a different corpus also found a 15% difference, but it did not reach significance: $p = .072$. The effect looks equal, but one is significant and the other is not. Why? It just so happens that the significant results come from a corpus of 90 million words and the other from a corpus of only 2 million. The takeaway from this isn't that p values are worthless and that we should abandon null hypothesis testing. Instead, it is important to realize that p values can be heavily influenced by sample size. Respect them for what they can tell us, but be careful not to use them inappropriately. For instance, a p value of .0001 does not mean more significant results than one of .05. Remember that *p* values help determine how unlikely the results are when we assume that the null hypothesis is right. They are not indicators of effect size.

What if you were a speech therapist looking through the literature for methods that you could use to improve your client's pronunciation of rhotics? You find one method that improved pronunciation by 1.5% with a *p* of .012. Another one reports improvements of 11% but is not significant (*p* = .059). If you believe that the ultimate truth rests in the level of significance, you'd implement the less efficient method. If you realize the inherent limitations of *p* values, you'd probably try the second one, since it seems to be more effective regardless of what the significance is. Furthermore, would your choice be influenced if you knew that the significant method that produced meager results entailed five times the number of hours to implement than the insignificant method? What if, on top of that, the significant method also entailed using expensive equipment that you don't have? In this situation, the takeaway is that statistical significance does not always equate with practical significance.

The question at this point is what to do about these limitations, especially in the context of an introductory text. The first thing you need to do is stop making decisions about the results of a study based solely on the fact that the *p* value is .05, or any other arbitrary cutoff point. In addition to using this traditional approach, spend more time looking at the guts of what is going on in the data. This can be done in a number of ways. First, include graphs of the data whenever possible, since they give a good sense of what is going on. Second, since *p* values don't indicate effect size, include a true measure of EFFECT SIZE. I'll discuss how to calculate these in the context of each statistical analysis. Third, include CONFIDENCE INTERVALS.

HINT
- When it comes to *p* values, small means significant.
- The *p* value indicates the chances of getting those particular results if the null hypothesis is considered to be true.
- A smaller *p* value doesn't indicate better results, or more important results, or a larger effect size. Measures of effect size do.
- In addition to *p* values, include graphs, measures of effect size, and confidence intervals to explain what is going on in the data.

2.8.4 Confidence intervals

All right, go back to the data in Table 2-1 and assume that they represent 17 people's scores on a language aptitude test. We know for a fact that those scores are completely representative of the 17 people who took the test, and that the mean score was 24.35. We also know that this value is probably somewhat close to the real mean score of the entire population represented (if we actually measured everyone), but not *exactly* the same. After all, what would the mean be if we administered the test to ten different groups of people? We'd expect each of the means from the different groups (or samplings of the population) to be somewhere around the real population mean, but none of them would equal it exactly.

Of course, it is impossible to test everyone to find out the real mean score of the entire population. However, we do know that sample means tend to fall into a normal distribution, and we do have one of those means from 17 members of that population. So, we can use those pieces of information to estimate what the mean would be for the population as a whole—that is, what the mean would be if we measured everyone, not just the 17 people we actually measured. This estimation is called the 95% CONFIDENCE INTERVAL.[7] It is not given as a single estimated mean but as an interval of scores that are very likely to contain the real mean. For the scores in Table 2-1, the 95% confidence interval is 20.75–27.95. What this means is that we can be 95% sure that this interval contains the true mean language aptitude score for the general population. Another way to see it is that if we tested 100 different groups and calculated a confidence interval for each one, chances are that 95 of those confidence intervals would contain the true mean.

Let's look at some data that I'll discuss again in a later chapter. Three different native language groups are given a test of their L2 abilities in English. The groups are speakers of Germanic languages, other European languages, and Asian languages. In Figure 2-13, the bars represent the high and low confidence intervals of the mean for each group. The line in the middle of each bar represents the mean score for each group. One thing to look for in confidence intervals is overlap. The confidence intervals for the Germanic and Asian groups overlap quite a bit. My eyeball tells me it's about a 75% overlap. What this means is that chances are pretty good that if we could give the test to the entire population of Germanic language speakers and to the entire population of Asian language speakers, their mean would fall into the 95% confidence interval, and since the confidence levels overlap a lot, in many cases it could fall into the confidence level of either group, which would make you suspect there's not really much difference between the scores the people in the two groups got.

---

[7] The use of 95% rather than some other percentage is a traditional level. In practice you can set it anywhere you want.

Figure 2-13. Confidence intervals of means for three groups on an L2 English test.

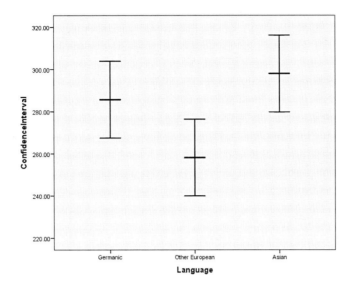

The situation is quite different for the Asian group and the other European group because they don't overlap at all. Chances are very slim that the population means would be similar if you gave the test to another set of language learners from these two groups. In other words, lack of overlap shows significance by itself. No p required. As we'll see in a later chapter, speakers of Germanic and of other European languages in this fictitious study don't differ significantly in their test scores. This shouldn't be surprising given the overlap there as well. Now, lest I lead you astray, a little bit of overlap between confidence intervals is okay and can still result in significant differences between the groups.

Now, imagine that the mean for the other European group stays the same, but that the range between the high and low confidence interval shrinks drastically to the point that none of the groups' confidence intervals overlap anymore. Can you see how this could happen without changing any of the group means? This change alone would mean that the other European group would be significantly different from the other two groups. This is so because the more narrow the confidence interval is, the closer it gets to the mean that we'd find if we measured everyone, not just the ones we actually did.

Up to this point we've been looking at the confidence intervals of the means of each group. Another informative way to use confidence intervals is to calculate them for the differences between the means of each group (mean of group X minus mean of group Y). These appear in Figure 2-14. There are three things a confidence interval of the difference between group means will tell you: (1) whether the difference is significant, (2) how precisely the mean is estimated, and (3) the size of the effect. Whenever the confidence interval of the mean difference between groups contains zero, the results are not significant at the .05 level. Conversely, mean difference confidence intervals that miss zero are significant. So, the mean difference between the Germanic and other European groups is not significant, nor is the mean difference between speakers of Germanic and Asian languages. The confidence interval of the mean difference between the other European and Asian groups doesn't include zero, so those two groups are statistically different from each other. Cool, huh?

Figure 2-14. Confidence intervals of differences between the means for three groups on an L2 English test.

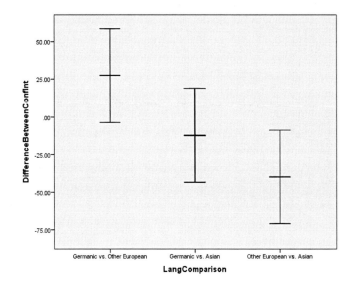

The second thing to look at when examining the confidence interval of the mean difference is the range of the confidence interval, or, in other words, how long it is in the graph. The smaller the range of scores in the 95% confidence interval, the more precise of an estimate it is of the real mean difference you'd find by measuring everyone if you could. Look at the different ranges in the confidence interval in Figure 2-15. (I've modified the data from what's in the previous graphs to make it more salient.) There, the most precise mean difference is when speakers of other European languages are compared to those of Asian languages. The least precise is when the scores of speakers of Germanic languages are compared with those of Asian languages. When you've got a really wide range, the chances that your mean differences are way off mark are much higher. That is something that you won't get by just inspecting the *p* value.

Figure 2-15. Modified confidence intervals of differences between the means for three groups on an L2 English test.

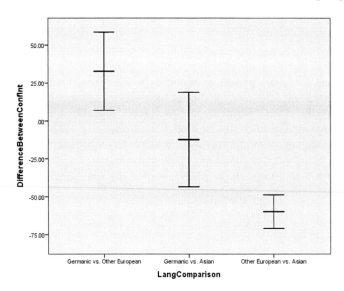

The third thing a confidence interval indicates is effect size. Remember that a *p* value of .05 and one of .00005 are both significant. They both indicate that getting such extreme scores is highly unlikely if you assume that the null hypothesis is true. But, you can't claim that the smaller one demonstrates that the independent variable influences the dependent variable to a greater extent. That is so because *p* values don't show the size of the effect. However, one way to find effect size is to compare the confidence intervals of the differences between the means. In Figure 2-15, two of the comparisons between groups are significant because their confidence intervals don't include zero. The effect size is seen as how far the confidence interval is from zero. The further from zero, the stronger the effect. As a result, there is a much larger effect of being in the other European versus the Asian group than there is of being in the Germanic versus other European group.

2.8.5 Type I and Type II errors

Let's say that you perform an analysis and find that there is a statistically significant relationship between grade point average (GPA) and scores on the TOEFL. People with low GPAs tend to score lower on the TOEFL than people with higher GPAs. What's more, your results are significant at the .05 level; there is only a 1-in-20 chance of getting those results if you are assuming that there is no relationship between TOEFL scores and GPAs. That is good, but the chances are still 1 in 20, not 0 in 20. What if your results represent the 1 instead of the 19 out of 20? This situation is known as a TYPE I error, or a false positive. It happens when you declare the hypothesis of your study to be correct: GPAs and TOEFL scores are related (because it looks like the null hypothesis is incorrect). But, when there is a Type I error, the sad truth is actually that the null hypothesis is correct: there is no significant relationship between the two scores.

TYPE II errors are just the opposite. They are called false negatives. This would happen if you find that there is no relationship between GPAs and TOEFL scores. People with high GPAs get both high and low TOEFL scores and people with low GPAs also get both high and low TOEFL scores. In other words, the null hypothesis seems to be right; there is no relationship. What makes it a Type II error is when there appears to be no relationship but there really is a relationship. That is, it looks like the null hypothesis is correct when it really isn't.

2.9 Using SPSS to Make Boxplots of Confidence Intervals

The data used in Figures 2-13 and 2-14 come from the results of an analysis in Chapter 6 (Tables 6-1 and 6-3).
1. Open SPSS and navigate to where you have downloaded the data files for this book. Choose *ConfidenceIntervals.sav > OK.* This opens up the *Data Editor* window in Figure 2-16.
2. Use the columns *ConfidenceInterval* and *Language* to reproduce Figure 2-13 and the columns *DifferenceBetweenConfInt* and *LangComparison* to reproduce Figure 2-14. Do this by clicking on *Graphs > Legacy Dialogs > Boxplot > Simple > Define.*
3. Highlight *ConfidenceIntervals* and move it into the *Variable* box by clicking on the arrow to the left of the *Variable* box.
4. Move *Language* into the *Category Axis* by highlighting it and clicking on the arrow to the left of the *Category Axis box > OK* (Figure 2-17).
5. Scroll down to the bottom of the *Statistics Viewer* window until you find the box plot in Figure 2-18 and double-click on it to open the *Chart Editor.* In the *Chart Editor*, double-click on one of the three bars in the boxplot to open the *Properties* window to the correct place (Figure 2-19). Choose the *Bar Options* tab and check *T-bar > Apply > Close.*
6. To rename the values on the bottom of the boxplot from *1, 2, 3,* to *German vs. Asian*, etc., double-click on each number and type in the name. Close the *Chart Editor* window and the modified boxplot will appear in the *Statistics Viewer* window.
7. If you want to copy the boxplot into another program, such as a word processor, right-click on it, choose *Copy*, then *Paste* in the other program.

Figure 2-16. Data for Figures 2-14 and 2-15.

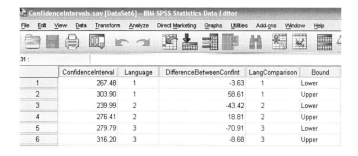

Figure 2-17. Boxplot dialog box.

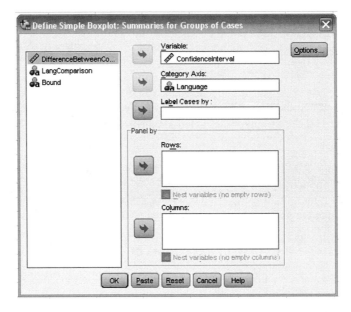

Figure 2-18. The unmodified boxplot.

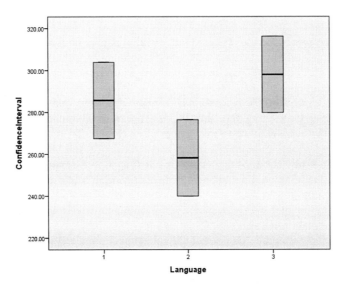

Figure 2-19. The *Properties* window of the *Chart Editor.*

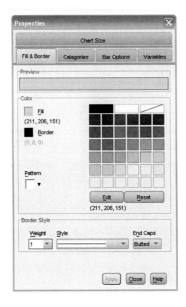

2.10 Hands-On Exercises for Descriptive and Inferential Statistics

Answers are available at http://linguistics.byu.edu/faculty/eddingtond/Data_Sets/answers.pdf

2.10.1 Descriptive statistics of pretest anxiety levels

Open the file *Nemati2012.sav.* It contains a measure of how anxious students were before taking an English language test. Use SPSS to calculate the mean, median, mode, standard deviations, skew, and kurtosis of the scores. Evaluate the normality of the distribution of the data with graphs and with statistical tests.

2.10.2 Variables and hypotheses

Identify the dependent variable and the independent variable(s) in the following studies. What kind of variable (ordinal, continuous, or categorical) is used in each study? What are the null and alternative hypotheses in each study?

2.10.2.1 English comparatives

Hilpert (2008) contrasted two different ways of expressing the comparative in English. It can be expressed by adding *–er* or by using *more* (e.g., *prouder, more proud*). Among other things, he tested the effect of the number of syllables a word has, whether *than* follows it or not, and how many times the word appears in a corpus—its frequency.

2.10.2.2 Morpheme recognition and semantic similarity

Derwing (1976) was interested in the effect semantics has on how people determine morphological relationships between words—that is, whether people perceive two words to have a morpheme in common. First, he got a bunch of people to rate how similar pairs of words were as far as meaning was concerned. They responded on a scale of 0 to 4 in which 0 meant *no connection in meaning whatsoever* and 4 meant *a clear and unmistakable connection in meaning.* The average response to that test became the semantic rating of the word pair. Some of the pairs he used were *spider/spin, dirty/dirt, necklace/lace,* and *month/moon.* Next, he put the word pairs into a question—for example, *Do you think the word* dirt *comes from the word* dirty*?* People responded on a four-point scale in which 4 was *no doubt about it* and 0 was *no way.*

2.10.2.3 Sentence length in first language acquisition

Miller and Chapman (1981) wanted to see how children's age is related to how complex their sentences are. They looked at the sentences that many different children of different ages produced and counted how many morphemes each sentence contained.

2.10.2.4 Classroom intervention and communication skills

Farber and Klein (1999) implemented a language enrichment program in 12 kindergarten and first-grade classes. At the end of the program, they tested the listening and writing skills of the children in those 12 classes as well as the listening and writing skills of children in 12 classes that didn't participate in the enrichment program. They wanted to see if the program improved the children's communication skills.

2.10.2.5 English syllabification

Eddington, Treiman, and Elzinga (2013) wondered what kinds of things people take into consideration when they choose to syllabify words like *camel* as either *cam-el* or *ca-mel.* They tested a large number of words by asking people to choose one of the two syllabifications. Some words had stress on the first syllable and others on the second. Some words, like *camel*, had a sonorant consonant such as /m/ in the middle, and others, like *attack*, had obstruents like /t/.

CHAPTER THREE

PEARSON CORRELATION

Question answered: What is the relationship between two variables?
Type of variables used: Both continuous.

A correlation is perhaps the statistic that is most easily grasped and visualized. It is used to determine what the relationship between two continuous variables is. Here are some examples:

- How are second language proficiency and degree of cultural adaptation related?
- How is word frequency related to the amount of time required to name a word?
- How does income relate to happiness?

Table 3-1. Percent of monophthong [a] versus [aɪ] and number of years spent living away from the South.

Speaker	Percent of [a]	Years living outside the South
1	98	1
2	82	1
3	99	2
4	65	3
5	90	3
6	85	5
7	75	5
8	50	5
9	75	6
10	55	6
11	85	7
12	70	8
13	30	8
14	55	9
15	80	9
16	25	10

Let's consider a sociolinguistic issue. One of the most salient aspects of southern US speech is the use of the monophthong [a] in words such as *pie* and *fight* rather than the diphthong [aɪ]. Do southerners who move away from the South lose this pronunciation over time? Table 3-1 contains made-up information about a number of American English speakers from the South.

Perhaps the best way to see the relationship between percent of monophthongs and years spent living away from the South is by plotting each pair of scores on a scatter plot. A scatter plot places each pair of scores as a single data point on a graph. In Figure 3-1, for each point, the percent of monophthongs is on the vertical axis and the number of years living away from the South is on the horizontal axis. The line in the chart is called a REGRESSION LINE. The placement of the regression line is determined by the data points themselves because it is fitted between them in such a way that the distance between the line and all of the data points is as small as possible. Notice that the line slopes downward. This indicates that there is a negative correlation between the percent of monophthongs and years away. A negative correlation means that people with more monophthongs have lived away for shorter periods of time. Inversely, people with fewer monophthongs have lived away for longer periods of time.

Figure 3-1. Scatter plot of percent of monophthongs and time spent living away.

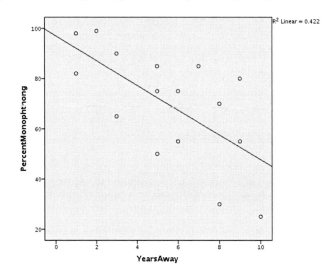

3.1 Using SPSS to Generate Scatter Plots

The monophthong and time away data are in the file *correlation.sav*. Once you have opened the file in SPSS, you will see the percent of monophthongs pronounced as [a] and the number of years spent away in two different columns of data. To create the scatter plot in Figure 3-1, click on *Graphs > Legacy Dialog > Scatter/Dot* (Figure 3-2) > *Simple Scatter > Define*.

Figure 3-2. Creating a scatter plot.

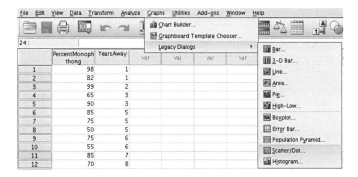

Click on *PercentMonophthong* and move it to the *Y-Axis* by clicking on the arrow to the left of the *Y-Axis* box. Move *YearsAway* to the *X-Axis* box in the same way > *OK* (Figure 3-3).

Figure 3-3. *Scatter plot* dialog box.

To place a regression line on the scatter plot, double click on the newly created scatter plot itself to open the Chart Editor. Click on *Elements > Fit Line at Total.* The *Properties* box will open. Choose *Linear > Apply > Close.*

3.2 Pearson Correlation Coefficient

Now let's consider another relationship.[1] A computational linguist develops a program to tag the words in a test document for part of speech. The program utilizes another corpus in which all of the words are pretagged for part of speech. That corpus is used to determine the part of speech of each of the words in the test document. Pretagged corpora of different sizes are used and the percent of correctly tagged words in the test document is recorded on each trial. This relationship is plotted in Figure 3-4. In this case, the regression line slopes upward, which indicates a positive correlation. The larger the pretagged corpus, the more accurately the program tags the words in the test document.

So, now that we've seen what positive and negative correlations look like on a scatter plot, we can see how a correlation analysis summarizes these kinds of relationships. The statistic we use in a correlation is called the Pearson correlation coefficient and is abbreviated *r*. The values of *r* range from +1 to −1. A negative relationship between variables, as we have between monophthongs and time spent living outside of the South, is represented as a negative value of *r*, which in that case is *r* = −.649. The positive relationship between percent of words tagged correctly in the test document and the size of the pretagged corpus used by the tagging program is calculated to be *r* = +.944. A correlation coefficient of zero would mean there is no relationship between the two variables. In that case, the regression line would be completely flat and the dots wouldn't cluster around it at all—just like the darts do on the dartboard (and wall) when I aim for the center. A perfect positive correlation, where *r* is equal to one, could be obtained by plotting the weights of different amounts of water on one axis and the volume of each amount of water on the other. In this case, the regression line would slope upward and all of the dots representing the volume and weight of water would fall directly on the regression line.

Inspecting the graph and the data points is a good way to see how strong the correlation is. One nice thing about correlations is that the value of *r* itself is a measure of the effect size of the correlation. As you add more data, the level of significance will change, but *r* is not directly dependent on how many data points are in the data. One way of looking at *r* is that if it is around .1 (or −.1) the correlation is weak. Correlations around .3 (or −.3) are considered moderate, and those around .5 and greater (or −.5 and smaller) are considered to indicate a strong relationship between the two variables (Cohen 1988). One word of caution—be careful when using these numbers to label an effect size as *weak*, *moderate*, or *strong*. The gauges are very rough estimates and may be best interpreted according to the field of research the data come from (Plonsky & Oswald forthcoming).

---

[1] These data are fictitious.

Figure 3-4. The relationship between pretagged corpus size and the percentage of words in the test document that are correctly tagged for part of speech.

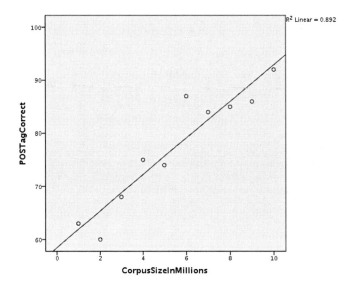

3.3 Using SPSS to Calculate Pearson Correlation (or a Spearman Rank-Order Correlation or a Kendall's Tau B)

To perform a Pearson correlation:

1. Open the *correlation.sav* file if it is not already open. Click on *Analyze > Correlation > Bivariate*. Move *PercentMonophthong* and *YearsAway* into the *Variables* box.
2. Make sure the *Pearson*, *Two-tailed*, and *Flag significant correlations* are checked, then click *OK*.
3. To perform a Spearman rank-order correlation, check *Spearman*. To perform a Kendall's *tau b*, check *Kendall's tau b* (Figure 3-5).

I'll explain Spearman rank-order correlations and Kendall's *tau b* later in this chapter. The outcome appears as in Table 3-2.

Figure 3-5. *Bivariate Correlation* dialog box.

3.4 Statistical Significance of a Correlation

As we've seen, the statistical program calculated that there is a negative correlation of $-.649$ between percent of monophthongs and years away from the South. The next question to ask is how possible it is that this correlation could be obtained by chance if we assume the null hypothesis, that there is no relationship, is true? The program calculates the level of significance, represented as p, to be .006. This appears on the row *Sig. (two-tailed)* on the SPSS output. Since p is smaller than .05, the possibility is smaller than 5%. Actually, the .006 p value shows that there is only a 0.6% probability, so we can reject the null hypothesis and assume that there is a relationship between time away and the use of monophthongs. Remember never to use the p value as an indicator of effect strength; that is what r shows you.

Table 3-2. Correlation statistics for percent of monophthongs and years spent living away.

Correlations		% Monophthong	YearsAway
% Monophthong	Pearson Cor.	1	$-.649^{**}$
	Sig. (2-tailed)		.006
	N	16	16
YearsAway	Pearson Cor.	$-.649^{**}$	1
	Sig. (2-tailed)	.006	
	N	16	16
**. Correlation is significant at the 0.01 level (2-tailed).			

3.5 One-Tailed or Two?

Table 3-2 mentions that the significance is two-tailed. What does that mean? Well, it has to do with what the initial hypothesis says about the relationship between the two variables. Generally, we have no prior assumption about whether the correlation between the two things is positive or negative. We leave that open and let the data tell us. If you don't assume that the correlation is positive or negative beforehand, you report the results as two-tailed. If you are completely sure that the correlation will be positive (or negative) before you carry out the study, and you just want to see how much so, you may choose a one-tailed level of significance. But, be careful. You will be considered a dirty, rotten cheater if you decide to use a one-tailed p value only after you see the results of the study. Notice that the r for both one- and two-tailed correlations is identical. The only difference is in the p value. Notice also that SPSS gives two-tailed p values by default. To get the one-tailed result you divide the p by two, or choose *One-tailed* in the *Bivariate Correlations* dialog box (Figure 3-5) and let SPSS do the advanced math for you.

3.6 Reporting the Results of a Correlation

These findings could be summarized in this way:

An analysis of the 16 Southerners in the study indicate that there is a negative relationship between the percent of monophthongs used by the speakers and the amount of time they have spent living outside of the South. This is shown by the correlation $-.649$, which is statistically significant with a p value of .006 (two-tailed).

Another way would be to say: "A strong negative correlation was found between the two scores that was statistically significant (r (14) $= -.649$, $p <$ .006, two-tailed)." The 14 in parenthesis after r is called the DEGREES OF FREEDOM. It is a measure of how much data the analysis is based on. For a correlation, the degrees of freedom is the number of paired scores used in the analysis minus two. If the results were of a Spearman rank-order correlation, then they would be reported using rho in this manner: (ρ (11) $= .376$, $p <$ .021, two-tailed). Results from a Kendall's *tau b* analysis would be reported with a *tau* rather than an r: (τ (14) $= -.649$, $p <$ .006, two-tailed). I promise I will explain Spearman and Kendall later.

3.7 Variance and r^2

Think again about the idea of weighing different volumes of water and correlating their weight against their volume. It would result in a perfect correlation of $r = 1$. Is there any variable, other than the volume of the water that influences its weight (assuming it is pure water, at the same temperature, on the same planet)? No, volume explains 100% of the differences in weight between the samples that are measured. In statistical terminology weight explains 100% of the variance, or in other words, 100% of the dispersion of the scores around the regression line. (Remember that variance is the standard deviation squared.) We can get this 100% figure by taking the r, which is 1, and squaring it, which yields an r^2 value of 1. In this case, 1 means everything, or 100%.

Now, what about the coefficient of −.649 that we observed between percent of monophthongs and time living away? Squaring that r value gives us an r^2 of .422. (Notice that number on Figure 3-1.) What this means is that the time living away from the South only accounts for 42% of the variance in the use of monophthongs. Beside time living away, there are a myriad of things that could be related to how often a speaker uses monophthongs: How much contact they have with other southerners, their age, how strong their sense of southern heritage is, how prestigious or stigmatized southern speech is in their workplace or social group, and so on. Those kinds of things make up the 58% of the variance we haven't accounted for. Even though we have found a significant correlation between the two variables, it is important to look at the r^2 in order to get a sense of how much of the variance is accounted for by the variable tested, or in other words, how strong an effect it has. A good rule of thumb is that an r^2 of .01 indicates a weak relationship, .09 a moderate one, and .25 or above a strong one. A significant correlation that accounts for a small portion of the variance is not something to write home about. Actually, people at home are probably not interested in your r^2 anyway.

3.8 Correlation Doesn't Mean Causation

I will offer one word of caution about correlations: they are dangerous when put into the wrong hands. For example, scientists have found a number of interesting correlations:

- Taller people have higher IQs than short people.
- Drownings are positively correlated with ice cream consumption.
- The more people there are in a country who believe in evolution, the wealthier people in that country are.

Does this mean that

- Height causes intelligence or intelligence causes height?
- People who eat more ice cream are more likely to drown?
- Believing in evolution makes you rich?

Correlations are only dangerous when people take them to show causation, because correlations show relationships, but not necessarily causes. Tall people are smarter because they are older and more experienced than people like children, who are short. People go into the water and eat ice cream more when it is warm outside; and in wealthy countries, there are more atheists, who are more likely to subscribe to the theory of evolution. Never use the results of a correlation to prove a cause, despite the fact that Al Gore gets away with it.

3.9 Assumptions of Correlation

There is an old adage, "Garbage in, garbage out," that applies very well to statistics. Although we may put numbers into a correlation analysis which yields some fancy results, it is extremely important to make sure that the data you put in fit the assumptions that an analysis of correlation is designed to work with. For example, the data for a Pearson's correlation must be continuous, not ordinal. If not, the output is highly suspect at least, and may be outright wrong. More technically, it may give you Type I or Type II errors or incorrect r or p values. I've noticed that it's not uncommon for books introducing statistics to mention the assumptions of a Pearson correlation in passing, but often they do not go on to explain how the assumptions are determined, nor what to do when the data do not fit the assumptions. My goal here is to provide basic guidelines for both of those issues, which is why this book is better. Pearson correlation assumes that

- The data are continuous.
- The relationship between the variables is linear.
- The data in both variables are normally distributed.
- The observations are independent.
- The data are homoscedastic.

Let's look at each of these in turn.

3.9.1 Continuous data

We've looked at correlations between continuous data, but what if you were interested in differences in the use of monophthongs between males and females? Gender is not continuous, so a correlation should not be performed. In this case, you would perform a t-test (see Chapter 5). What if you wanted to see if monophthongization rates correlated with the order someone ranked in their graduating class? Although rank is numeric, it is not continuous. With ordinal data the Spearman rank-order or Kendall's *tau b* analyses that I keep mentioning would be appropriate instead. The nice thing about both of these analyses is that the data are organized and the results are interpreted in the same way that a Pearson correlation is. In any event, only continuous data may be analyzed in a Pearson correlation.

3.9.2 Linear relationship

When two variables are linear, the relationship between them is roughly equal across all of their values. That is, the degree that one variable changes should be about the same for all values of the other variable. One way to see if the data are linear is by plotting them on a scatter plot. Figure 3-6 comes from the data in the columns labeled *EndUpVerbing* and *Decade* in the file *correlation.sav*. These data have to do with how often expressions such as *end up going, ended up dropping,* and *ends up shooting* are in various corpora from the 1930s to the 2000s.[2] As you can see, this expression has ended up being used more often in recent decades.

The straight regression line represents the best fit between all of the data points when taken together. The curved LOESS LINE differs from the regression line in two ways. First, it isn't named after a Dr. Loess but is an abbreviation for "local regression line." Second, rather than fitting the line based on all of the data at once, the Loess line is essentially calculated by taking the first few data points and creating a line based on it. The next few data points are considered, and a line calculated based on it, and this continues until all of the subsets of the data have been considered. That is why the Loess line may not be straight. When the data are linear the Loess line should be fairly straight and follow the regression line quite closely. Because it doesn't in this case, these data may not be linear. Bends or curves in a Loess line often indicate lack of linearity. In these data, the use of *EndUpVerbing* started to increase slowly in the first part of the twentieth century. The curvature in the line shows that growth has not been steady, but has increased more quickly in the latter half of the century.

3.9.2.1 Using SPSS to generate graphs for visualizing linearity in the data

To test for linearity, inspect the scatter plot,
Open *end up VERBing.sav.* Click on *Graphs > Legacy Dialog > Scatter/Dot > Simple Scatter > Define*. Click on *EndUpVerbing* and move it to the *Y-Axis* by clicking on the arrow to the left of the *Y-Axis* box. Move *Decade* to the *X-Axis* box in the same way > *OK*.

To place a regression line on the scatter plot,
Double click on the scatter plot itself to open the *Chart Editor*. Click on *Elements > Fit Line at Total*. The *Properties* box will open. Choose *Linear > Apply > Close*.

To place a Loess line on the scatter plot,
Double click on the scatter plot itself to open the *Chart Editor*. Click on *Elements > Fit Line at Total*. The *Properties* box will open. Choose *Loess > Apply*. Adjust *% of points to fit* to smooth Loess line if desired > *Apply > Close*.

This yields the scatter plot in Figure 3-6.

Figure 3-6. Scatter plot of *EndUpVerbing* by decade.

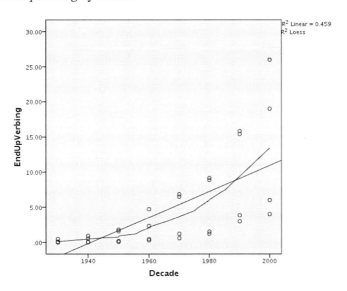

---

[2] Taken from http://corpus.byu.edu.

3.9.2.2 What to do if the data are not linear

First of all, lack of linearity could simply mean that there is no significant relationship between the two variables. In the same vein, sometimes the relationship simply isn't linear. Imagine graphing the amount of caffeine intake against a measure of "How good do you feel?" Feeling good may go up at the smaller doses of caffeine, but once you hit the megadoses, the line will probably turn down abruptly as people get overly jittery. In that case, there is a u-shaped curve that we wouldn't want to straighten out. The shape is very telling of the effect.

Another thing that may cause a lack of linearity is the existence of OUTLIERS. A visual inspection of the scatter plot for the data should help identify any extreme values. If the existence of outliers is making the data nonlinear, you may sometimes delete them if there is a good justification for it, but not just to make things work the way you want them to. One possible justification would be that the scores are two and a half or three standard deviations away from the mean. (See Chapter 7 for other methods of calculating this.) In essence, what you are claiming is that those scores are so extreme that they are not likely to be representative of what is really going on. Imagine that one extremely high outlying score comes from a study that measures reaction times. That particularly long reaction time could have been due to the participant's being distracted and not paying attention to the test instead of answering right away. An extremely short reaction time, on the other hand, could be due to a "Whoops, I didn't mean to hit the key right then" moment.

Two other methods for addressing the issue of nonlinearity are using a different statistic and transforming the data.[3] Kendall's *tau b* is a statistic that does not require linearity as a Pearson correlation does, and is often used in cases when unresolvable nonlinearity arises. Transforming the data, which is covered later in this chapter, is also a method of addressing data that are not linear.

3.9.3 Normally distributed data

Another assumption of a Pearson correlation is that the data are fairly normally distributed. This means that a histogram of the data should somewhat approximate a bell curve. In Chapter 1, I discussed how histograms, boxplots, and Q-Q plots give graphic representations of degree of normality, and how measures of skew and kurtosis also indicate deviations from normality. If you don't put too much stock in them, tests such as Kolmogorov-Smirnov or Shapiro-Wilk can be used in addition to the graphic representations in order to calculate how much the distribution of the data differs from normal. When they give conflicting results, trust the graphics over the tests. In any event, if the distribution turns out to be close to normal you are justified in using a Pearson correlation.

Let's look at the distribution of *EndUpVerbing* used in the above example. The data appear skewed both in the boxplot in Figure 3-10 and the Q-Q plot in Figure 3-11, since many of the dots vary from the line. In the histogram in Figure 3-12 the distribution is seen to clearly deviate a great deal from normal as well. The results of the tests of normality appear in Table 3-7. Deviation from normality is significant in the Shapiro-Wilk and the Kolmogorov-Smirnov tests. Skew and kurtosis are also out of the stringent +1 to −1 range.

Figure 3-10. Boxplot of *EndUpVerbing*.

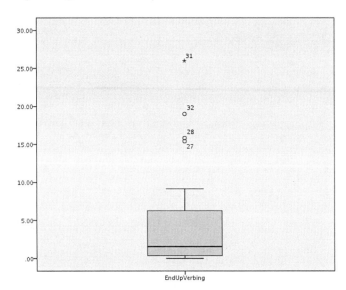

---

[3] Other methods for eliminating or accounting for nonlinearity which are beyond the scope of this book are referred to as robust regression (Anderson 2007) and curvilinear regression (George & Mallery 2011).

Figure 3-11. Q-Q plot of *EndUpVerbing*.

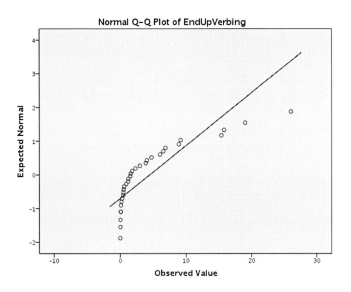

Figure 3-12. Histogram of *EndUpVerbing*.

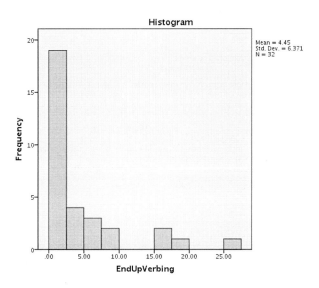

Table 3-7. Tests of normality for *EndUpVerbing*.

	Number	Significance	Standard Error	Number / Std. Err.
Shap.-Wilk	.720	.0005		
Kol.-Sm.	.242	.0005		
Skew	1.990		.414	4.806
Kurtosis	3.736		.809	4.618

The fact that all of the measures and graphs point to non-normality means that we should not perform a Pearson correlation on these data. If there were only a small degree of non-normality (notice the judgment call) you could choose to ignore it and report the results of the Pearson correlation, since Pearson is resistant to a small degree of non-normality (Edgell & Noon 1984). Another option would be to try transforming one or both of the variables. The last option is to simply recognize the lack of normality and use Kendall's *tau b* instead. Results of both a Pearson correlation and Kendall's *tau b* appear in Table 3-8. Now you see why I kept bringing up Kendall's *tau b* in the previous pages.

Table 3-8. Pearson and Kendall's *tau b* correlation for frequency of *EndUpVerbing* and decade.

	Coefficient	Significance
Pearson correlation	.677	.0005
Kendall's *tau b*	.669	.0005

Both statistics result in a positive correlation between the frequency of *EndUpVerbing* and decade. Given the fact that the assumptions of linearity and normality required for a Pearson correlation are violated, the results of the Pearson correlation should not be used unless those issues can be resolved.

HINT
When SPSS gives the significance of .000, it should be reported as $p < .0005$, not $p < .000$.

3.9.3.1 Using SPSS to generate graphs and measures of normal distribution

Use the following steps to generate the boxplot in Figure 3-10, the histogram in Figure 3-11, the Q-Q plot in Figure 3-12, and the results of the Shapiro-Wilk and Kolmogorov-Smirnov tests in Table 3-7:

1. Click on *Analyze > Descriptive Statistics > Explore*.
2. Click on the variable name, *EndUpVerbing*, and move it to the *Dependent List* by clicking on the arrow between the boxes.
3. Click on *Statistics* > check the box next to *Descriptives > Continue*.
4. Click on *Plots*, check the boxes next to *Histogram* and *Normality plots with tests > Continue > OK*.
5. To superimpose the normal distribution curve on the histogram, double click on the histogram itself, then in the *Chart Editor* choose *Elements > Show Distribution Curve*.

3.9.4 Independence of observations

Pearson correlations also require the observations to be independent of each other. The idea here is that there should be only one score per participant. If one person is measured twice, the answers given the first time are not independent of those provided the second time. This is generally a problem in longitudinal studies, where the research question has to do with what the effect of time is. When people are tested at different points in time, the answers they give on a later test are likely to be influenced by their answers on an earlier one. Giving a pretest or a posttest could result in lack of independence of the observations. The best way to deal with this lack of independence is to design your study beforehand to avoid it. Otherwise use a statistical test that is designed for repeated measures (see Chapter 8). Now, what about the *EndUpVerbing* data? They are taken from the same four corpora at different points in time. If we treat a corpus as a subject, then the observations are not independent, which is strike three against analyzing it with a Pearson correlation.

3.9.5 Homoscedasticity

This tongue-twister, and its opposite, *heteroscedasticity* (along with its alternate spelling *homoskedasticity*), is also known as equal variances and homogeneity of variances. (Why can't we all just decide on one name and stick to it?) Since a picture is worth a thousand words, the idea behind this can clearly be seen in Figure 3-13 where the vertical axis represents foreign language ability and the horizontal axis is the number of years the person has lived in the foreign country.

Notice that the data points are about evenly dispersed from the regression line all along the length of the line. It doesn't matter that they are close or far from the line, just evenly spread along the length of the line. This indicates that regardless of how many or how few years people have lived in the second-language country, their second-language ability scores have about an equal spread (or variance) from the regression line—that is, they are homoscedastic.

The situation in Figure 3-14 is quite different. There, the variance of the scores is not constant across the spectrum of years living in a foreign country. More specifically, the variance is smaller on the left-hand side of the plot compared to the right-hand side. The longer people have lived in the foreign country, the more widely spread out their language abilities become, or in other words these data are heteroscedastic. This is evident in the fan shape of the data points. If your data are heteroscedastic you don't need to throw your hands up in despair. Grab your mouse and either run them through a Kendall's *tau b*, or transform the data to see if you can eliminate it that way.

Figure 3-13. Scatter plot showing homoscedastic variance.[4]

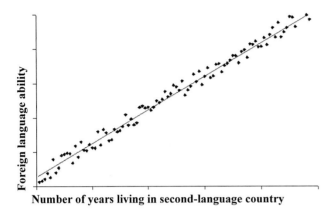

Figure 3-14. Scatter plot showing heteroscedastic variance.[5]

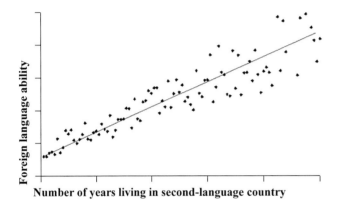

3.10 Parametric versus Nonparametric Statistics

I've mentioned several times that when the assumptions of a Pearson correlation cannot be met, one way around that is to use a Kendall's *tau b*. If that's the case, why worry about meeting all those assumptions and performing all those tests of regularity and linearity at all? Dude, wouldn't it be simpler to do Kendall's *tau b* to begin with? In order to answer this question we need to contrast and compare PARAMETRIC and NONPARAMETRIC STATISTICS. Pearson correlation is parametric and Kendall's *tau b* is nonparametric. Parametric statistics rely on the parameters of mean and standard deviation and are designed around a particular distribution of the data. They are better than nonparametric statistics in a number of ways, which is why we try as hard as possible to use them and only revert to nonparametric statistical procedures as a last-ditch resort.

3.10.1 Disadvantages of nonparametric statistics

In many nonparametric analyses, continuous data are transformed into ordinal data. For example continuous 231, 433, 501, 503, 789 would be converted into ordinal 1, 2, 3, 4, 5. This results in a great deal of information being lost, which ultimately makes the outcome less precise. At the same time, because nonparametric statistics are less precise, they often require much more data than a parametric analysis does to achieve statistical significance. Effect sizes for nonparametric statistics are much harder to come by as well.

So far we've only looked at one independent variable at a time, but we often want to know how several different variables influence the dependent variable. For example, we may be interested in not only whether the number of years living abroad influences second-language learning, but whether the student's gender plays a part as well. In these cases, it is imperative to determine whether years abroad and gender affect test scores independently of each other, or on the contrary, gender and number of years abroad interact with each other. Nonparametric statistics do not allow you to see whether the independent variables are interacting or not, which is another reason we try to use parametric statistics whenever possible.

---

[4] Image retrieved from http://upload.wikimedia.org/wikipedia/commons/9/93/Homoscedasticity.png.
[5] Image retrieved from http://upload.wikimedia.org/wikipedia/commons/a/a5/Heteroscedasticity.png.

3.10.2 Advantages of nonparametric statistics

One of the advantages of nonparametric statistics is that they can handle ordinal and categorical data, unlike most parametric statistics. Chalk up one for the nonparametric team. Many studies in linguistics involve tests with scales that could be treated as ordinal:

- *strongly agree, agree, disagree, strongly disagree*
- *never, sometimes, often, always*
- *best accent, second-best, third-best, worst accent*

Studies with these kinds of questions produce data that call for nonparametric analysis (although for a differing perspective, see Carifio & Perla 2007). Counts of things in different categories, such as number of adjectives used in different genres of speech involve categorical data, which is why they are not amenable to parametric statistics. They are also not as affected by outliers because they don't depend on the mean, but the median, in their calculations.

So, to make a long story short, the best practice is to use parametric statistics if at all possible. Transforming the data into a different scale, and eliminating outliers should be tried if it means that a parametric analysis may be performed and is justified. Use nonparametric statistics only when the assumptions of the parametric test can't be met or when there is no other way to make the data amenable to parametric analysis.

3.11 Data Transformation

Transformations essentially convert the data into numeric data on a different scale. While it may sound like cheating or data massaging, it is completely legitimate since the transformed data are mathematically equivalent to the original untransformed data, but the new scale that they are transformed into may result in data that can be analyzed parametrically. Performing a transformation on the data may sound technical and complex. In reality, it is just a matter of letting the computer apply a formula to each of the scores, and then placing the transformed scores into a new column on the spreadsheet. The data in the new column can then be tested to see if they help eliminate the problems of nonlinearity, non-normal distribution, or heteroscedasticity. If so, then the statistics are redone using the transformed scores instead of the original scores.

There are quite a few different transformations that can be applied, so which one is best? Some commonly suggested transformations appear in Table 3-9 (Velleman & Hoaglin 1981).[6] When using these transformations it is important to find the lowest number in your data. If it is below 1, modify the formula to make the lowest value equal to one instead (Osborne 2002). This is done to eliminate zeros, which are problematic for some transformations like logarithmic transformations. For example, if the lowest number is -3, add 4 to each value so that the lowest value is now 1. If you were doing a square transformation, the modified formula would be (4+*variable*)**2. If you were calculating a negative reciprocal root the new formula would be $-1/(SQRT(4+variable))$. This adjustment is not needed for an arcsine transformation where the values are proportions. A value like 25% needs to appear as 0.25 in the spreadsheet in that case.

Table 3-9. Common transformations.

When to Use	Transformation Name	SPSS Syntax
Negative skew	Fourth Power	*variable**4*
Negative skew	Cube	*variable**3*
Negative skew	Square	*variable**2*
Positive skew	Square Root	*SQRT(variable)*
Positive skew	Cube Root	*Variable**(1/3)*
Positive skew	Natural Logarithm	*Ln(variable)*
Positive skew	Base 10 Logarithm	*LG10(variable)*
Positive skew	Negative Reciprocal Root	$-1/(SQRT(variable))$
Positive skew	Negative Reciprocal	$-1/(variable)$
Data are proportions	Arcsine	*ARSIN(Variable)*

---

[6] Some other less common transformations I have run across are $-1/(variable*variable)$, *EXP(variable)*, *Ln(variable)/(1−Ln(variable))*, $-1/(variable**(1/3))$, and *LG10(X−variable)* where X is the highest value of the variable plus one.

These same transformations can be tried if you encounter problems with heteroscedasticity or lack of linearity. While these transformations often work in the cases listed above, finding a transformation that makes your data normal often entails trying several different options, and checking to see which one solves the problem—in other words, good ol' trial and error. Comparing the histograms of the untransformed data and the transformed data is one way of getting a sense of whether they have helped. Is the histogram of the transformed data more bell shaped? Of course, along with visual inspection we can always consider the measures of normality such as Shapiro-Wilk to determine if the transformation has made the data more normal.

As a test case, I applied a number of transformations to the non-normal data from the *correlation.sav* data under the *EndUpVerbing* column. I then applied a number of measures of normal distribution to the resulting transformed data. The results appear in Table 3-10. The transformation column contains the name of the transformation along with the formula used in SPSS to carry out the transformation. The *p* value of the Shapiro-Wilk test for the untransformed data is .0005, showing that the distribution differs significantly from normal. The same measures were applied to the transformed data. It should be clear that when the cube root transformation is applied, the *p* value of the Shapiro-Wilk and Kolmogorov-Smirnov tests become insignificant and the skew and kurtosis numbers also move closer to falling between +1 and −1. However, the best indication that the transformation has been successful is comparing the histogram of the untransformed data (Figure 3-15) with the data transformed with the cube root (Figure 3-16).

Figure 3-15. Histogram of untransformed *EndUpVerbing* data.

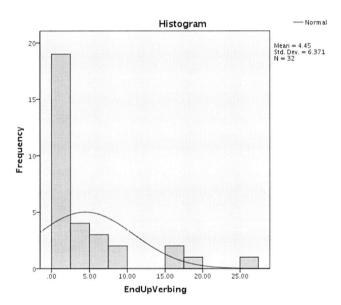

Figure 3-16. Histogram of the *EndUpVerbing* data after the cube root transformation was applied to them.

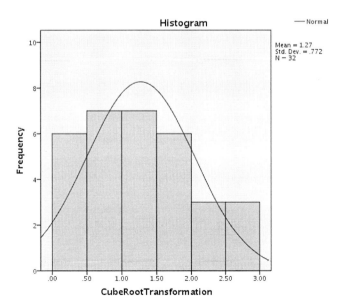

Table 3-10. Tests of normal distribution of *EndUpVerbing* and of several transformations of the data.

Transformation	Shapiro-Wilk *p*	Kolmogorov-Smirnov *p*	Skew Standard Error	Kurtosis Standard Error
Untransformed	.0005	.0005	4.806	4.605
Square Root *SQRT(variable)*	.0005	.0005	8.062	15.061
Base 10 Logarithm *LG10(variable)*	.015	.145	1.393	−1.037
Negative Reciprocal Root *−1/(SQRT(variable))*	.031	.200	.079	−1.726
Natural Logarithm *Ln(variable)*	.015	.145	1.393	−1.037
Cube Root *Variable**(1/3)*	.447	.200	1.045	−.710

What is nice about this transformation business is that, in addition to making the distribution more normal, the transformed data have also resolved the issues of heteroscedasticity and lack of linearity that we saw before. Compare the curve in the Loess line in the untransformed data in Figure 3-6 with the linear Loess line in Figure 3-17. In those same graphs notice the fan shape distribution of the data points indicative of heteroscedasticity in Figure 3-6. It has been eliminated in Figure 3-17 where the data points are about equally spread from the line in each decade. If all of the rest of the assumptions have been met, it would now be kosher to perform a Pearson correlation on the transformed data. However, the fact that the data consist of measurements from the same four corpora at different points in time means that they aren't independent, which is another requirement for a Pearson correlation. Dang it.

3.11.1 Using SPSS to transform data

Let's use the data in the *correlation.sav* file under the *EndUpVerbing* column to demonstrate how a transformation is done. The transformed values of this variable were used to calculate the measures of normality in Table 3-10.

1. Click on *Transform > Compute Variable*. In the *Function group* box choose *Arithmetic*. This fills the *Functions and Special Variables* box with transformations (Figure 3-18). Look back at Table 3-9. The formula for each of the transformations used there appear under the transformation name. For example, the formula for a base 10 logarithm is *LG10(variable)*.
2. To choose this transformation double click on *LG10* in the *Functions and Special Variables* box. This puts *LG10(?)* in the *Numeric Expression* box.
3. Click on *EndUpVerbing* then move it into the formula in the *Numeric Expression* box by clicking on the arrow. This produces *LG10(EndUpVerbing)*.
4. Give the transformed variable a new name, such as *Logarithm*, in the *Target Variable* box > OK. The transformed variables are placed in a new column in the spreadsheet entitled *Logarithm*.

Figure 3-17. Linearity in the cube root transformed data.

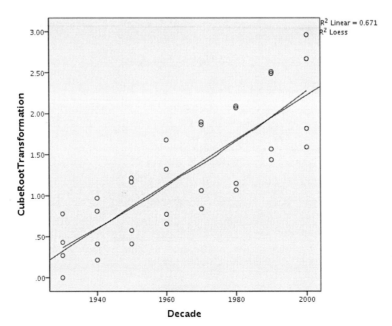

Remember that some transformations cannot be carried out on zero or negative numbers. Doing this will produce an error. Remember to add a number to each value so that none is zero or smaller. In the example above this is achieved with the modified formula *LG10(1+EndUpVerbing)*. Note also that not all transformations appear as prefabs in the *Functions and Special Variables* box. In some cases you will need to use the calculator pad under the *Numeric Expression* box to modify a formula in the box.

It should be clear how you could use scatter plots to determine whether a particular transformation of data could eliminate lack of linearity in your data. One thing to remember is that linearity results from plotting two variables on a graph. So, if transforming the data for one variable does not make the data more linear, it is possible that transformation of the other variable will. Sometimes both need to be transformed in order to achieve linearity and make the data fit the assumptions of a Pearson correlation.

Figure 3-18. The *Transform > Compute Variable* menu.

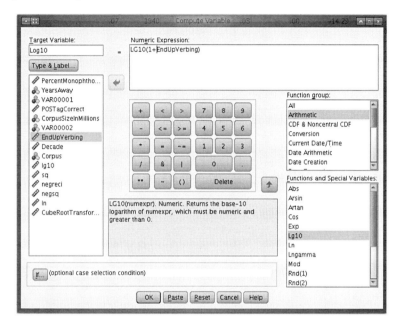

A word of caution is warranted at this point. When reporting the results of an analysis that has been done on transformed data, it is essential to explicitly state what transformation you have performed. Some researchers report the results of the analysis of both the untransformed and transformed data. What's more, any descriptive statistics that are given about the data need to be based on the untransformed values. Transformed data are very difficult to interpret. For example, a data point that represents a frequency of 19.01 instances per million words in a particular corpus is interpretable, but when that number is transformed into a cube root, it becomes 2.67 and no longer means number of instances per million words.

3.12 Recipe for a Correlation

1. Make sure both variables are continuous. If one or both are ordinal, do a Kendall's *tau b* instead.
2. Make sure the data are independent, if not use a mixed-models approach (Chapter 8).
3. Perform tests of linearity, homoscedasticity, and normal distribution.
4. Address any problems with linearity, homoscedasticity, and normal distribution by dealing with outliers, transforming the data or both.
5. Rerun the tests of linearity, homoscedasticity, and normal distribution. If these are still violated consider using a Kendall's *tau b* instead.
6. Run the Pearson correlation, and report the results in the correct format (e.g., Pearson: *r* (30) = .67, *p* < .0005, two-tailed; Kendall's *tau b*: τ (30) = .669, *p* < .0005, two-tailed).

3.13 Hands-On Exercises for Correlation

Answers are available at http://linguistics.byu.edu/faculty/eddingtond/Data_Sets/answers.pdf

3.13.1 Corpus frequency

Keller and Lapata (2003) wanted to use the web to measure the frequencies of sequences of certain nouns followed by adjectives such as *educational material*. They wondered how related the frequencies they get from the web are to the frequencies in a structured corpus such as the British National Corpus. The file *Keller&Lapata.sav* contains frequency data for a number of the adjective-noun collocations they used.

1. Check the BNC and Google frequencies for normal distribution, linearity, and homoscedasticity. What do you find?
2. Corpus frequencies are known to have non-normal distributions. Transform the BNC and Google data using a base 10 logarithm (*LG10*) and recheck for normality, homoscedasticity, and linearity. Does this take care of issues with linearity, homoscedasticity, and normality for both the BNC and Google frequencies?
3. Given what you found, are you justified in performing a Pearson correlation on the data? If not, what's your other option?
4. Perform a correlation analysis using the correct statistical procedure. Give the results of the analysis in standard format. Interpret the results in prose.

3.13.2 Sonority

The data in the file *Parker.sav* come from a study by Parker (2008). Many linguists suggest that speech sounds can be categorized according to how sonorous they are. According to the sonority scale, stops are the least sonorous sounds, and vowels the most. Sonority has been criticized because it does not seem to relate to any phonetically measurable property. However, Parker hypothesizes that sonority is related to volume (more or less) where vowels are the loudest and stops are the softest, and all other sounds fall between these two extremes. He uses the most-open vowel /ɑ/ as a baseline for his measurements and subtracts the measurements of volume for all other sounds from the volume of /ɑ/. That is why all of the numbers in the column *Mean sound level value relative to sound level of /ɑ/* are negative. His goal is to compare his measures of volume for each class of sounds (laterals, glides, affricates, etc.) to the sonority scale. How related are the two? The *Sonority Scale Ranking* column contains the rankings of the sounds by sonority from lowest to highest.

1. What kind of data are the numbers that appear in the *Sonority Scale Ranking* column?
2. What kind of data are the numbers in the *Mean sound level value relative to sound level of /ɑ/* column?
3. What does this tell you about the kind of correlation to perform?
4. Perform a correlation analysis using the correct statistical procedure. Give the results of the analysis in standard format. Interpret the results in prose.

CHAPTER FOUR

CHI-SQUARE (χ^2)

Question answered (goodness of fit χ^2): Is the actual distribution of items into categories different from what you could get by chance?
Only one independent variable is considered, which is a count of categorical data.

Question answered (test of independence χ^2): Do the observed counts show an interaction between two or more independent variables, which would mean that they are related to each other?
Dependent variable: Counts of categorical data
Independent variable: Categorical data

CHI-SQUARE (pronounced [k^{h}aɪ] square) can be used to answer questions such as the following:
1. Is synesthesia real as it relates to vowels and colors? In other words, do people match the colors yellow, red, and blue to the vowels [i], [ɑ], and [u] in a particular pattern (e.g., [ɑ] is red)?
2. In what register (spoken, academic, or newspaper) is *turn the Noun on* versus *turn on the Noun* more common?

4.1 Goodness of Fit Chi-Square

Perhaps the best way to illustrate the idea behind chi-square is with data from an old experiment of mine (Eddington 2001). Consider the words *coffee* and *caffeine*. They have similar spelling and pronunciation, and are also related by association. I wondered if they are so closely related that the mention of *coffee* could subconsciously trigger an association with *caffeine* as well. If so, one piece of evidence of this is that the vowel [æ] in *caffeine* could be used in creating a new word that is related to *coffee* even when the word *caffeine* is not explicitly mentioned. I tested this by presenting the following sentence to participants that contained the new word *c__ffify*.

Jill loves the taste of coffee; if she could, she would c__ffify everything so it tasted like coffee.

The participants also heard three possible pronunciations of the new word *c__ffify*, each with a different vowel, and then they chose which of the three sounded best to them. Counts of the three responses appear in Table 4-1.

Table 4-1. Results of *coffee/caffeine* study.

Response Choices	Vowel in Response Choice	# of Observed Responses	# of Expected Responses
c[ʌ]ffify	Vowel not found in *coffee* or *caffeine*	70	123
c[ɑ]ffify	Vowel found in *coffee*	113	123
c[æ]ffify	Vowel found in *caffeine*	186	123

These data illustrate a goodness of fit chi-square because there is only one variable—choice of vowel. There were 369 total responses, and you would expect those 369 responses to be about equally distributed among the three response options if their distribution were random. In other words, you would expect 123 responses to each of the three possibilities. The question a goodness of fit chi-square answers is whether the number of observed responses to each of the three possible pronunciations (70, 113, 186) differs significantly from the expected responses (123, 123, 123). Eyeballing the differences between observed and expected responses shows that the responses with the [æ] vowel (as in *caffeine*) occur more often than expected, but the responses with the [ʌ] and [ɑ] vowels were given less often than predicted. However, is the difference significant and how strong is the effect?

A chi-square analysis shows that there are differences—which should elicit shouts of elation if you are the researcher. Chi-square produces two numbers, a χ^2 value and a p value. The data we are considering yield a χ^2 of 55.92 and a p value of .0005. The small p value indicates that the chances of getting the 70, 113, 186 distribution by chance (e.g., having a chimp randomly throw 369 banana peels into one of three boxes), when you assume that there should be no difference, is extremely unlikely, so it must be due to something else besides chance.

4.1.1 Standardized residuals and effect size in a goodness of fit chi-square

The fact that the analysis is significant just means there are differences in the data, but it doesn't specify which observed numbers differ from their expected values significantly. This is easily derived from the output of the analysis in Table 4-2. The numbers in the residual column are just the observed minus the expected values, so it's a simple thing to calculate the STANDARDIZED RESIDUALS using this formula:

$$Standardized\ Residual\ for\ one\ cell = \frac{Residual}{\sqrt{Expected}}$$

$$Standardized\ Residual\ for\ c\text{\textasciicircum}ffify = \frac{-53}{\sqrt{123}} = \frac{-53}{11.09} = -4.77$$

$$Standardized\ Residual\ for\ cahffify = \frac{-10}{\sqrt{123}} = \frac{-10}{11.09} = -0.90$$

$$Standardized\ Residual\ for\ caeffify = \frac{63}{\sqrt{123}} = \frac{63}{11.09} = 5.68$$

Now that we've got the standardized residuals, we can assess the significance of the differences between the observed and expected values of each of the three possible test choices. A standardized residual that is 1.96 or higher or −1.96 or lower is significant at $p < .05$, while those that are higher than 2.58 or lower than −2.58 are significant at $p < .01$ (Sheskin 2003:226–227).

In this case, it appears that people did not choose the [ɑ] vowel from *coffee* in the new word *c__ffify* more than at a chance level since the standard residual is −0.90. This is odd since that was the vowel in *coffee* that appeared in the explicit definition of the new word they were given. However, the [æ] vowel does appear in the answers more than chance would have it, yet the word *caffeine* was not used in the definition of the word *c__ffify*. This high number of [æ] responses is purportedly because *coffee* and *caffeine* are so closely related in people's heads that hearing one activates the other. In this case, the choice of the [æ] of *caffeine* is thought to be evidence of that relationship. Notice that the [ʌ] vowel was chosen significantly less often than predicted ($SD = -4.77$). This would be expected since there don't appear to be words with that vowel that are closely related to *coffee*.

At this point we know that there are differences and we know which ones are significant, but one crucial bit of information that is missing is a measure of effect size that will tell us how strong the effect that we've found is. This is where Cramer's V comes in handy. It requires a bit of hand calculation since SPSS doesn't give it to you for a goodness of fit chi-square. Never fear though, SPSS does give you all the numbers you need to plug into the formula (Table 4-2): chi-square, total number of observations, and the degrees of freedom.

$$Cramer's\ V = \sqrt{\frac{2}{Total + df}}$$

$$Cramer's\ V = \sqrt{\frac{55.919}{369 + 2}} = .388$$

Cramer's V ranges from 0 to 1. A weak effect is often considered to be from .1 to .2, a moderate effect is from .2 to .4, a strong effect is from .4 to .6, and a very strong effect is over .6 (Rea & Parker 1992). Remember that these are not set-in-stone cutoff points but rough estimates. The .388 we got here indicates a moderate effect of vowel preferences. Remember that this is something that you can't get from simply inspecting the *p* value.

4.1.2 Reporting the results of a goodness of fit chi-square

Reporting the results of a chi-square analysis entails giving a few pieces of information. First, show the overall significance and effect size of the analysis by providing the χ^2 value, the *p* value, the degrees of freedom, and the Cramer's *V*. In this case, $\chi^2(2) = 55.92$, $p < .0005$, Cramer's $V = .388$. I would also give the standardized residuals of each cell along with an explanation of what they tell you. The *2* in parentheses following χ^2 indicates the degrees of freedom. Here it tells you how many cells the table has. For a chi-square, it is one less than the number values the variable has ($3 - 1 = 2$, see Table 4-2).

Table 4-2. SPSS goodness of fit chi-square output for the *coffee/caffeine* study.

Vowel				Test Statistics	
	Observed N	Expected N	Residual		Vowel
c^ffify	70	123.0	−53.0	**Chi-Square**	55.919
cahffify	113	123.0	−10.0	*df*	2
caeffify	186	123.0	63.0	**Asymp. Sig.**	.000
Total	369				

4.1.3 Using SPSS to calculate a goodness of fit chi-square

The analyses in this chapter come from the file *ChiSquare.sav.* In that file, the columns *Vowel* and *VowelCount* are the data for the *coffee/caffeine* experiment, while the columns *Corpus*, *Answer*, and *CorpusCount* are for the *sneaked/snuck* study, which is a chi-square test of independence that we'll see soon.

Even though we are dealing with categorical data, SPSS requires us to use numbers rather than words in the *Data View* spreadsheet page to specify categories such as *Vowel* (*c^ffify*, *cahffify*, *caeffify*) and *Answer* (*sneaked* or *snuck*). These numbers are given names on the *Variable View* sheet. Click on the *Variable View* tab on the bottom left of the *Data Editor* sheet, and you will notice in the *Names* column that all the variables are specified as numeric in the *Type* column (Figure 4-1).

Figure 4-1. Variable view of chi-square data.

However, what those numbers mean is specified in the *Values* column (e.g., 1 = *c^ffify* and 2 = *cahffify*). Clicking on a cell under the *Values* column brings up the dialog box in which the numeric values may be given names (Figure 4-2). The *Measure* column is where we specify whether a variable is categorical or continuous. Continuous variables are called *Scale* here.

Figure 4-2. Value labels dialog box.

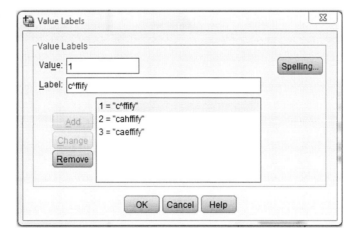

To analyze the *coffee/caffeine* data:

1. Specify the dependent variable by clicking on *Data > Weight Cases.*
2. Click on *Weight Cases by* and then on the *VowelCount* variable in the left-hand window.
3. Click on the arrow to move it to the box under *Frequency Variable > OK* (Figure 4-3).
4. Carry out the goodness of fit chi-square by clicking on *Analyze > Nonparametric Tests > Legacy Dialogs > Chi Square* (Figure 4-4).
5. Move *Vowel* to *Test Variable List* by clicking on *Vowel* and then on the arrow between the boxes > *OK* (Figure 4-5).

SPSS produces the data in Table 4-2. (Disregard the error about the weight value if you get one. SPSS just doesn't like the fact that the data columns in the spreadsheet don't have equal numbers of rows.)

Figure 4-3. *Weight Cases* dialog box.

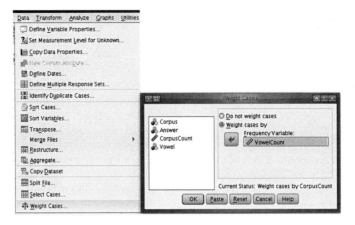

Figure 4-4. Finding the chi-square menu.

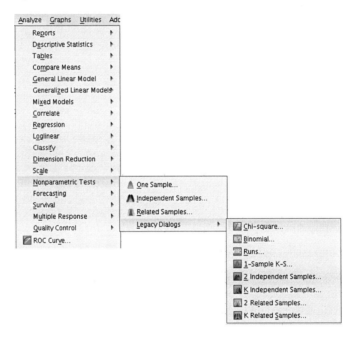

Figure 4-5. Chi-square dialog box.

4.2 Chi-Square Test of Independence

The above example is an instance of using a goodness of fit chi-square to analyze data with a single variable. It is also possible to analyze data with more than one independent variable using a chi-square test of independence. Here we'll consider a chi-square test of independence in which the independent variables are the language variety (American or British) and the past tense of *sneak* (*sneaked* or *snuck*). The research question is whether the two variables are dependent on each other. In other words, is there any effect of the variety of English on the use of *snuck* versus *sneaked*. If there is an influence, then they are dependent on each other; if not, then they are independent. The specific research question is whether *snuck*, the irregular past tense of *sneak*, is an Americanism. The data in Table 4-3 come from the British National Corpus (BNC) and the Corpus of Contemporary American English (COCA).[1]

Table 4-3. Frequencies of *sneaked* and *snuck* in COCA and the BNC.

	sneaked	*snuck*
COCA	869	896
BNC	125	10

As you can see, there are quite a few more cases of both variants of the past tense of *sneak* in COCA. This is not surprising since COCA is about four and a half times larger than the BNC. However, there is no need to compensate for the size difference between the corpora since we are testing whether the proportions of the two past tense forms are different in COCA and the BNC.

The chi-square on these data comes out significant ($\chi^2(2) = 94.50$, $p < .0005$), meaning that the two variables are not independent. But what exactly is significant? To answer this, it is important to compare the observed scores with the expected scores that the program calculates. It should be clear that the expected scores in a two-dimensional table like this are not calculated by dividing the total number of responses ($869 + 896 + 125 + 10 = 1900$) by the number of cells (4). Instead, the expected values here are what are expected if corpus and past tense type are truly independent of each other. I will forgo explaining exactly how the calculations are made. Let the computer do it for you.

In Table 4-4, boldface numbers indicate observed counts that are larger than expected counts. Regular fonts, on the other hand, show counts that are smaller than expected. One way of viewing this is as an interaction between past-tense type and speech variety such that *sneaked* appears more often than expected in British English and *snuck* more often than expected in American English.

4.2.1 Effect size and standardized residuals in a chi-square test of independence

A chi-square test of independence answers these questions: Do the observed counts show an interaction between the two independent variables? Are the variables related to each other or are they independent? The results of our chi-square are significant, but that fact doesn't give any sense of which individual words are significant nor the degree to which the uses of *sneaked* and *snuck* are related to British or American English. This is a question that Cramer's *V* can answer. As we saw above, it measures strength of relationship on a 0-to-1 scale: 0 indicates no relationship, and numbers close to 1 indicate an extremely strong one. The nice thing is that SPSS gives the Cramer's *V* to you, with no calculations on your part. In the case of *sneaked* and *snuck*, the Cramer's *V* is fairly weak at .223 (see Table 4-6), so

---

[1] See http://corpus.byu.edu.

the relationship between the different past-tense forms and the variety of English is not very strong, regardless of the fact that it is significant.

Determining which cells account for most of the significance of the chi-square is a matter of looking at the standard residual for each cell in Table 4-5, which SPSS again calculates for you. You'll recall that observations with standardized residuals that are 1.96 or higher or −1.96 or lower fit this bill at the .05 level, while the more stringent +/−2.58 corresponds with the .01 level of significance. As far as British usage is concerned, *sneaked* appears significantly more than expected and *snuck*, significantly less than expected, judging by their standardized residuals (6.5 and −6.8; see Table 4-5). However, the standardized residuals from the American data don't reach significance. This suggests that Americans don't use *snuck* significantly more than *sneaked* (standardized residuals are −1.8 and 1.9) and that the overall results of the chi-square are principally due to the differences between the two in British English.

4.2.2 Reporting the results of a chi-square test of independence

The main effect of the *sneaked/snuck* study could be reported as follows: $\chi^2 (2) = 94.50$, $p < .0005$, Cramer's V = .223. A discussion of what the standardized residuals say about the data is also in order.

Table 4-4. Observed and expected frequencies of *sneaked* and *snuck* in COCA and the BNC.

	Observed		Expected	
	sneaked	*snuck*	*sneaked*	*snuck*
COCA	869	**896**	923.4	**841.6**
BNC	**125**	10	70.6	64.4

4.2.3 Using SPSS to calculate a chi-square test of independence

1. Specify the dependent variable by clicking on *Data > Weight Cases*. Click on *Weight Cases by* and then on the *CorpusCount* variable in the left-hand window.
2. Click on the arrow to move it to the box under *Frequency Variable > OK*.
3. Carry out the chi-square by clicking on *Analyze > Descriptive Statistics > Crosstabs*.
4. Move *Corpus* into *Row(s)* and *Answer* into *Column(s)*.
5. Click on *Cells*, check *Observed, Expected, Standardized > Continue* (Figure 4-6).
6. Click on *Statistics*, choose *Chi-square* and *Phi and Cramer's V > Continue > OK* (Figure 4-7). SPSS generates the data in Tables 4-5, 4.6, and 4.7:

Figure 4-6. *Crosstabs* dialog box.

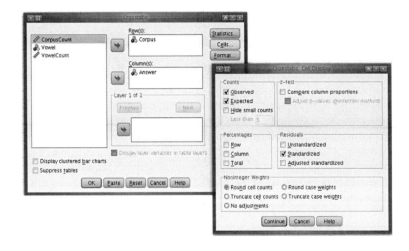

Figure 4-7. *Crosstabs Statistics* dialog box.

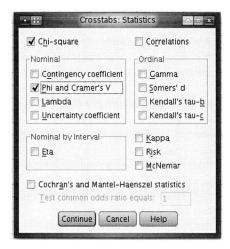

Table 4-5. SPSS Table of observed and expected frequencies for the *sneaked/snuck* study.

Corpus * Answer Cross tabulation			Answer		Total
			sneaked	*snuck*	
Corpus	BNC	Count	125	10	135
		Expected Count	70.6	64.4	135.0
		Std. Residual	6.5	−6.8	
	COCA	Count	869	896	1765
		Expected Count	923.4	841.6	1765.0
		Std. Residual	−1.8	1.9	
Total		Count	994	906	1900
		Expected Count	994.0	906.0	1900.0

Table 4-6. SPSS chi-square output for the *sneaked/snuck* study.

Chi-Square Tests	Value	df	Asymp. Sig. (2-sided)	Exact Sig. (2-sided)	Exact Sig. (1-sided)
Pearson χ^2	94.503[a]	1	.000		
Continuity Correct.[b]	92.773	1	.000		
Likelihood Ratio	112.191	1	.000		
Fisher's Exact Test				.000	.000
Linear-by-Linear Assoc.	94.453	1	.000		
N of Valid Cases	1900				

a. 0 cells (0.0%) have expected count fewer than 5. The minimum expected count is 64.37.
b. Computed only for a 2 × 2 Table

Table 4-7. SPSS Chi-square measures of effect size for the *sneaked/snuck* study.

Symmetric Measures		Value	Approx. Sig.
Nominal by Nominal	Phi	.223	.000
	Cramer's *V*	.223	.000
N of Valid Cases		1900	

4.3 Assumptions of Chi-Square

Since chi-square is not a parametric statistic, the data do not need to follow a normal distribution. However, the observations must be independent of each other. In an experiment, this would mean that one response should not be related to another response. In the *sneaked/snuck* study, I interpret this to mean that the data can only come from one corpus, not both. Studies that test people at two different points in time shouldn't be analyzed with chi-square because they would violate independence. Their earlier responses are highly related to their later ones. The numbers in a chi-square analysis must also be whole-number counts, never percentages or proportions, or you will have your hand slapped with a ruler because if you use anything other than whole numbers, the results are garbage. The problem with using percentages or proportions is that 4/5 is .2 and so is 400/500. You lose the fact that there is more data in one case when you convert them to proportions. Lastly, in a 2 × 2 chi-square the expected value in each cell must be at least five. When the test involves a table larger than 2 × 2 no more than 20% of the cells may have cells with expected values under five.

But wait, what if the expected values don't meet this assumption? Look back at the bottom of Table 4-6. For that particular chi-square, it indicates that *0 cells (0.0%) have expected count fewer than 5*, so we are safe using chi-square. However, if the assumption wasn't met we could use a Fisher's exact test instead. The *p* value for the Fisher's test appears in Table 4-6 and has a *p* value of .000 (read .0005). Note that SPSS does not give the Fisher's test a value or a number of degrees of freedom, just a *p* value. Treat one-sided vs. two-sided in the same way as one-tailed and two-tailed (see section 3.5).

4.4 Recipe for a Chi-Square

1. Make sure the data are counts of categorical data and not percentages or proportions. (A t-test or an ANOVA would be appropriate for percentages or proportions.)
2. Make sure the data are independent.
3. Use a goodness of fit chi-square if there is only one independent variable and a chi-square test of independence if there are two or more independent variables.
4. Run the chi-square and check to see if it meets the assumption about expected counts under five. If that assumption isn't met, give the *p* value from the Fisher's exact test and the Cramer's *V*; otherwise, report the results of the chi-square in this format: $\chi^2(2) = 94.50, p < .0005$.
5. Report the values of effect size (Cramer's *V*) and the standardized residuals.
6. Describe in prose what the results of the analyses mean.

4.5 Hands-On Exercises for Chi-Square

Answers are available at http://linguistics.byu.edu/faculty/eddingtond/Data_Sets/answers.pdf

4.5.1 Judeo-Spanish sibilant voicing

At an earlier stage in its history, Spanish distinguished between /s/ and /z/ in words such as [kaza] *house* and [kasa] *hunt*. Later, [s] and [z] merged into [s], making *house* and *hunt* homophones: [kasa]. However, in Judeo-Spanish, these two phones are thought to remain distinct. But are they? To test this hypothesis, Bradley and Delforge (2006) recorded a Judeo-Spanish speaker saying 72 words that historically had [s] and another 72 that historically had [z]. They analyzed the words and categorized the pronunciations as either voiced, partially voiced, or voiceless. Their results appear in Table 4-8.

Table 4-8. Results of Bradley and Delforge's (2006) study on sibilant voicing in a Judeo-Spanish speaker.

	Historically voiceless /s/	Historically voiced /z/
# of voiceless realizations	49	2
# of partially voiced realizations	6	6
# of fully voiced realizations	17	64

1. Enter the data in Table 4-8 into SPSS. These data result in a 2 × 3 chi-square. You will need a column for number of realizations, a column for degree of voicing, and a column for the historical pronunciation. The values of the independent variables needs to be numeric, and you need to specify the meaning of the number you decide to give them as in Figure 4-2.
2. Follow the above instructions for performing a chi-square test of independence in SPSS.

3. Examine the observed counts of voiced, partially voiced, and voiceless pronunciations. Compare them with the expected counts SPSS calculates. How do they help prove or disprove Bradley and Delforge's hypothesis?
4. Are the results significant?
5. What does the Cramer's *V* statistic tell you?
6. What do the standardized residuals tell you?
7. How would you report the results of this chi-square in standard format?
8. Does this analysis meet the assumptions of chi-square?

4.5.2 /r/ to /R/ in Canadian French

Canadian French is undergoing a change from /r/ to /R/. Speakers who retain /r/ are considered traditionalist speakers, while speakers who use /R/ are early adopters. Sankoff and Blondeau (2007:571) claim that "eight of ten early adopters are female; and seven of ten traditionalists are male, a statistically significant difference."

1. Enter these data into SPSS. You'll have to extrapolate some numbers that aren't specifically given. One column contains the number of speakers, another gender, and a third pronunciation ([R] vs. [r]). The values of the independent variables needs to be numeric, and you need to specify the meaning of the number you decide to give them as in Figure 4-2.
2. What is the research question the data intend to answer?
3. Perform a chi-square. It looks significant, but what do the standardized residuals tell you?
4. Check the assumptions of chi-square. Which is not met?
5. How can you address this problem? Run the appropriate analysis.
6. Are the results significant?
7. What does Cramer's *V* tell you?
8. How would you report the results of this analysis?

CHAPTER FIVE

T-TEST

Question: Are scores from two groups significantly different from each other?
Dependent Variable: Continuous.
Independent Variable: Categorical with two values.

One of the most common types of research questions involves testing whether two groups differ from each other in some regard. For example,

- Who uses a broader range of intonational pitch? Men or women?
- Are stressed vowels longer in Argentine or Mexican Spanish?
- Do French-English bilinguals recognize French words that have English cognates faster than French monolinguals?
- Who eats more ramen noodles? College students or CEOs?

5.1 Comparing Groups with an Independent T-Test

In studies such as these, comparing the mean scores of the two groups is the beginning point of answering the question, but just because the mean score of one group is larger than the other doesn't necessarily mean that there is a statistically significant difference between the two. Here's why: the mean only tells you the middle point of the scores. It says nothing about how spread out the scores are from that middle point. Determining whether there is a true difference involves looking at the distribution of the scores in each group.

Consider the four distributions in Figure 5-1, labeled A, B, C, and D. The A distribution has a mean of 145, while B, C, and D all have the same mean of 159. The difference between B, C, and D has to do with the dispersion of the scores from the mean. Let's say that the research question asks how likely group A, with a mean of 145, and a group with a mean of 159 are to be statistically different from each other when the null hypothesis says they aren't. If the comparison is between A and B, chances are that the difference is significant. The two distributions hardly overlap. If the comparison is between A and D, on the other hand, there is so much overlap that the difference between 145 and 159 probably isn't significant.

Figure 5-1. Example distributions.[1]

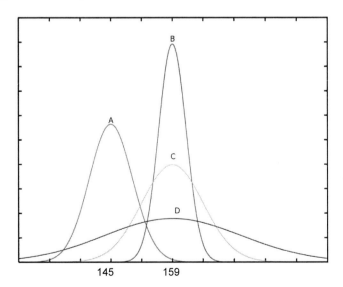

The question that remains is how do you take into consideration both the means and the distributions of the two groups? The answer is (drumroll, please) by using an independent t-test! Let's illustrate this with a simple fictitious example. The research question is whether surfers in California front the /u/ in *dude* to a greater extent than nonsurfing

---

[1] Image retrieved from http://commons.wikimedia.org/wiki/File%3ANormal_Distribution_PDF.svg.

Californians. So you go to Doheny beach and pester 100 surfers into saying *dude* into your recorder, and you manage not to get yourself kicked off the beach in the process. You also manage to get another 93 nonsurfers to say *dude* (see file *surfer_F2.sav*). Since F2 is a good measure of tongue fronting, it is used as the continuous dependent variable. The categorical independent variable is surfer versus nonsurfer.

The mean F2 for surfers is 1811.73, and for nonsurfers, it is lower, at 1702.62. The boxplot in Figure 5-2 shows the distribution of the scores. Since higher F2 values indicate a more fronted position for the tongue, it looks like surfers do front more, but would you get the same results if you tested another group of surfers? A t-test produces numbers that help us answer that (Table 5-1). The *t* value is the raw outcome of a t-test that can't be interpreted alone. The degrees of freedom (*df*) is a measure of how much data the t-test is based on. For a t-test, the *df* is the number of scores minus two for the kind of data we are looking at. We have 193 measurements of F2, so the *df* is 191. The mean difference between the surfers' and nonsurfers' F2s is 109.109 Hz. The low *p* value of .0005 lets us know that we can reject the null hypothesis and assume that getting the difference we got between the surfers and nonsurfers is highly unlikely if the null hypothesis held true.

Figure 5-2. Boxplot of distribution of surfer and nonsurfer F2 measurements.

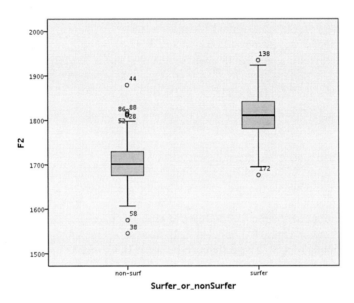

Table 5-1. Outcome of the t-test for the F2 differences between surfers and nonsurfers.

t	14.924
df	191
p	.0005
Mean difference	109.109

5.1.1 Calculating effect size

Getting a significant outcome doesn't tell us anything about the magnitude of the effect of surfing on vowel fronting. We need a measure of effect size, and for an independent t-test, a Cohen's *d* comes to the rescue. To calculate it, you just need two pieces of information, the *t* value and the *df*, which you can get from Table 5-1 or from the SPSS output in Table 5-3. This is the formula:

$$Cohen's\ d = \frac{2(t)}{\sqrt{degrees\ of\ freedom}} = \frac{2(14.924)}{\sqrt{191}} = \frac{29.848}{13.820} = 2.159$$

The values for Cohen's *d* range from +∞ to −∞. Values around +/− .2 indicate a small effect size, values around +/− .5 indicate a medium effect size, and those at +/− .8 or that are more extreme indicate a large effect size (Cohen 1988). It should go without saying that the effect of surfing on fronting the /u/ in *dude* is extremely large in our toy data set. One final thing to inspect is the confidence intervals (CI) of the differences in surfer and nonsurfer means (Table 5-3). They have only a 28.842 hertz range (lower: 94.688; upper: 123.530), which tells us that the mean difference between the two groups we measured is pretty close to the real mean we'd find if we measured all the surfers and nonsurfers on Doheny beach.

5.1.2 How to report the results of an independent t-test

Reporting the results of this study could be done in this way:

We observed that surfers had an F2 that was on average 109 Hz higher than nonsurfers. A t-test revealed that this difference was statistically significant (t (191) 14.924, $p < .0005$, 95% CI [94.688, 123.530]). Additionally, the effect size was quite large (Cohen's $d = 2.159$). Therefore, it appears that surfers have a much more fronted /u/ in *dude* than nonsurfers. The data used for the analysis were normally distributed and homoscedastic.

We'll look at the assumptions of t-tests below.

5.1.3 Using SPSS to perform an independent t-test

Setting up the data

1. Open the *surfer_F2.sav* file. Notice that the categorical variable for *surfer* or *nonsurfer* is given as the numbers 1 and 0 rather than as a name such as *surfer* or *nonsurfer*, or *S* or *N*.
2. Click on the *Variable View* tab at the bottom of the window. In order to treat those numbers as the categorical data they really are, make sure that the variable is specified as *String* by selecting the *String* entry under the *Type* column of the row where the variable *Surfer_or_nonSurfer* appears. This means that the variable is not to be treated as a real number. The entry under the *Measure* column also needs to read *Nominal*.
3. In order to specify what 1 and 0 mean, click on the *Values* column where it intersects with the S*urfer_or_nonSurfer* row. The *Value labels dialog box* will open.
4. Put *1* in the *Value* box if it is not there already and *surfer* in the *Label* box > *Add*. Put *0* in the *Value* box if it is not there already and *nonSurfer* in the *Label* box > *Add* > *OK*.

Running the analysis

1. Click on *Analyze > Compare Means > Independent-Sample t-test*. Click on *F2* and move it to the *Test Variable(s)* box by clicking on the arrow.
2. Move the *Surfer_or_nonSurfer* variable into the *Grouping Variable* box by clicking on it and then on the arrow.
3. Click on *Define Groups* and type the variable values of *1* in the *Group 1* box and *0* in the *Group 2* box > *Continue > OK*.

SPSS produces Tables 5-2 and 5-3.

To make the boxplot of the surfers' and nonsurfers' F2 scores from Figure 5-2,
1. Click on *Graphs > Legacy Dialogs > Boxplots > Simple > Define*.
2. Move *F2* into the *Variable* box and *Surfer_or_nonSurfer* into the *Category Axis* box > *OK*.

Table 5-2. Means of F2 for surfer versus nonsurfer data.

Group Statistics					
	Surfer_or_nonSurfer	N	Mean	Std. Deviation	Std. Error Mean
F2	surfer	93	1811.73	47.969	4.974
	nonSurfer	100	1702.62	53.207	5.321

Table 5-3. T-test results of F2 for surfer versus nonsurfer data.

Levene's Test for Equality of Variances			T-test for Equality of Means					95% CID	
	F	Sig.	t	df	Sig. (2-tailed)	Mean dif.	Std. error dif.	Lower	Upper
F2 Equal variances assumed	.061	.805	14.924	191	.000	109.109	7.311	94.688	123.530
Equal variances not assumed			14.980	190.821	.000	109.109	7.284	94.742	123.476

CID = Confidence Interval of the Difference

5.1.4 The assumptions of an independent t-test

As we saw with Pearson correlations, parametric statistics require certain assumptions to be met or the results they produce may not be valid. Of course, the first assumption is that the dependent variable must be continuous and the independent must be categorical with two values. T-tests are parametric, and as a result, they require that the data in both groups approximate a normal distribution. The tests for normality described in Chapter 2 apply to t-tests as well.

If you find that the distribution is not normal, you should try transforming the data as described in that chapter. If nothing that you try yields a distribution close to normal, never fear: there are two paths to take. One is to use BOOTSTRAPPING, which I discuss at the end of this chapter. The other is to use a MANN-WHITNEY TEST, which is a nonparametric replacement for an independent t-test. Mann-Whitney is also appropriate for ordinal data.

Remember our tongue-twisting friend, homoscedasticity (Section 3.9.5)? He must be satisfied in a t-test as well but in a bit different way. The idea here is that the variances in the two groups you are testing must be similar. Luckily, figuring this out is fairly simple. Look back at the boxplot in Figure 5-2 (not at Table 5-2). The boxes and their whiskers are about equally proportioned. That suggests homoscedasticity. It is not relevant that the boxes are not at equal heights, just that they have about the same shape. Unequally proportioned boxes, on the other hand, indicate heteroscedasticity.

SPSS also gives a statistical test of homoscedasticity, which appears in the output of the surfer data in Table 5-3. It is called a LEVENE'S TEST for equality of variance. Any time you do a t-test, SPSS makes life easier for you by automatically performing this test, which you see reported in Table 5-3 with an F of .061 and a p of .805. What does this mean? Well, the Levene's test asks whether the variances between the surfers' and nonsurfers' F2s are significantly different from each other. The high p value of .805 tells us that they are not significantly different. The lack of difference is a good thing in this case because it means that the data fit the parameters for a t-test; they have roughly equal variances. In this case, reporting the t of 14.924 and the p of .0005 from the top row is warranted. But what if the Levene's test found a significant difference between the variances of the surfer and nonsurfer groups, or if the boxplots of the two had very different shapes? In that case, an independent t-test can't be relied upon. Instead, a WELCH'S T-TEST is used since it does not require equal variances. The results of the Welch's t-test appear in the row titled *equal variances not assumed* in Table 5-3.

Another assumption of an independent t-test is that the observations must be independent of each other. This means that no one should give more than one score in a group because the two scores would be correlated. It also means that if you are comparing two groups for differences, no one person should be a member of both groups. That would make their scores in one group dependent on their scores in the other group. In like manner, if you are comparing something like a noun group to an adjective group, there should be no adjectives in your noun group.

However, there are some times that you need to look at observations that are not independent. For example, if you are interested in how people vary their rate of speech when speaking with strangers versus people they know, you would want to measure the same people's speech rate under two different conditions. In like manner, if you wanted to see how quickly people respond to *walk* as a verb compared to *walk* as a noun, the reaction times to each are surely not independent. In such cases, a paired t-test is called for, as described later on in this chapter.

I have been putting a lot of emphasis on making sure that the assumptions of the analysis are met. If they are not, it opens up the possibility that your analysis may have Type I or II errors. In other words, your study may be wrong. It is a sad reality that many researchers don't even bother to check the assumptions; this is even true in psychology (Hokstra, Kiers, & Johnson 2012), where there is much more emphasis on statistics than in linguistics. I would not only urge you, with all the concern of a loving parent, to check assumptions and also to state in the summary of your statistical analysis that you did check them and what you found.

5.1.5 Performing multiple t-tests

We used a t-test to determine whether surfers front the /u/ in *dude* more than nonsurfers do. What if we also supposed that there may be differences in the degree of /u/ fronting in surfers of different ages, or surfers from Southern versus Northern California? Now we'd be testing the effect of three different independent variables on vowel fronting. It would be extremely tempting to do three t-tests on the same data with three different independent variables (surfer vs. nonsurfer, older vs. younger, Northern vs. Southern), but that is a no-no. The first problem with it is that by considering each independent variable all alone, you cannot test whether there are interactions between variables. Sometimes two independent variables work together instead of separately in how they affect the dependent variable, and such interactions are often the most interesting result of a study and are something you surely don't want to miss. What's more, when each individual independent variable is tested in isolation, it doesn't account for the influences the other variables have. You need a test that can hold the influence of all the other independent variables steady while testing for the individual effect of each independent variable, one at a time, and a t-test is not it, mate. When you want to see how multiple variables affect a dependent variable, use one of the multifactorial statistics such as Two-Way ANOVA (Chapter 6), Multiple Linear Regression (Chapter 7), Logistic Regression (Chapter 9), or a repeated measured analysis such as a Mixed-Effects Model (Chapter 8). Don't let the names scare you; these guys are your friends.

Another problem with performing multiple t-tests is that the possibility of getting erroneous outcomes becomes more likely. Remember that the minimal level of significance is that there is only a 1 in 20 chance of getting the results by chance when you are supposing the null hypothesis holds. So if you did a bunch of different t-tests with different independent variables and the same dependent variable, it is quite possible that one of those would be obtainable by chance rather than by the effect of the independent variable.

However, there are times when doing more than one t-test is unavoidable. In that case, the BONFERRONI ADJUSTMENT saves the day. It is an adjustment to the p value of the t-tests. It is done by dividing the p value you have chosen, say .05, by the number of t-tests you are doing. For example, if you are doing three t-tests on the same data with the same dependent variable and you have decided on a .05 level of significance, then .05 divided by 3 is .016. This means that each of your three t-tests must now achieve a p value of .016 rather than .05 in order for you to be able to claim statistical significance. If you choose this route, be sure to indicate that you used a Bonferroni adjustment when describing your results so you don't get slammed by the statistics police.

5.2 Using SPSS to Perform a Mann-Whitney Test

A Mann-Whitney test is appropriate if your data are not normally distributed, are skewed, or contain outliers. Instead of comparing means or medians, the test looks at whether the distribution of scores is shifted to the left or right. It is a great test to use with ordinal data. Along with a Welch's t-test, it can be used to analyze data in which there are unequal variances between the two groups. Let's skew the surfer data (not skewer the surfers) with some outliers. Add these four rows to the surfer data:

F2	Surfer_or_nonSurfer
2952	1
2973	1
2939	1
2985	1

1. Click on *Analyze > Nonparametric Tests > Legacy Dialogs > Two Independent Samples*. Place *F2* in the *Test Variable List* and *Surfer_or_nonSurfer* in the *Grouping Variable* box using the arrow. Check *Mann-Whitney U* in the *Test Type* box (Figure 5-3).
2. Click on the *Grouping Variable* box > *Define Groups* and put *0* in the *Group 1* box and *1* in the *Group 2* box > *Continue > OK.* This tells SPSS that *0* means "nonsurfer" and *1* means "surfer."

SPSS generates Tables 5-4 and 5-5. The F2 measurements have been converted into rank order scores. For example, scores of 45, 33, 21, and 12 would be converted into 4, 3, 2, and 1. The mean rank for surfers is 142.55 and for nonsurfers it is 56.76, so surfers' scores are higher at a significance of .0005. You would report this as: $U = 626$, $p = .0005$.

Figure 5-3. *Two Independent Samples dialog box.*

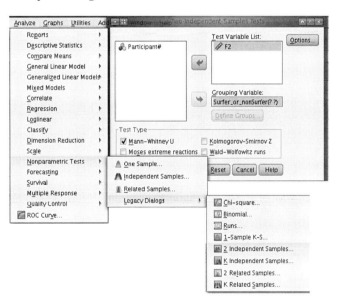

Table 5-4. Rank means of the skewed surfer data.

Ranks				
	Surfer_or_nonSurfer	N	Mean rank	Sum of ranks
F2	Nonsurfer	100	56.76	5676.00
	Surfer	97	142.55	13827.00
	Total	197		

Table 5-5. Results of the Mann-Whitney test of the skewed surfer data.

Test Statistics[a]	
	F2
Mann-Whitney U	626.000
Wilcoxon W	5676.000
Z	−10.558
Asymp. Sig. (2-tailed)	.000

a. Grouping Variable: Surfer_or_nonSurfer

5.3 Paired (or Dependent) T-Tests

The t-tests described so far are independent t-tests. They are independent because each person only contributed one F2 score to one group, either the surfer group or the nonsurfer group. What if we were interested in whether surfers keep their fronted *dude* /u/ when they get older, put down their surf boards, lose their hair, and get real jobs? We could measure them at one point in time, then wait ten years and measure them again. (Imagine trying to track them down again in ten years!) The initial measurements and those taken after ten years are not independent. A person's initial score and their score ten years later are probably more related to each other than the scores from two different individuals. We have now done a repeated-measures study on the same participants, which violates the assumption of independence required for an independent t-test. The solution to this sticky predicament is to perform a PAIRED T-TEST, which is also called a DEPENDENT T-TEST.

The data for independent and paired t-tests must be organized differently on the spreadsheet. In an independent t-test, there is a column that specifies which group the observation belongs to (see Table 5-6). This is called the LONG FORMAT.

Table 5-6. Data format for an independent t-test.

Participant #	F2 measurement	Surfer or nonsurfer
1	1713	0
2	1759	0
3	1642	0
19	1839	1
20	1873	1

For a paired t-test, on the other hand, both of the measurements for the same item (or same participant if participants are measured more than once) must be put on the same row under different columns that represent the two groups of the independent variable (Table 5-7). This is called the WIDE FORMAT.

Table 5-7. Data format for a paired t-test.

Listening Comprehension Scores		
Participant #	(Before treatment)	(After treatment)
1	264	240
2	240	232
3	198	239

A classic example of a paired t-test is a longitudinal study in which the participants are tested at two different points in time. Let's take the case of an English teacher whose L2 students complained that they understood everything that she said in class but had comprehension problems when they dealt with other English speakers. The teacher hypothesized that her students were too accustomed to her speech alone and needed to hear a wider variety of idiolects and English varieties. In order to address this issue, she first tested her students' listening comprehension, and then for three weeks, she incorporated some activities that required her students to listen to and interact with a number of speakers who spoke different varieties of English. After that treatment, she retested the students' listening comprehension. Their hypothetical scores appear in *PairedT-test.sav*.

As you can see in Tables 5-8 and 5-9, the students' scores went from a mean of 242.77 to 263.69 after the three-week treatment. This increase of 20.92 is statistically significant at $p < .005$. The confidence interval tells us that if we repeated the study with different students' scores, we'd expect the difference to be somewhere between 6 and 37 points. One other thing to notice is that if the confidence interval of the difference between means included zero (e.g., −12 to 8), that would be an indication that the difference is not significant.

Table 5-8. Means of the before and after listening comprehension scores.

Paired Samples Statistics				
	Mean	N	Std. Deviation	Std. Error Mean
BeforeScore	242.77	30	57.437	10.486
AfterScore	263.69	30	60.238	10.998

5.3.1 Calculating effect size for a paired t-test

One other important figure to have is a measure of effect size. One measure that is easy to calculate is Pearson's r—yes, the same r as in correlation. The formula is

$$Pearson's\, r = \sqrt{\frac{t^2}{t^2 + degrees\, of\, freedom}} = \sqrt{\frac{-3.072^2}{-3.072^2 + 29}} = \sqrt{\frac{9.437}{38.437}} = .495$$

Small effects hover around .1, medium effects around .3, and large effects are .5 or larger (Cohen 1988), so the effect of the dialect training on the students was fairly large, with an r of .495.

In any case, it is important to keep in mind that in a paired t-test, the scores are compared for each individual speaker who gives two different scores. It is the difference between each pair of scores that is used in the calculation. This differs from an independent t-test, in which participants give one score in only one group, and then the two groups are tested to see if the scores they contain differ significantly from each other as a whole. Individuals in one group are not directly compared to individuals in the other.

Table 5-9. Results of the paired t-test of before and after listening comprehension scores.

	Paired Differences							
			Std. Error Mean	95% CID				Sig. (2-tailed)
	Mean	Std. Dev.		Lower	Upper	t	df	
BeforeScore - AfterScore	-20.921	37.301	6.810	-34.849	-6.993	-3.072	29	.005

CID = Confidence Interval of the Difference

5.3.2 Using SPSS to perform a paired t-test

1. Open the file *PairedT-test.sav.* Click on *Analyze > Compare Means > Paired-Samples t-test.*
2. Move *BeforeScore* under *Variable 1* and *AfterScore* under *Variable 2 > OK* (Figure 5-4).

This produces the outcome in Tables 5-8 and 5-9.

Figure 5-4. *Paired t-test dialog box.*

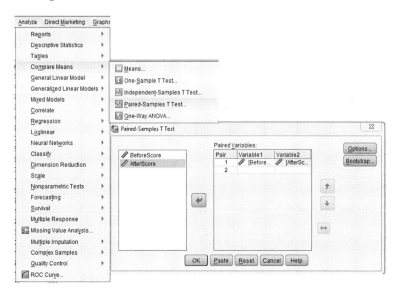

5.3.3 How to report the results of a paired t-test

These results could be reported in this way:

After the training sessions that included speech from a number of different varieties of English, the students' listening comprehension scores increased by about 20 points. A paired t-test indicates that the differences between their before and after scores were statistically significant (t (29) = −3.072, $p < .005$, 95% CI [−34.849, −6.993]). The magnitude of the effect was fairly large as well (Pearson's $r = .495$). The differences between the pairs of scores were normally distributed.

5.3.4 Assumptions of a paired t-test

Except for independence and homoscedasticity, the assumptions of a paired t-test are the same as those of an independent t-test. One is that the data must be normally distributed. For an independent t-test, the data must have a normal distribution. However, for a paired t-test, the differences between the pairs of scores must have a normal distribution. If they don't, and you have tried transforming the data in order to make them normal, you could either try bootstrapping, as I'll explain later, or use the nonparametric equivalent to the paired t-test, the WILCOXON SIGNED-RANK TEST, which is explained below. T-tests also require a continuous numeric dependent variable; ordinal data may not be used in a t-test but may be used in a Wilcoxon signed-rank test.

5.4 Using SPSS to Perform a Wilcoxon Signed-Rank Test

If you look at the histograms and boxplots of your data and see some indications of a distribution that is way out of whack, that is a sign that a Wilcoxon signed-rank test is more appropriate than a paired t-test. As an example of how this is done, let's use the listening comprehension data.

1. Open *PairedT-test.sav*. Click on *Analyze > Nonparametric Tests > Legacy Dialog > Two Related Samples* (Figure 5-5).
2. Move *BeforeScore* into the *Variable 1* box using the arrow. Move *AfterScore* into the *Variable 2* box.
3. Check *Wilcoxon* in *Test Type box > OK* (Figure 5-6).

This produces the output in Tables 5-10 and 5-11.

Figure 5-5. The *Two Related Samples* menu.

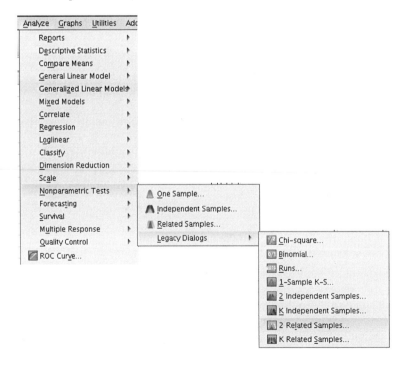

Figure 5-6. The *Two Related Samples* dialog box.

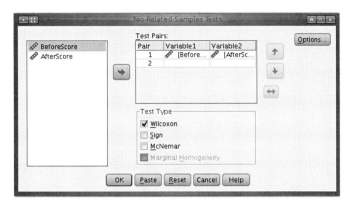

Table 5-10. Rank means of the listening comprehension data.

Ranks		N	Mean rank	Sum of ranks
AfterScore − BeforeScore	Negative ranks	8[a]	12.13	97.00
	Positive ranks	22[b]	16.73	368.00
	Ties	0[c]		
	Total	30		

a. AfterScore < BeforeScore
b. AfterScore > BeforeScore
c. AfterScore = BeforeScore

Table 5-11. The results of a Wilcoxon signed-rank test of the listening comprehension data.

Test Statistics[a]	AfterScore − BeforeScore
Z	−2.787[b]
Asymp. sig. (2-tailed)	.005

a. Wilcoxon signed-ranks test
b. Based on negative ranks.

5.4.1 How to report the results of a Wilcoxon signed-rank test

Notice in Table 5-10 that for 22 of the 30 pairs of scores, the after score was larger than the before score. In eight cases, the opposite was true. These results would be reported as $Z = -2.787$, $p = .005$.

5.5 Bootstrapping a T-Test

A lot of statistical tests assume that there is a normal distribution and that there is homoscedasticity. When these assumptions are violated, the results of the test can be slightly inaccurate to outright wrong. I've already mentioned some ways of handling this, but here I want to introduce another way, called bootstrapping (see Ch. 14 in Moore & MacCabe 2006). It falls under the rubric of robust statistics because it allows you to toss the requirements of normal distribution and homoscedasticity out the window. I won't try explaining exactly how bootstrapping works, but it's pretty computationally intense, as you will see when you use it. That is why it has only recently been included in statistical programs. The reason I mention it here at the end of the chapter is that only the more recent versions of SPSS have it (version 18 and newer), and even then, it doesn't come as part of the base program but as an add-on you have to get separately. You can tell you have it because the *Bootstrap* button will show up when you run a t-test, as in Figure 5-7.

To run a bootstrapped t-test of the surfer data, you follow the same protocol as I described above, but when you get to the step depicted in Figure 5-7, click on *Bootstrap*, which will bring up the *Bootstrap dialog box* (Figure 5-8).

Figure 5-7. The *Bootstrap* button in the *T-test dialog box*.

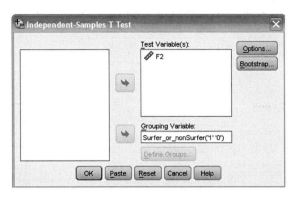

Figure 5-8. The *Bootstrap dialog box*.

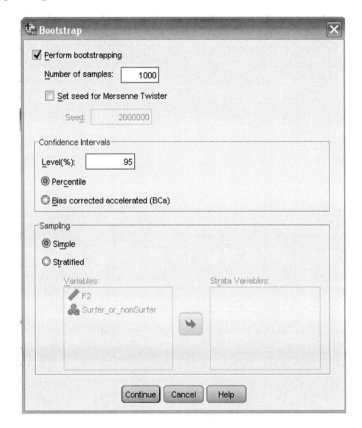

There are many different parameters to mess with here, but generally, the only thing you need to do is check *Perform bootstrapping* and make sure *Number of samples* is the default 1000 > *Continue*.

The results of the bootstrapped t-test appear in Table 5-12, and the results without bootstrapping appear back in Table 5-3. You would report the bias, standard error, significance, and 95% confidence intervals. Now, a word of caution: if you run the t-test with bootstrapping several times, the bootstrapped results will usually differ a bit. This is normal and expected. Notice that regardless of whether the variances are assumed to be equal, the bootstrapped t-test results are the same because equal or unequal variances don't matter anymore. The other numbers in the table vary a bit, but regardless of whether you bootstrap or not, the results are significant in this case. If you carry out a bootstrapped t-test, be sure to mention that in the discussion of your results.

Table 5-12. Results of the bootstrapped t-test of the surfer data.

Bootstrap for Independent Samples Test			Bootstrap[a]			95% CI	
		Mean difference	Bias	Std. error	Sig. (2-tailed)	Lower	Upper
F2	Equal variances assumed	109.109	.411	7.219	.001	94.086	123.752
	Equal variances not assumed	109.109	.411	7.219	.001	94.086	123.752

a. Unless otherwise noted, bootstrap results are based on 1000 bootstrap samples
b. CI = Confidence Interval

5.6 Recipe for an Independent T-Test

1. Make sure that your dependent variable is continuous and your independent variable is categorical with only two values. If it has more than two values, perform an ANOVA. If the dependent variable is ordinal, use a Mann-Whitney test instead. Make sure the data are in the format shown in Table 5.6.
2. Check the variances of the two groups. If they are unequal, bootstrap or use a Welch's t-test.
3. Check the distributions of the two groups. If they are non-normal, try transforming the data to make it normal, bootstrap, or use a Mann-Whitney test.
4. Report the results in the correct format (e.g., $t(9) = 2.920$, $p < .017$, 95% CI [−32.345, −12.988], Cohen's $d = .299$).

5.7 Recipe for a Paired T-Test

1. Make sure that your dependent variable is continuous and your independent is categorical with only two values. If it has more than two values, use a mixed-model approach. If the data are ordinal, use a Wilcoxon signed-rank instead. Make sure the data are in the format shown in Table 5.7.
2. Check the distributions of the two groups. If they are non-normal, try transforming the data to normalize it, do a bootstrapped paired t-test, or use a Wilcoxon signed-rank.
3. Report the results in the correct format (e.g., $t(9) = 2.920$, $p < .017$, 95% CI [−32.345, −12.988], Pearson's $r = .201$).

5.8 Hands-On Activities for T-Tests

Answers are available at http://linguistics.byu.edu/faculty/eddingtond/Data_Sets/answers.pdf

5.8.1 Word order comprehension by English speakers learning Spanish

In English, subjects usually precede the verb (SV; e.g., Bob$_S$ kicked$_V$ the ball). In Spanish, on the other hand, subjects may either precede or follow the verb (e.g., Juan$_S$ vino$_V$. Vino$_V$ Juan$_S$, "Juan came"). Tight (2012) wondered how well English speakers learning Spanish were able to comprehend Spanish sentences with VS word orders. He tested how well students who had had one, three, or five semesters of Spanish understood eight VS and eight SV sentences. The dependent variable here is how many SV and VS sentences each individual participant understood. Tight reports that the participants were much better at understanding SV sentences than VS sentences. Let's just look at the results from the students who have been studying Spanish for three semesters.

1. Download and open *Tight2012.sav.*
2. Perform a t-test. The subject numbers for students with three semesters of Spanish are in *Subject_3Sem*, and their test results are in *TotalSV_3Sem*, and *TotalVS_3Sem*. Give the results in the correct format.
3. What is the mean number of VS and SV sentences correctly understood?
4. What kind of t-test is this? How do you know?
5. Check for homoscedasticity by comparing the boxplots of the SV and VS data. What do you find?
6. Calculate the difference between the SV and VS for each subject and put it into a different column (i.e. # of SV sentences correct minus # of VS sentences correct). Check the normality of the distribution of the differences you just calculated. Is it normally distributed?
7. What can you do to take care of the heteroscedasticity and lack of normal distribution you observed?
8. Run an analysis of the data once you have taken care of the issues in # 5 and #6 and report the results in the correct format.
9. Calculate Pearson's r to check the effect size.

5.8.2 L2 contact hours during study abroad

Dewey et al. (2014) were interested in what sorts of things were related to how much students used their L2 while on a study abroad. One question they had was whether males or females spent more hours using their target language. Use the data in *Dewey_et_al.sav* to answer this question.

1. What are the mean number of hours each group spent using the L2.
2. Check the data to see if they follow the assumptions of an independent t-test (homoscedasticity, normal distribution). What do you find?
3. What can you do to address any violations of the assumptions?
4. Run the appropriate analysis and report the results in the correct format.
5. Calculate Cohen's *d* to check the effect size.

CHAPTER SIX

ANOVA (ANALYSIS OF VARIANCE)

6.1 One-Way ANOVA

Question: Are the means scores from two or more groups significantly different from each other?
Dependent variable: Continuous.
One independent variable: Categorical with two or more values.

One-way ANOVA can be used to answer questions such as the following:
1. Do voice onset times differ significantly after /p, t, k/?
2. Three teaching methods are applied in three different ESL classrooms. Which one results in higher reading comprehension scores?
3. Nonnative speakers are judged according to how fluent they are perceived to be by native listeners. How does the listeners' level of education (high school graduate, college graduate, advanced degree) affect their judgments?

You'll remember that a t-test is used to determine whether the scores or observations in one group differ significantly from another group. One-way ANOVA is kind of like a t-test on steroids because it can be used to see if two *or more* groups differ from each other. Are you impressed yet? Say you are an English teacher and you wonder if it is easier for speakers of languages that are more similar to English to learn English as a second language. You divide your students into three groups: speakers of Germanic languages, speakers of other European languages, and speakers of Asian languages. (Alright, I know that there are so many other variables that may influence the experiment. But this example gets the idea across. Okay?) You administer a test to the students and get the following means for each group: Germanic, 286; Other European, 258; and Asian, 298.

Now, you should know by now that a simple inspection of the means is not enough to let you know which group scored significantly higher. Like a t-test, ANOVA not only takes the mean of each group into consideration, but also considers how much the scores are spread out from the mean—the variance of the scores—hence the fancy name ANALYSIS OF VARIANCE.

6.1.1 The results of a one-way ANOVA

Now, let's see how our hypothetical Germanic, Other European, and Asian groups fared. The one-way ANOVA analysis of these data produces a table of the descriptive statistics, which includes the mean score for each group (Table 6-1). It also produces the statistical results of the ANOVA in Table 6-2. Focus on the *NativeLang* row, where native language is the independent variable we're interested in. There are a number of important things to look for in Table 6-2. First is the F statistic, which is analogous to t in a t-test. The second thing is the degrees of freedom. In an ANOVA, there are two different degrees of freedom, (in this case, 2 and 27), which are calculated for you. The between subjects df of 2 appears in the *NativeLang* row, and the within subjects df of 27 appears in the *Error* row.

Table 6-1. Descriptive statistics for the test scores data.

Estimates				
Dependent variable: TestScore				
			95% confidence interval	
NativeLang	Mean	Std. error	Lower bound	Upper bound
Germanic	285.690	8.874	267.482	303.899
OtherEuropean	258.202	8.874	239.993	276.410
Asian	297.994	8.874	279.785	316.202

Table 6-2. Results of the one-way ANOVA for the test scores.

Tests of Between-Subjects Effects						
Dependent variable: TestScore						
Source	Type III sum of squares	df	Mean square	F	Sig.	Partial eta^2
Corrected model	8301.412^a	2	4150.706	5.271	.012	.281
Intercept	2362569.770	1	2362569.770	3000.006	.000	.991
NativeLang	8301.412	2	4150.706	5.271	.012	.281
Error	21263.088	27	787.522			
Total	2392134.271	30				
Corrected total	29564.500	29				

a. R^2 = .281 (adjusted r^2 = .228)

The third thing to look at is the *p* value, which in this case is .012. This *p* value only tells you that there is some significant difference somewhere between the three groups of test scores, but there are two crucial pieces of information the *p* value doesn't give you. One is which of the three groups (Germanic, Other European, and Asian) differ from each other. The other is how strong the effect of native language is on the test scores. We'll tackle these one at a time.

6.1.1.1 Post hoc analysis

At this point, we know that there is a significant difference between the groups; however, we are still clueless about which of the three language groups are actually different from each other. That is what a POST HOC ANALYSIS can tell us. In a t-test there are only two groups, so when the analysis is significant, it's a no-brainer that the group with the higher mean scored significantly higher than a group with a lower mean score. On the other hand, in ANOVA, you need to run a post hoc analysis to compare each group to all of the other groups and to test whether they are significantly different. There's a smorgasbord of different post hoc analyses to choose from. I suggest using TUKEY if the number of scores in each group is the same (like they are in the data we are considering) if not, use a SCHEFFÉ test. You may have a control group that you are comparing a number of test groups to. If this is the case, a DUNNETT is your best choice.

Look at the *significance* column in Table 6-3, which displays the results of the Tukey post hoc test. When you compare each of the three groups to each of the other groups and look at the *significance* column, the only comparison that is significant is *Asian* versus *OtherEuropean*. In the *Mean difference (I − J)* column, you can see that Asians scored 39.79 points higher than members of the *Other European* group on average. Notice also that the confidence intervals that pass through zero indicate a lack of significance, too.

Now a word of caution: the post hoc analysis compares the test scores in each of the three groups to each other. Wouldn't it be tempting to just avoid ANOVA altogether and just do a bunch of t-tests to compare the three groups to each other? Don't give into this temptation. It's bad stats.

6.1.1.2 Effect size with partial eta^2

In Table 6-2, we see a *p* value of .012. The only thing that *p* value says is that there are significant differences. If it were .00002 instead, you may want to think that the smaller value means that the effect of native language on the scores is stronger. Actually, *p* values can't be used in this way. You need a true measure of effect size instead. Think back to correlations. They give a nice *r* value. When you square the *r*, you get an *r^2*, which tells you how much of the variance the independent variable has accounted for. Knowing the effect size is a very useful thing. An *r^2* of .53 is exciting, but one of .02 lets us know that we aren't accounting for very much. For ANOVA, there is a similar measure of effect size known as PARTIAL ETA^2. For these data, it is .281 (see Table 6-2), and it can be loosely interpreted in this way: values around .01 show a weak effect, those around .06, a medium effect, and values of about .14 and larger, a large effect (Cohen 1988). Here the value of .281 indicates a large effect size.

6.1.1.3 Reporting the results of a one-way ANOVA

Now we've got all the information we need to report the outcome. The main effect of native language type and effect size in terms of partial eta^2 could be summarized and reported as F (2, 27) = 5.271, p < .012, η2 = .281. The results of the post hoc analysis always need to be reported when using an ANOVA. In this case, you could state that the only significant difference is that Asians scored significantly higher than other Europeans, as shown by a Tukey post hoc test at a significance level of p = .010.

Table 6-3. Tukey post hoc tests for the test scores.

Multiple Comparisons							
Dependent variable: TestScore							
Tukey HSD							
		Mean difference (I − J)	Std. error	Sig.	95% CI		
(I) NativeLang	(J) NativeLang				Lower bound	Upper bound	
Germanic	OtherEuropean	27.49	12.550	.091	−3.63	58.61	
	Asian	−12.30	12.550	.595	−43.42	18.81	
OtherEuropean	Germanic	−27.49	12.550	.091	−58.61	3.63	
	Asian	−39.79*	12.550	.010	−70.91	−8.68	
Asian	Germanic	12.30	12.550	.595	−18.81	43.42	
	OtherEuropean	39.79*	12.550	.010	8.68	70.91	

Based on observed means.
The error term is Mean Square (Error) = 430.401.
CI = Confidence interval
* = The mean difference is significant at the 0.05 level.

6.1.2 Residuals

Before we get into the assumptions of ANOVA, I need to introduce the concept of RESIDUALS, which is sometimes shrouded in mystery and explained in cryptic terms in statistics texts. A residual is the actual score minus the predicted score. Once again, I'm going to use the water volume and water weight idea. Figure 6-1 shows you what plotting different volumes of water and their weights on a scatter plot would look like. Since the regression line represents the predicted values, all of the data points fall smack dab on the regression line, which means that the distance from the data points to the line is zero. The actual weights are exactly the same as the predicted weights. Since the distance between the actual data point and the predicted value is zero, the residuals would all be zero, too. Therefore, the volume explains 100% of the variability in the weight of the water. There is no other variable that explains the weight of the water other than the volume.

Of course, human behavior (at least for most people) is much more complex than that of water. Any measure of behavior is going to have a lot more variability, so the data points aren't all going to fall neatly on the regression line. So, there are residuals that can be measured.

Figure 6-2 shows a plot of the transformed frequency of the *EndUpVerbing* data by decade. I've drawn in lines representing the residuals for the COHA and GoogleUS corpora. All of the COHA frequencies are larger than the predicted values on the line, so those residuals are positive. On the other hand, the GoogleUS residuals are all negative because they lie below the line. What the residuals tell you is that there is some variability that is not being accounted for by time (the decade variable). Something else that we haven't accounted for has a hand in the frequency of *EndUpVerbing* expressions and is responsible for the residuals.

Now that is fine and dandy for continuous variables, which let you draw a nice regression line, but how do you calculate the residuals for a categorical variable? Let's go back to the differences in test scores between speakers of Germanic, other European, and Asian languages. The individual scores appear in Figure 6-3, where native language 1 = Germanic, 2 = Other European, and 3 = Asian. The means for these groups are 286, 258, and 298, respectively, and the means are used to calculate the residuals, so if a speaker of a Germanic language got a score of 275, then the residual of that particular score is that score minus the group mean of 286 (e.g., 275 − 286 = −11).

Figure 6-1. Scatter plot of water weight and water volume.

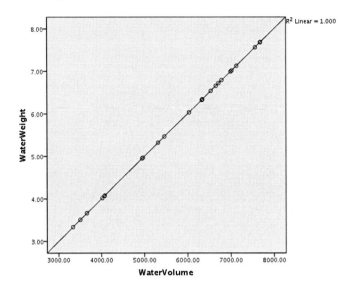

Figure 6-2. Some residuals of the *EndUpVerbing* data.

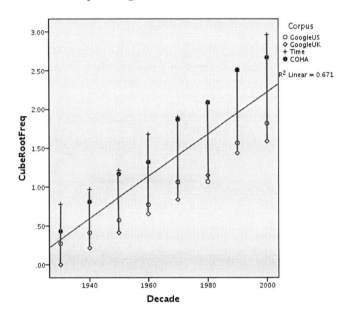

Figure 6-3. Scatter plot of scores by native language group.

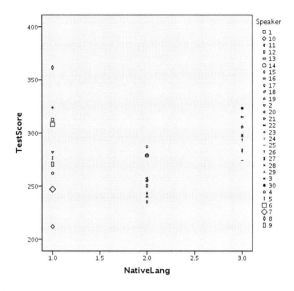

6.1.3 Assumptions of one-way ANOVA

It should not surprise you that the data that can be analyzed with an ANOVA are the same kinds that can be used with a t-test. The assumptions of both statistics are also quite similar. Of course, there must be independence between the groups, and the dependent variable must be continuous. Now, some of the assumptions don't have to do with the actual scores but with the residuals of those scores, which is why I just got through explaining what residuals are in section 6.1.2. You won't need to figure out what the residuals and the expected values are by hand. SPSS is nice enough to do that for you. If you need to review how to check a distribution for normality, go back to Chapter 3. When you follow the instructions in that chapter, SPSS will calculate and save the residuals for you in the *Statistics Data Editor* spreadsheet in a new column called *RES_1* (or *RES_2* if there is already a *RES_1* on the spreadsheet). It will also create a new column called *PRE_1* that contains the predicted values.

ANOVA assumes that residuals are distributed normally. You can check the normality of the residuals by inspecting the Q-Q plots and histograms of the residuals that SPSS puts in the newly created *RES* column. Because the independent variable is categorical in the case we're considering, the predicted values are just the group means, and the residuals are fairly normal. (Take my word for it, and we can save printing a few graphics to make the tree-huggers happy.) Residuals that are not normally distributed may be made normal by transforming the dependent variable (see Chapter 3). If doing that does not make the residuals normal, try bootstrapping the analysis (see Section 6.5). Another option you can try is using the nonparametric alternative to the one-way ANOVA test, the KRUSKAL-WALLIS test. This test is also appropriate for ordinal data. I'll explain how to perform those tests later.

Another assumption of ANOVA is that the variances of the residuals for each group need to be roughly equal, as well. (Homoscedasticity strikes again.) This process can be eyeballed by making a boxplot of the residual values by language group. (First, go to *Graphs > Legacy Dialogs > Boxplot > Simple > Define*. Then, put *RES_1* in the *Variable* box and *Native Language* in the *Category Axis* box > *OK*). When the boxes for each group are about the same size and shape, we should be ecstatic because that means that the residuals are homoscedastic. However, in this case, the boxplot—consisting of the residuals from speakers of Germanic languages—is much longer than the other two, which suggests problems. Besides a visual check, the residuals also may be tested with a Levene's test of equality of error variances. The results of this test appear in Table 6-4. The *p* value of .014 tells us that there is a significant difference in the variances between the groups. Unfortunately for us, running an ANOVA on heteroscedastic data like these can result in inaccurate outcomes, so we may not use the results reported in Tables 6-2 and 6-3, (☹). If you experience this problem, try bootstrapping the ANOVA or performing a Welch's ANOVA instead. I promise I'll get to all that soon.

As a final note, do you remember the problems that I discussed would arise if you carried out multiple t-tests on the same dependent variable data but with different independent variables? The same holds true of one-way ANOVAs. That kind of analysis is a job for a factorial ANOVA or one of the multifactorial analyses I will discuss in Chapters 7 and 8.

Table 6-4. Results of the Levene's test for the test scores.

Levene's Test of Equality of Error Variances			
F	*df*1	*df*2	Sig.
4.978	2	27	.014

6.1.4 Using SPSS to perform a one-way ANOVA

1. Open the data set *TestScores.sav*.
2. Click on *Analyze > General Linear Model > Univariate* (Figure 6-4).
3. Place *TestScore* in the *Dependent Variable* box and *NativeLang* in *Fixed Factor(s)* box.
4. Click on *Post Hoc*. The *Post Hoc* dialog box appears (Figure 6-5). In that box, move *NativeLang* to *Post Hoc Tests for* box. Check *Tukey* and *Bonferroni > Continue*.
5. Click on the *Save* button and check *Unstandardized* in the *Predicted Values* box and *Unstandardized* in the *Residuals* box > *Continue*.
6. Click on *Options*. In the *Options* box, move *NativeLang* to *Display Means for* box. Check *Compare main effects*. From the *Confidence interval adjustment* drop-down menu, choose *Bonferroni*. Check *Descriptive statistics*, *Estimates of effect size*, and *Homogeneity tests > Continue > OK* (Figure 6-6).

Figure 6-4. The *one-way ANOVA* dialog box.

Figure 6-5. The *post hoc* dialog box.

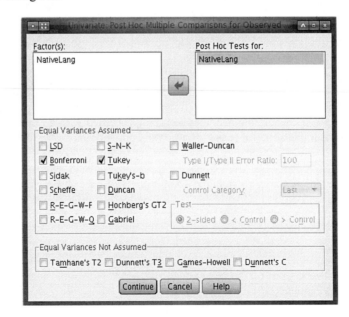

Figure 6-6. The *One-Way ANOVA Options* box.

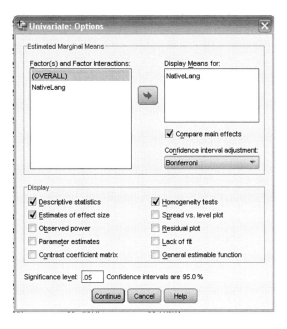

6.1.5 Using an ANOVA or t-test in studies that compare two groups

In the previous chapter, we looked at F2 differences in the word *dude* between surfers and nonsurfers. The means of the data can be summarized in a table with one row (for F2) and two columns (one for surfer and one for nonsurfer). T-tests are specifically designed for such cases, but one-way ANOVA can handle them, too. So, what is the difference between a one-way ANOVA and a t-test? Well, *t-test* starts with *T* and *ANOVA* with *A*. In other words, take your pick. Compare the results of the t-test for the surfer data and an ANOVA of the same data in Table 6-5. The two tests use different degrees of freedom and result in a different statistic (*t* or *F*). However, the important thing is that the *p* values are both indicating the same results and the effect sizes are both strong.

Table 6-5. T-test and one-way ANOVA of surfer data.

	df	*t*	*F*	*p* <	Effect size
T-test	191	14.924	–	.0005	Cohen's $d = 2.159$
ANOVA	1, 192	–	222.713	.0005	Partial eta^2 = .538

6.2 Welch's ANOVA

If you run into issues of heteroscedasticity, one solution is to use a Welch's ANOVA, which does not assume homoscedasticity. It requires running the ANOVA in a slightly different way, as described below. Because the variances of the Germanic, other European, and Asian language groups differ significantly, as the Levene's test shows (Table 6-4), a Welch's ANOVA is a much better statistic to use on them. The results for the Welch's ANOVA appear in Table 6-6.

Table 6-6. Results of the Welch's ANOVA for the test scores.

Robust Tests of Equality of Means				
TestScore				
	Statistic	*df1*	*df2*	Sig.
Welch	13.826	2	16.575	.000

6.2.1 Reporting the results of a Welch's ANOVA

The results of this Welch's ANOVA could be reported like this: F (2, 16.575) = 13.826, p < .0005. Since we have unequal variances, we must also use a different post hoc test because tests like Tukey and Scheffé are not appropriate when there is heteroscedasticity. In Figure 6-5, you will see that you can choose a number of post hoc tests, such as TAMHANE'S T2, that are designed for data with unequal variances. The results of this post hoc appear in Table 6-7. They mirror the previous post hoc analyses because they also show that Asians significantly outscored other Europeans.

Table 6-7. Tamhane's T2 post hoc analysis of the test scores.

Multiple Comparisons							
Dependent variable: TestScore							
Tamhane							
		Mean difference (I − J)	Std. error	Sig.	95% CI Lower bound	Upper bound	
(I) NativeLang	(J) NativeLang						
Germanic	OtherEuropean	27.489	14.589	.231	−12.89	67.87	
	Asian	−12.304	14.297	.792	−52.31	27.70	
OtherEuropean	Germanic	−27.489	14.589	.231	−67.87	12.89	
	Asian	−39.792*	7.433	.000	−59.40	−20.19	
Asian	Germanic	12.304	14.297	.792	−27.70	52.31	
	OtherEuropean	39.792*	7.433	.000	20.19	59.40	

*. The mean difference is significant at the 0.05 level.
CI = Confidence interval

6.2.2 Using SPSS to perform a Welch's one-way ANOVA

1. Click on *Analyze > Compare Means > One-way ANOVA*.
2. Move *TestScore* to the *Dependent List* and *NativeLang* to *Factor* box.
3. Click on *Options* button and check W*elch > Continue*.
4. Click on *Post Hoc*, check *Tamhane's T2 > Continue > OK*.

Be sure that your independent variable is coded as a number—not a string—or SPSS won't let you put it in the *Dependent List.*

6.2.3 Using SPSS to perform a Kruskal-Wallis H test

Let's assume that the test score analysis results in a non-normal distribution of the residuals, so we need to perform a Kruskal-Wallis H test on the data.

1. Open the file *TestScores.sav*. Click on *Analyze > Nonparametric Tests > Independent Samples*. Click on *Objective* tab and make sure *Automatically compare distributions across groups* is checked (Figure 6-7).
2. Choose the *Fields* tab. Move *Test Score* into the *Test Fields* box and *NativeLang* into the *Groups* box > *Run* (Figure 6-8).

Figure 6-7. Kruskall-Wallis *Objective* tab.

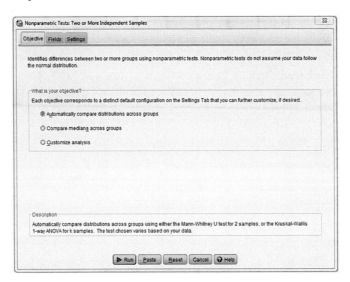

The results of the Kruskal-Wallis H test appear as in Figure 6-9. To see the results, double click on the *Hypothesis Test Summary* box (Figure 6-10). The results would be reported as H (2) = 10.315, *p* < .006, two-tailed.
To see the post hoc test:

At the bottom of the screen, below Figure 6-9, in the *View* drop-down box, choose *Pairwise Comparisons* (Figure 6-11). The post hoc results appear as in Figure 6-12.

Figure 6-8. Kruskal-Wallis *Field* tab.

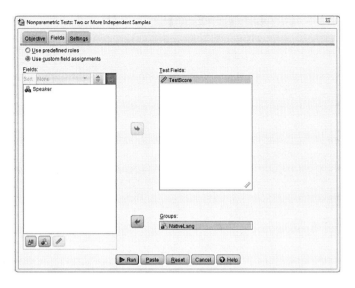

Figure 6-9. Results of the Kruskal-Wallis H test on the test score data.

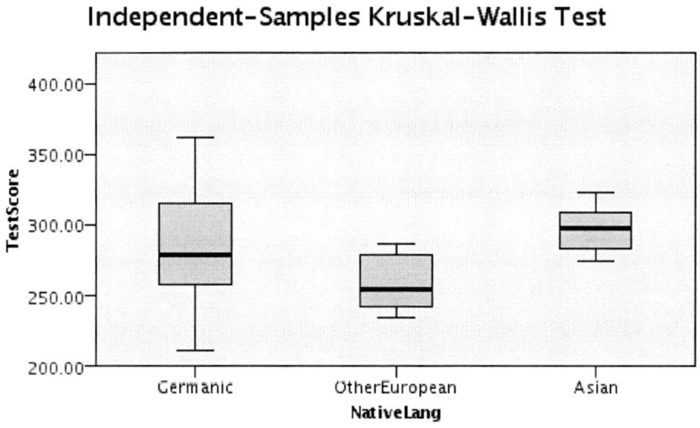

Independent-Samples Kruskal-Wallis Test

Total N	30
Test Statistic	10.315
Degrees of Freedom	2
Asymptotic Sig. (2-sided test)	.006

1. The test statistic is adjusted for ties.

Figure 6-10. *Hypothesis Test Summary* box.

Hypothesis Test Summary

	Null Hypothesis	Test	Sig.	Decision
1	The distribution of TestScore is the same across categories of NativeLang.	Independent-Samples Kruskal-Wallis Test	.006	Reject the null hypothesis.

Asymptotic significances are displayed. The significance level is .05.

Figure 6-11. *View* drop-down box.

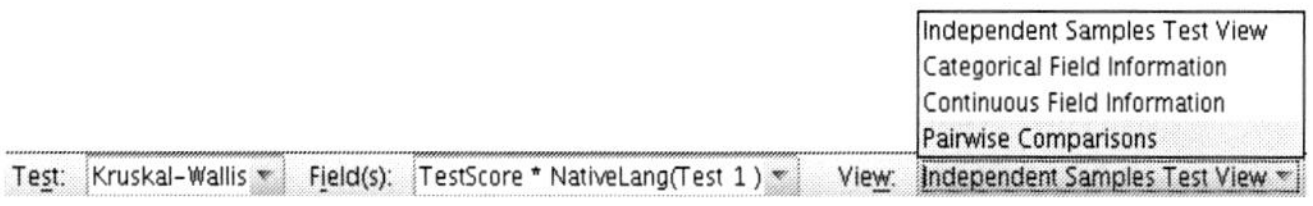

Independent Samples Test View	
Categorical Field Information	
Continuous Field Information	
Pairwise Comparisons	

Test: Kruskal-Wallis ▼   Field(s): TestScore * NativeLang(Test 1) ▼   View: Independent Samples Test View ▼

Figure 6-12. Kruskal-Wallis post hoc results.

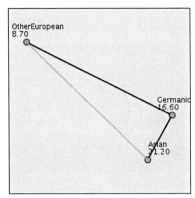

Each node shows the sample average rank of NativeLang.

Sample1-Sample2	Test Statistic	Std. Error	Std. Test Statistic	Sig.	Adj.Sig.
OtherEuropean-Germanic	7.900	3.937	2.007	.045	.134
OtherEuropean-Asian	-12.500	3.937	-3.175	.001	.004
Germanic-Asian	-4.600	3.937	-1.168	.243	.728

6.3 Factorial ANOVA

So far, most of the statistical tests we've looked at (e.g., t-test, correlation, and one-way ANOVA) only consider the effect of a single independent variable on a dependent variable; however, in linguistic studies, it is often the case that several independent variables may come into play. Factorial ANOVA is designed to handle many independent variables. It can be used to answer questions such as

1. How do gender, marital status, and native country relate to how much one speaks during casual conversation in a group setting?
    Dependent variable: Number of words spoken per minute.
    Independent variable 1: Gender (male, female).
    Independent variable 2: Marital status (married, unmarried).
    Independent variable 3: Country (Ireland, New Zealand, England, United States, Canada).

2. How do learning style and first language relate to reading comprehension abilities in English as an L2?
    Dependent variable: Score on reading comprehension test.
    Independent variable 1: Learning style (auditory or visual).
    Independent variable 2: First language (Korean, Portuguese, Arabic).

In theory, a factorial ANOVA could investigate many independent variables, but the more you add, the harder it is to interpret the results and the interactions between the variables. Remember to keep it simple, and stick to two or three at the most.

Consider the last example involving reading comprehension scores. Students of English would fit into one of the cells in Table 6-8 based on their learning style and native language. Notice that an individual's score would go into only one box, never more than one. This is important because factorial ANOVA requires the scores to be independent of each other.

Table 6-8. Cells in the 2 x 3 reading comprehension test.

	Auditory	Visual
Korean		
Portuguese		
Arabic		

Let's look at a hypothetical study that examines how preferred learning style (visual, auditory) and native language (Korean, Portuguese, Arabic) influence the students' scores on a reading comprehension test. We are actually testing a number of different hypotheses. The first two hypotheses are about the main effects of the independent variables on reading comprehension. First, does learning style affect reading comprehension scores? Second, does native language affect reading comprehension scores? The third question is about the INTERACTION EFFECT: do learning style and L1 interact with each other in some way to influence reading comprehension?

Our factorial ANOVA gives us the results in Table 6-9. Notice that *NativeLang* and *LearnStyle* are both significant at the .0005 level. However, since we are dealing with more than one independent variable, the possibility exists that there is interaction between the participants' L1 and learning style and that the interaction is significant, as well. It is important to consider all possible interactions by including them as independent variables. In this case, the interaction of *NativeLang* and *LearnStyle* is significant at .020.

Table 6-9. Factorial ANOVA results for the reading comprehension data.

Tests of Between-Subjects Effects						
Dependent Variable: TestScore						
Source	Type III sum of squares	df	Mean square	F	Sig.	Partial eta^2
Corrected model	387888.177[a]	5	77577.635	13.303	.000	.735[a]
Intercept	5476176.668	1	5476176.668	939.045	.000	.975
NativeLang	194909.431	2	97454.716	16.711	.000	.582
LearnStyle	138995.976	1	138995.976	23.835	.000	.498
NativeLang* LearnStyle	53982.770	2	26991.385	4.628	.020	.278
Error	139959.470	24	5831.645			
Total	6004024.315	30				
Corrected total	527847.647	29				

a. R^2 = .735 (adjusted R^2 = .680)

6.3.1 Interactions

The interaction between native language and learning style is significant. But what exactly is the interaction? How are the two variables related? The best way to examine the interaction is with a good ol' line chart, as shown in Figure 6-13. The two main effects are significant, so how does that show up on the line chart? The fact that auditory learners do better than visual learners is clear because the auditory scores are all higher regardless of the student's L1. In the same way, L1 is clearly significant. The Portuguese speakers outscore the Korean speakers, who outscore the Arabic speakers. This pattern holds for both the auditory and visual learners. Now, if there were no interaction, we would expect the lines to be roughly parallel, showing that the effect of native language is completely unrelated to that of learning style.

However, the lines are not parallel. This suggests that learning style and native language do not act independently on the test scores but work in tandem and are interconnected. It is true that the visual learners, regardless of L1, score lower than the auditory learners. However, the Portuguese speakers who are visual learners score much higher than visual learners who speak Korean and Arabic. The line representing the Portuguese speakers' scores is not parallel to the other lines. This is where the interaction is apparent. Native language interacts with learning style so that Arabic and Korean visual learners score far below their Portuguese-speaking counterparts, while the differences among the three groups of language speakers is not as great among the auditory learners.

Figure 6-13. Line chart of mean reading comprehension scores by language and learning style.

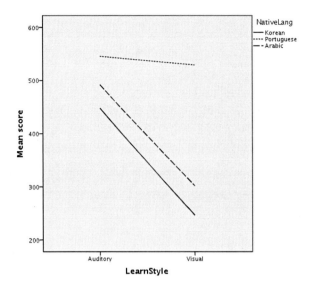

I'd like to contrast the interaction in Figure 6-13 with another hypothetical one in Figure 6-14. In that graph, notice that auditory learners still outscore visual learners. There is a main effect of learning style, but it clearly is not completely separate from L1 since auditory Portuguese speakers do worse on the test than speakers of the other languages, while visual Portuguese speakers do better. The fact that the line for the Portuguese speakers crosses the lines for the other speakers means that native language is inseparably tied to learning style and you can't really assert a main effect of L1 all by itself. So in this case, the main effect of L1 is not what is important. What *is* crucial, and what should be the focus of the results, is that the interaction between the two variables is significant.

Figure 6-14. Line chart of mean reading comprehension scores by language and learning style with crossing lines.

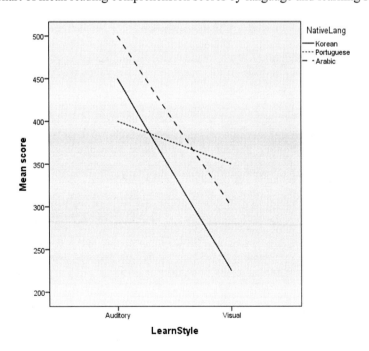

6.3.2 Reporting the results of a factorial ANOVA

So far, we have seen that learning style, native language, and the interaction between these are significant (Table 6-9). When reporting the results of a factorial ANOVA, the statistical results of all of the independent variables and all of the interactions between them need to be reported. You should also report partial eta^2 to show effect size. For these data, you could state that learning style was significant (F (1, 24) = 23.835, p < .0005, η^2 = .498),[1] as was the native language of the speaker (F (2, 24) = 16.711, p < .0005, η^2 = .582); however, there was a significant interaction

---

[1] There are multiple variables, so there are multiple η^2. If you add the partial eta^2 for all of the individual independent variables, they often total more than one. Don't freak out; this is normal.

between the two (F (2, 24) = 16.711, p < .020, η^2 = .278). (Notice that the second degrees of freedom number comes from the *Error* row in Table 6-9.) A good visual summary of the data, like the graph in Figure 6-13, does a lot to explain what the interaction is all about, so be sure to include one.

6.3.3 Post hoc analysis of a factorial ANOVA

Okay, so we have seen there are significant differences between speakers depending on their L1, their learning style, and the interaction between the two, but that doesn't gives us all the details we need to interpret the results. For example, as far as L1 is concerned, we don't know if all three of the L1s are different from each other, or if just one or two are significantly different. The results of the Tukey's post hoc analysis (Table 6-10) help us answer that question. It shows that the Portuguese speakers' scores differ significantly from Arabic and Korean speakers' scores, while the Arabic and Korean speakers' scores don't differ from each other. That is pretty obvious from the graphs, but that particular post hoc collapses the scores for both the visual and auditory learners. What we really need to be able to examine are the differences between the participants who are visual versus auditory learners and to separate these out by L1. This post hoc appears in Table 6-11.

Table 6-10. Post hoc analysis of the reading comprehension test by language.

Pairwise Comparisons						
Dependent variable: TestScore						
(I) NativeLang	(J) NativeLang	Mean difference (I − J)	Std. error	Sig.[b]	95% CI for difference[b] Lower bound	Upper bound
Korean	Portuguese	−190.325*	34.152	.000	−278.219	−102.431
	Arabic	−49.680	34.152	.476	−137.574	38.214
Portuguese	Korean	190.325*	34.152	.000	102.431	278.219
	Arabic	140.645*	34.152	.001	52.751	228.539
Arabic	Korean	49.680	34.152	.476	−38.214	137.574
	Portuguese	−140.645*	34.152	.001	−228.539	−52.751

Based on estimated marginal means.
CI = Confidence interval
*. The mean difference is significant at the .05 level.
b. Adjustment for multiple comparisons: Bonferroni.

The post hoc analysis in Table 6-11 helps us determine which differences in line height at both the visual and auditory side are significant (Figure 6-13). If you inspect the significance column, you will see that the only pairwise comparisons that are significant are that visual learners who speak Korean score an average of 283.077 points lower than visual learners who speak Portuguese. The average difference in points is given in the *Mean difference (I − J)* column. In like manner, visual learners who speak Arabic score an average of 227.582 points lower on the reading comprehension exam than Portuguese speakers who are visual learners.

Table 6-11. Post hoc analysis of the reading comprehension test by language and learning style.

Pairwise Comparisons							
Dependent Variable: TestScore							
LearnStyle	(I) NativeLang	(J) NativeLang	Mean difference (I − J)	Std. error	Sig.[b]	95% CI for difference[b] Lower bound	Upper bound
Auditory	Korean	Portuguese	−97.573	48.298	.164	−221.874	26.728
		Arabic	−43.865	48.298	1.000	−168.166	80.435
	Portuguese	Korean	97.573	48.298	.164	−26.728	221.874
		Arabic	53.708	48.298	.831	−70.593	178.008
	Arabic	Korean	43.865	48.298	1.000	−80.435	168.166
		Portuguese	−53.708	48.298	.831	−178.008	70.593
Visual	Korean	Portuguese	−283.077*	48.298	.000	−407.378	−158.777
		Arabic	−55.495	48.298	.786	−179.796	68.805
	Portuguese	Korean	283.077*	48.298	.000	158.777	407.378
		Arabic	227.582*	48.298	.000	103.281	351.883
	Arabic	Korean	55.495	48.298	.786	−68.805	179.796
		Portuguese	−227.582*	48.298	.000	−351.883	−103.281

Based on estimated marginal means
CI = Confidence interval
*. The mean difference is significant at the .05 level.
b. Adjustment for multiple comparisons: Bonferroni.

Now it is clear why the interaction between the two variables is significant, and exactly what the interaction is, is also clear. We can now speculate about the interaction. There are no significant differences between the three languages for auditory learners, but Portuguese visual learners outperform Arabic and Korean visual learners. Why? Well, Portuguese is written in the Latin alphabet, as is English, the second language they are studying. Learners who depend more on visual information, and whose native language does not use the Latin alphabet (Arabic and Korean speakers), may be at a disadvantage in comparison to Portuguese speakers who also use the Latin alphabet.

Now, there is one point I'd like to make before moving on. What if our research question involved testing the students from different countries on their reading comprehension abilities at the beginning and end of the semester (pre- and posttests)? We would need to design our table to have cells like the ones in Table 6-12. Each student would contribute two scores to the study. Be careful: now the scores in the cells are no longer independent from each other, since students' scores on the pretest are related to their posttest scores. In other words, there are repeated measures of each student in the design. The point I'm trying to make here is that studies with repeated measures may not be analyzed with the kind of factorial ANOVA we are discussing here. Chapter 8 explains how to deal with repeated measure studies; you can skip forward if you just can't contain yourself any longer.

Table 6-12. A repeated measures experimental design.

| | Reading Score | |
	Pre	Post
Korean		
Portuguese		
Arabic		

6.3.4 Using SPSS to perform a factorial ANOVA

1. Open the file *ReadingComp.sav*. Click on *Analyze > General Linear Model > Univariate*. Place *score* in the *Dependent Variable* box and *NativeLang* and *LearnStyle* in the *Fixed Factors* box (Figure 6-15).

Figure 6-15. Factorial ANOVA dialog box

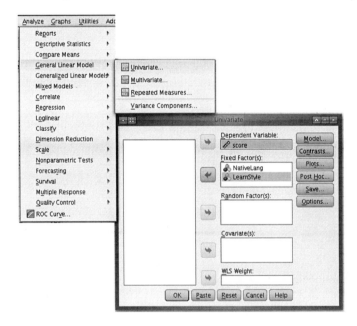

2. Click on *Post Hoc*. Move *NativeLang* to the *Post Hoc Tests for* box. (Remember that post hoc analysis is only needed for variables with three or more values. *LearnStyle* only had two values, so we don't need to include it here.)
3. Check *Tukey > Continue* (Figure 6-16). Click on *Options*, and fill in the dialog box as in Figure 6-17 > *Continue > Paste*. This will open the *Syntax Editor* window (Figure 6-18) which reads as follows:

```
DATASET ACTIVATE DataSet1.
UNIANOVA score BY NativeLang LearnStyle
    /METHOD=SSTYPE(3)
    /INTERCEPT=INCLUDE
    /POSTHOC=NativeLang(TUKEY)
    /EMMEANS=TABLES(NativeLang) COMPARE ADJ(BONFERRONI)
    /EMMEANS=TABLES(LearnStyle) COMPARE ADJ(BONFERRONI)
    /EMMEANS=TABLES(NativeLang*LearnStyle)
```

```
/PRINT=ETASQ HOMOGENEITY
/CRITERIA=ALPHA(.05)
/DESIGN=NativeLang LearnStyle NativeLang*LearnStyle.
```

Figure 6-16. *Post hoc* dialog box for factorial ANOVA.

Figure 6-17. *Options* dialog box for factorial ANOVA.

Figure 6-18. *Syntax Editor* window for factorial ANOVA.

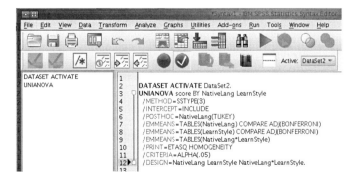

To perform post hoc analyses on the interactions between variables (Table 6-11), you must do the following by modifying the code in the *Syntax Editor* window. It's something you can't do in the menus.

1. In the *Syntax Editor* window, delete the period at the end of the line that reads
    `/DESIGN=NativeLang LearnStyle NativeLang*LearnStyle.`
2. Add this line below the last line in the *Syntax Editor* window:
    `/EMMEANS=TABLES(NativeLang*LearnStyle)COMPARE(NativeLang)adj(Bonferroni).`
3. Be sure a period follows the last line.

4. With the cursor somewhere in the code, press the run button, which is a green arrow located in the top center of the *Syntax Editor* window. Among other things, this generates Tables 6.9–6.11.

To produce the line chart in Figure 6-13,

1. Click on *Graphs > Legacy Dialogs > Line > Multiple.* Make sure option *Summaries for groups of cases* is checked > *Define.*
2. Fill out the line chart dialog box as in Figure 6-13 > *OK.* Note that when you move *score* to the *Variable* box it is renamed *Mean([score]).*
3. To change the lines from the default colors or to change them to dashed lines, double-click on the line chart in the SPSS output to bring up the *Chart Editor* window.
4. Double-click on the line in the chart's legend under *NativeLang*, and a dialog box where you can make those modifications will appear.

Figure 6-19. Line chart dialog box.

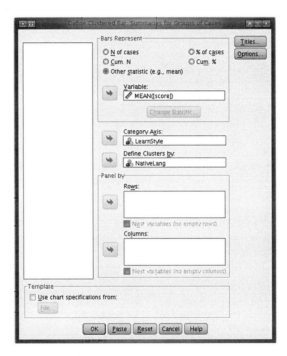

6.3.5 Assumptions of factorial ANOVA

Data analyzed in a factorial ANOVA must satisfy the same assumptions as those of a one-way ANOVA. When the variances are a little heteroscedastic, ANOVA is fairly robust if the groups are all of the same size, so you don't need to worry too much. If group sizes vary a lot, you can remedy the problem by transforming the data or using bootstrapping.[2] If the residuals are not normally distributed and cannot be made normal by transformation, and if you can't bootstrap the analysis, there is no easily implemented nonparametric equivalent of a factorial ANOVA that can deal with that. However, if bootstrapping isn't available, the next section describes one quick and dirty method for analyzing data of this sort that may arise.

6.3.6 Using SPSS to perform a nonparametric analysis in place of a factorial ANOVA

If your analysis results in residuals that cannot be made to fit a normal distribution by transforming the dependent variable, I suggest analyzing it the way I'm about to show you. But I emphasize that this is a last-ditch method that some statistically savvy people may frown upon. Combine the two independent variables into one new variable. Let's use the reading comprehension data as an example. Learning style and native language are combined as in Table 6-13. (You can probably figure out how to use the transform dialog box to do this, or do it by hand.)

---

[2] Another method for dealing with this is using weighted least squares (Pryce 2002).

Table 6-13. Combining two variables into one new variable.

NativeLang	LearnStyle	NewVariable
1	1	11
2	1	21
3	1	31
1	2	12
2	2	22
3	2	32

Now it is possible to perform a Kruskal-Wallis analysis. Follow the instructions in this chapter for carrying out a Kruskal-Wallis H test and you will see that there are significant differences (H (5) = 21.361, $p < .001$). The post hoc reveals three pairwise comparisons that are significant at the .05 level. Korean-speaking and Arabic-speaking visual learners score lower than Portuguese-speaking visual learners. We could see this from the factorial ANOVA, as well. However, Arabic-speaking visual learners were also seen to score significantly higher than Portuguese-speaking auditory learners.

This is quite surprising given the fact that it was not significant in the post hoc of the ANOVA. The means tell a different story: Arabic visual = 301.816, Portuguese auditory = 545.741. There are two reasons for this difference.

First, the data have been converted from continuous scores into ordinal scores, a change that entails a loss of important information. Second, by collapsing two variables into one, we have further muddled the data. Now you should see why it is important to use parametric tests or bootstrapping if at all possible, and only resort to this kind of analysis using collapsed variables if there is no other option. If this kind of analysis were the only option, a discussion of the actual means would be appropriate.

6.4 Repeated Measures ANOVA

With the exception of paired t-tests, one of the assumptions of all of the statistics we have looked at so far is that the data must be independent, meaning that we can't have scores or observations from one person in more than one group in the study. If the experiment is designed to contrast two types of treatment, one person may not belong to both treatment groups, nor may he or she give more than one score or observation in the same treatment group. In like manner, no test items may belong to more than one group. There are, however, many experimental designs in linguistics that entail getting measurements from the same people (or test item) more than once, or putting participants into more than one group.

Suppose that we want to know how voice onset time differs for /p, t, k/ in word-initial position. We could record participants saying a number of different words that contain each of these three phones. Notice that this means that each participant provides data for each of the three groups that are going to be contrasted statistically. In essence, each participant belongs to all three experimental groups. What's more, each participant pronounces a number of different words in each group, not just one word. There is nothing inherently wrong with this experimental design. In fact, studies of this sort are extremely common. What is important is that the data are analyzed properly. Repeated measures studies should not be examined with statistics that are not designed to handle repeated measures such as independent t-tests or ANOVAs.

It is fairly standard for most textbooks to introduce REPEATED MEASURES ANOVA at this point. But I'm going to break with tradition, not because I am naturally rebellious, but because in recent years, better methods of analyzing repeated measures have become available, mainly due to the computational power of contemporary computers, which makes performing repeated measures studies more feasible. For this reason, I will suggest that repeated measures data should be examined in a mixed-effects model (see Chapter 8).

6.5 Bootstrapping in ANOVA

When you run across residuals that are not normally distributed or are not homoscedastic, don't throw up your hands in desperation. A simple way around this problem is to use bootstrapping, which does not assume normally distributed residuals and homoscedasticity. As I mentioned before, not all versions of SPSS include this option, and it is a component that is added onto the base program, rather than an integral part of it. But, if it is available to you, take advantage of it.

Let's look at how bootstrapping affects the reading comprehension data. The first thing to notice is that when you bootstrap, the overall results of the main and interaction effects aren't affected by bootstrapping (Table 6-9). The results of bootstrapping are only evident in the pairwise comparison of the means (compare Table 6-14 and 6-15). Keep in mind that every time you run a bootstrap analysis, the results will always be a little different. This difference between the results is normal, considering the way bootstrapping does its calculations. When you compare the two tables below, you will see that the major difference is that when that data are bootstrapped, there is a significant difference between Korean and Portuguese speakers who are auditory learners, which doesn't reach significance in the unbootstrapped analysis. Which analysis is correct then? The unbootstrapped or the bootstrapped? When I checked the residuals of the unbootstrapped analysis, they were not normally distributed, and they were heteroscedastic, so the results of that analysis are not reliable. Since the bootstrapped analysis doesn't assume that the residuals are normally distributed or homoscedastic, the results it produces are reliable, so those results should be reported instead. This example shows us how an analysis with poorly distributed residuals produces incorrect results. A word to the wise: always check the assumptions!

Table 6-14. Pairwise comparisons of the reading comprehension scores without bootstrapping.

Pairwise Comparisons
Dependent variable: TestScore

LearnStyle	(I) NativeLang	(J) NativeLang	Mean difference (I − J)	Std. error	Sig.[b]	95% CI for difference[b] Lower bound	Upper bound
Auditory	Korean	Portuguese	−97.573	48.298	.164	−221.874	26.728
		Arabic	−43.865	48.298	1.000	−168.166	80.435
	Portuguese	Korean	97.573	48.298	.164	−26.728	221.874
		Arabic	53.708	48.298	.831	−70.593	178.008
	Arabic	Korean	43.865	48.298	1.000	−80.435	168.166
		Portuguese	−53.708	48.298	.831	−178.008	70.593
Visual	Korean	Portuguese	−283.077*	48.298	.000	−407.378	−158.777
		Arabic	−55.495	48.298	.786	−179.796	68.805
	Portuguese	Korean	283.077*	48.298	.000	158.777	407.378
		Arabic	227.582*	48.298	.000	103.281	351.883
	Arabic	Korean	55.495	48.298	.786	−68.805	179.796
		Portuguese	−227.582*	48.298	.000	−351.883	−103.281

Based on estimated marginal means
CI = Confidence interval
*. The mean difference is significant at the .05 level.
b. Adjustment for multiple comparisons: Bonferroni.

6.5.1 Using SPSS to perform a one-way ANOVA with bootstrapping

The only difference between carrying out a regular one-way ANOVA and one with bootstrapping is that you have to add one step to the process. Once you get to the main dialog box (Figure 6-20), if bootstrapping is available, there will be a *Bootstrap* button. Click on it to bring up the *Bootstrap* dialog box, and fill it out as in Figure 6-21. Continue with the rest of the steps of the analysis. For some reason, bootstrapping won't work if you have chosen to save anything with the *Save* button, so make sure nothing is checked in that dialog box.

Table 6-15. Pairwise comparisons of the reading comprehension scores using bootstrapping.

Pairwise Comparisons
Dependent variable: TestScore

LearnStyle	(I) NativeLang	(J) NativeLang	Mean difference (I − J)	Bootstrap Bias	Std. error	Sig.	95% CI for difference Lower bound	Upper bound
Auditory	Korean	Portuguese	−97.573	−.158	40.342	.018	−178.777	−24.088
		Arabic	−43.865	−.110	45.227	.345	−127.215	49.354
	Portuguese	Korean	97.573	.158	40.342	.018	24.088	178.777
		Arabic	53.708	.121	50.077	.296	−44.697	156.216
	Arabic	Korean	43.865	.110	45.227	.345	−49.354	127.215
		Portuguese	−53.708	−.121	50.077	.296	−156.216	44.697
Visual	Korean	Portuguese	−283.077	−.961	52.483	.001	−382.847	−179.449
		Arabic	−55.495	−.982	51.052	.287	−155.004	46.065
	Portuguese	Korean	283.077	.961	52.483	.001	179.449	382.847
		Arabic	227.582	.051	46.273	.001	137.484	318.418
	Arabic	Korean	55.495	.982	51.052	.287	−46.065	155.004
		Portuguese	−227.582	−.051	46.273	.001	−318.418	−137.484

CI = Confidence interval

Figure 6-20. Dialog box for ANOVA with *Bootstrap* button.

Figure 6-21. *Bootstrap* dialog box.

6.5.2 Using SPSS to perform a factorial ANOVA with bootstrapping

Follow the instructions for performing a factorial ANOVA, but add bootstrapping, as described in the preceding section and illustrated in Figures 6-20 and 6-21. When you click on *Paste*, the code in the *Syntax Editor* window should now read like the text below, except that you need to type the underlined line of code in by hand. In fact, the whole reason for opening the code in the *Syntax Editor* window is to add that line of code that you can't put in via the menus. That code is what produces Table 6-15.

```
BOOTSTRAP
/SAMPLING METHOD=SIMPLE
/VARIABLES TARGET=score INPUT=NativeLang LearnStyle
/CRITERIA CILEVEL=95 CITYPE=PERCENTILE  NSAMPLES=1000
/MISSING USERMISSING=EXCLUDE.
UNIANOVA score BY NativeLang LearnStyle
/METHOD=SSTYPE(3)
/INTERCEPT=INCLUDE
/POSTHOC=NativeLang(TUKEY)
/EMMEANS=TABLES(NativeLang) COMPARE ADJ(BONFERRONI)
/EMMEANS=TABLES(LearnStyle) COMPARE ADJ(BONFERRONI)
/EMMEANS=TABLES(NativeLang*LearnStyle)COMPARE(NativeLang)ADJ(Bonferroni)
/EMMEANS=TABLES(NativeLang*LearnStyle)
/PRINT=ETASQ HOMOGENEITY
/CRITERIA=ALPHA(.05)
/DESIGN=NativeLang LearnStyle NativeLang*LearnStyle.
```

Make sure that nothing is checked in the *Save* dialog box. Now highlight the entire block of code and press the green arrow to carry out the analysis. Sometimes in other applications you can get away with just clicking the green arrow if the cursor is somewhere in the code, but that doesn't work here. Remember that if you run the exact same bootstrapped ANOVA more than once, the outcomes will not be exactly identical, so your results will probably differ a little from those in Table 6-15.

6.6 Recipe for a One-Way ANOVA

1. Make sure that your dependent variable is continuous and your independent is categorical with two or more values. If the data are ordinal, use a Kruskal-Wallis instead.
2. Make sure that the data are independent, if they are not, use mixed-effects (see Chapter 8).
3. Run the ANOVA and then check the residuals to make sure their distribution is normal. If they are not normal, try transforming the dependent variable to achieve normality. If that is unsuccessful, try bootstrapping, or perform a Kruskal-Wallis test instead.
4. Check the variances of the residuals in each group for large differences. If they vary quite a bit, bootstrap, or use a Welch's ANOVA.
5. Run the ANOVA once the assumptions have been met.
6. Report the results in the correct format (e.g., $F(3, 89) = 3.921, p < .029, \eta^2 = .32$).

6.7 Recipe for a Factorial ANOVA

1. Make sure that your dependent variable is continuous and your independent variables are categorical with two or more values.
2. Make sure that the data are independent. If not, use mixed-effects (see Chapter 8).
3. Remember to include all possible interactions as independent variables.
4. Rerun the ANOVA and then check the residuals to make sure their distribution is normal. If they are not normal, try transforming the dependent variable to achieve normality, or run a bootstrapped analysis. If you don't have the bootstrap option, try combining the independent variables into a single new variable and running a Kruskal-Wallis test on those data as a last resort.
5. Check the variances of the residuals in each group. Transform the dependent variable if the residuals are very different from each other to achieve similar variances in each group, or use bootstrapping.
6. Run the ANOVA once the assumptions have been met.
7. Report the results of all independent variables and interactions in the correct format (e.g., Learning style: (F (1, 24) = 23.835, $p < .0005$, $\eta^2 = .498$), native language (F (2, 24) = 16.711, $p < .0005$, $\eta^2 = .582$), learning style by native language (F (2, 24) = 16.711, $p < .020$, $\eta^2 = .278$).

6.8 Hands-On Exercises for One-Way ANOVA

Answers are available at http://linguistics.byu.edu/faculty/eddingtond/Data_Sets/answers.pdf

6.8.1 Does language experience affect how well English speakers learning Spanish understand Verb + Subject sentences?

Once again, we'll use Tight's (2012) data in this exercise (*Tight2012.sav*). Remember that in Spanish, subjects may follow the verb (e.g., *Vino$_V$ Juan$_S$.* "Came Juan.") whereas in English, subjects usually precede the verb. Tight tested how well English speakers learning Spanish were able to comprehend Spanish sentences with Verb + Subject (VS) word orders. He wondered if having more experience with Spanish would help students understand sentences with VS word order. His participants had one, three, or five semesters of Spanish. Of the eight test sentences, the number each student understood correctly appears in the *TotalVS_all* column. The number of semesters of Spanish each student had appears in the *Num_Semesters_all* column. How did the number of semesters the students had studied influence how well they understood sentences in Spanish with VS word order?

1. Download and open *Tight2012.sav*.
2. Perform a one-way ANOVA with a Tukey's post hoc test on the data, and report the results of both in standard format.
3. The data do not meet all of the assumptions of ANOVA. Which assumptions are violated?
4. Address these violations by transforming the data. Which transformation, if any, takes care of the violations? If the transformation takes care of the violation, rerun the ANOVA using the transformed variable and compare the new results with your original ANOVA; if not, bootstrap.
5. If you can't bootstrap, perform a Kruskall-Wallis H test and post hoc test on the untransformed data. Report the results in the standard format. How do they compare with the ANOVA you performed on the transformed data or with the bootstrapped analysis?

6.8.2 Test anxiety in ESL learners

Nemati (2012) was interested in what factors are related to the test anxiety that students of English as a foreign language experience. She administered a test of anxiety level right before her students took their final English exam. (Talk about adding to the already-present stress!) The students were divided according to their majors: preuniversity, general studies, MA in literature, MA in sociology. The purpose of the study is to determine if test anxiety is related to major.

1. Open *Nemati2012.sav*.
2. Perform a one-way ANOVA and post hoc test on the data, and report the results in the standard format.
3. Summarize the results of the ANOVA and the post hoc test in prose.
4. Test the data to make sure they fit the assumptions of ANOVA. Do they?
5. If the assumptions are violated, what can you do to deal with those violations? If they are violated take appropriate steps, and run the appropriate analysis. Report the results of that analysis in the standard format.

6.9 Hands-On Exercise for Factorial ANOVA

Answers are available at http://linguistics.byu.edu/faculty/eddingtond/Data_Sets/answers.pdf

6.9.1 Vowel fronting in California English

Hall-Lew (2011) was interested in the fronting of /u/ in California English. She measured /u/ after noncoronal consonants, which she calls the KOO context. She compared the F2 in these words with the F2 of words with /i/, which is the vowel that /u/ is moving toward. The difference in F2 between the /u/ and /i/ appears in the KOO column in the file *Hall-Lew2011.sav*. That is the dependent variable. What is the effect of gender (male, female), age (young, old), and the interaction of gender and age on the fronting of /u/?

1. Perform a factorial ANOVA test on the data. (There are only two values per independent variable, so no post hoc test is needed.)
2. Test the data to make sure they fit the assumptions of ANOVA. If not, try transformations, or bootstrap and rerun the analysis.
3. Report the results in the standard format.
4. Describe the results in prose. Remember that higher F2s mean more fronting.
5. The F2 values in the table are not the F2 of a single word produced by a single speaker but the mean F2 value for a particular speaker. That is, each speaker produced a number of words with /u/ and these were averaged together. What problem does this present for the assumptions of this analysis? How could it be addressed?

CHAPTER SEVEN

MULTIPLE LINEAR REGRESSION

Question: What is the relationship between a dependent variable and several independent variables?
Dependent variable: Continuous
Independent variables: Any number of continuous or categorical variables

MULTIPLE LINEAR REGRESSION is a great tool for linguistic analysis. It allows us to see how a number of different independent variables are related to the dependent variable. Here's the good news: one of the best features of multiple linear regression is that you can use both continuous and categorical independent variables. Here's the less-than-good news: once you start using more complex data with more than one independent variable, things get a bit tricky. Interactions can occur between them. They can be correlated with each other to the point that it is impossible to tease out their individual relationships to the dependent variable. In other words, there are a lot of potential issues to deal with. When you've got complex data, you will most likely need to run several different multiple regressions before you arrive at the final one that you will report.

Multiple linear regression can be used to answer these types of questions:

- How do gender (Male or Female), number of years living in a foreign language country, native language (Spanish, Chinese, or Japanese), grade-point average, and type of motivation (extrinsic or intrinsic) relate to a person's score on the TOEFL exam?
- How is voice onset time influenced by phone (/p, t, k/), speech rate (syllables per second), gender (Male or Female), and stress (primary, secondary, or none)?

7.1 Simple Regression

Before getting into a complex multiple regression, it is a good idea to see how a simple regression with only one independent variable works. A nice linguisticy (linguistiky? linguisticky?) thing to model is the effect of word frequency on reaction time, as graphed in Figure 7-1. The regression line in Figure 7-1 is the line that most closely fits the data points and represents the values that the model predicts. The line is defined by two values: the INTERCEPT and the SLOPE.

The intercept specifies how high or low the line is. Of course, the line is not flat and is higher and lower at different points along its length, so to make things simple, you measure the intercept at the point it crosses (or intercepts) the vertical axis at zero. You can see in Figure 7-1 that when frequency is zero, the line is at about 900 milliseconds (ms) on the reaction-time axis. The results of this simple regression appear in Table 7-1, which indicates that the exact value of the intercept is 906.415. This appears in the *Constant* row under column *B*.

Figure 7-1. Reaction time and word frequency.

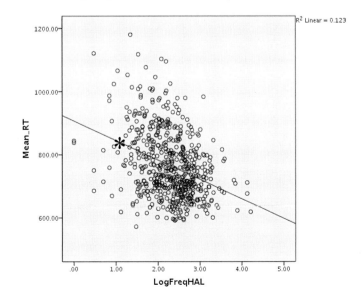

Lines that slope down have negative slopes, and lines that slope up have positive slopes. For these data, the slope is -61.588, as you can see in the *LogFreqHAL* row in Table 7-1. The slope is important because it has a very specific interpretation: for every one-unit increase in the independent variable, the dependent variable changes by -61.588, on average. In other words, for every increase of one in log-word frequency, the average of the reaction times decreases by about 62ms, so higher-frequency words generally result in lower reaction times.

One way to make sense of this is to see how these numbers work together on the graph. If you look carefully at the regression line in Figure 7-1 you'll see that I've placed an asterisks on it at a frequency of 1. If you follow the asterisk horizontally over to the vertical reaction-time axis, you'll see that it corresponds to a reaction time of about 860ms. If you look at the line about the frequency of 2, it corresponds to a reaction time of about 800ms. So, when you increase frequency by 1, the reaction time decreases by about 60ms, which is exactly what the slope (or UNSTANDARDIZED COEFFICIENT or B) of -61.588 in Table 7-1 indicates.

The regression line represents which line fits best, but because most of the data points don't fall right on it, it isn't a perfect fit to the actual data. Table 7-2 contains a measure that should be familiar to you—R square (r^2). The r^2 of .123 shows that frequency accounts for 12.3% of the variability in the reaction times. The closer to the regression line the data points fall, the higher the r^2. The fact that several data points fall far from the line means that a lot of the variation is due to something other than word frequency. The r^2 of .123 tells us that frequency exerts a moderate effect on reaction time. The rule of thumb is that an r^2 around .01 indicates a weak effect, an r^2 around .09 a moderate effect, and an r^2 at .25 or higher a strong effect.

Table 7-1. Coefficients table when word frequency is used to predict reaction time.

Coefficients[a]						
	Unstandardized Coefficients		Standardized Coefficients		
Model	B	Std. Error	Beta	t	Sig.
1 (Constant)	906.415	15.903		56.997	.000
LogFreqHAL	-61.588	6.720	-.351	-9.165	.000

a. Dependent Variable: Mean_RT

Table 7-2. Model Summary when word frequency is used to predict reaction time.

Model Summary				
Model	R	R Square	Adjusted R Square	Std. Error of the Estimate
1	.351a	.123	.122	97.93888

a. Predictors: (Constant), LogFreqHAL

7.1.1 Using SPSS to perform a simple regression

1. Open *RTData.sav*. Click on *Analyze > Regression > Linear*. Move *Mean_RT* to the *Dependent* box and *LogFreqHAL* to the *Independent(s)* box > *OK*.
2. To produce the scatter plot in Figure 7-1, click on *Graphs > Legacy Dialogs > Scatter/Dot > Simple Scatter > Define*. Move *Mean_RT* into *Y Axis* and *LogFreqHAL* into *X Axis > OK*.
3. Double-click on the scatter plot to open the *Chart Editor*. Click on *Elements > Fit line at total > Close*.

7.2 Multiple Linear Regression

Now that we've seen how a simple regression works, let's consider a few more variables. I will illustrate this process with the kinds of variables that are common in psycholinguistic studies, such as reaction times, word length, word frequency, and so on. The English Lexicon Project (ELP; Balota et al. 2007) is packed with these kinds of data that are just begging to be used in a statistics text, so I extracted 600 words from it to use as an example data set. The idea behind the ELP was to create a large database of words that can be used as test items. In the database, each word includes lexical information, such as word length, part of speech, and frequency, and average reaction times. Knowing these kinds of information is crucial when choosing test items to include in an experiment, as well as when factoring out characteristics that need to be controlled for.

Why was the ELP created? The major reason is that reaction times to English words are a staple in psycholinguistics. A study may claim that a particular word is processed differently in people's brains than another word because they responded to it more quickly or more slowly than they did to the other word. However, there are many characteristics of the words that may influence reaction times besides mental-processing differences, so these need to be controlled for.

In order to determine average reaction times, approximately 400 subjects were asked to name words shown on a computer screen as quickly as possible. Each subject saw about 2,500 words, and about 25 subjects responded to each of the 40,000 words in the database, so the reaction times reported in the database for each word is the mean of those 25 measurements.

So why am I describing this process in so much detail? Well, I really want to use these data, but I have to justify it for this reason: in a multiple regression, subjects should give only one response, otherwise the data will not be independent, and independence is an assumption of regression. Normally, when you are using data to test a hypothesis, it isn't kosher to collapse reaction times by subject or item and use those means in a multiple regression. Repeated measures such as these should be analyzed with mixed models. However, since the purpose of this chapter is to describe how to perform a multiple regression, and not to test a hypothesis, I'm going to let those requirements slide a bit and pretend that each reaction time comes from a single person. In your own studies, however, you don't have the liberty to do this.

Figure 7-2. Venn diagram of various relationships.

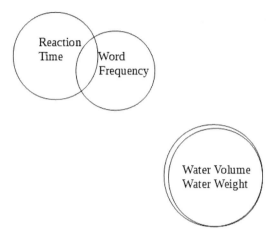

In the simple regression just demonstrated, we looked at the effect of word frequency on reaction time. Now we will add another independent variable: word length. The independent variables in a regression analysis, and the way they relate to the dependent variable can be visualized in a number of different ways. We already saw that frequency accounts for 12% of the variability in reaction times. We can envision this variability as the amount of reaction time that word frequency covers in Figure 7-2. Now, let's contrast this statistic with the hypothetical study I keep coming back to in which the volume of water is used to predict the weight of the water. In Figure 7-2, pretend that the circles overlap completely, which indicates that water volume explains 100% of the variability in the weights of the different volumes of water. Another way of looking at this is with a scatter plot, shown in Figure 7-3. All of the data points fall directly on the line, so the volume explains all of the variance in the weight of the water (r^2 is 1).

Figure 7-3. Scatter plot of water weight and water volume.

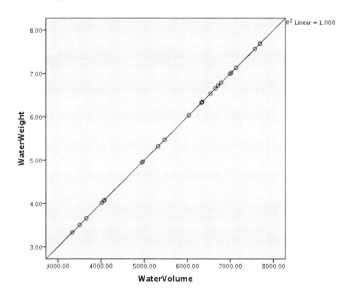

The process becomes a bit more involved when there's more than one independent variable. If you consider how the variables *word frequency* and *number of syllables in a word* affect reaction time, it's possible that they are completely unrelated to each other, with no overlap (Figure 7-4, top). It is much more likely that there is some overlap

(Figure 7-4, middle). In the case of *number of syllables* and *word length*, the overlap may be enormous (Figure 7-4, bottom), in which case it may be hard to figure out whether there is any difference at all between their influence on reaction times. These are the kinds of issues that must be dealt with in multiple regression.

Figure 7-4. Relationships between other variables.

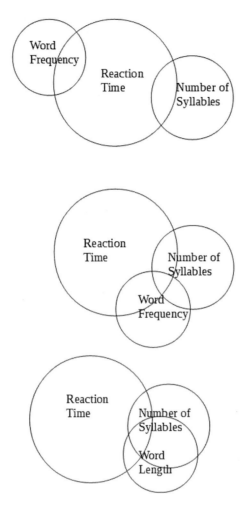

7.2.1 Running the initial analysis

The first step in performing a multiple regression is to run the analysis with all of the variables. Mind you, this process will rarely yield the final analysis you want to report. However, you can't address issues that may come up, nor can you make sure that the assumptions are met, until this step is completed. Remember that the dependent variable is *reaction time*, and the independent variables are *word length* and *word frequency*. I will break with my self-imposed protocol in this chapter and explain how to perform the analysis in SPSS at this point in the discussion rather than later so that you can follow along more easily.

7.2.2 Using SPSS to perform a multiple linear regression

1. Open the file *RTData.sav*. Click on *Analyze > Regression > Linear*. Move *Mean_RT* into the *Dependent* box and *Freq_HAL* and *Length* into the *Independent(s)* box.
2. Click on *Statistics* and check the boxes named *Estimates, Covariance matrix, Model fit,* and *Collinearity diagnostics*, then click *Continue* (Figure 7-5).
3. Click on *Plots*. Enter *SRESID* in the *Y* box and *ZPRED* in the *X* box. Check *Histogram, Normal probability plot,* and *Produce all partial plots*, then click *Continue > OK* (Figure 7-6).

Figure 7-5. Linear Regression dialog box.

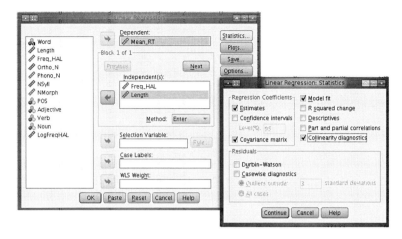

Figure 7-6. Linear Regression Plots dialog box.

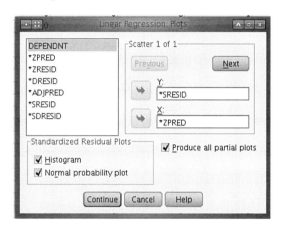

7.2.3 Interpreting the outcome of the initial multiple linear regression analysis

To interpret the outcome of the initial multiple linear regression analysis, begin by inspecting the model summary table (Table 7-3). It gives an r^2 of .135 and an adjusted r^2 of .133. ADJUSTED R^2 values are slightly lower than the r^2 because they take into account the fact that there is more than one independent variable in the equation. We interpret these two different kinds of r to mean that the variables included in the analysis account for about 13% of the variance in reaction times. The ANOVA table (Table 7-4) indicates that some independent variable is significantly influencing the reaction time, but it doesn't indicate which specific independent variables are significant or insignificant. That's why you've got to look at the Coefficients table (Table 7-5).

Table 7-3. Model Summary of the initial multiple regression analysis.

Model Summary[b]				
Model	R	R Square	Adjusted R Square	Std. Error of the Estimate
1	.368[a]	.135	.133	97.33347

a. Predictors: (Constant), Length, Freq_HAL
b. Dependent Variable: Mean_RT

Table 7-4. ANOVA of the initial multiple regression analysis.

ANOVA[a]					
Model	Sum of Squares	df	Mean Square	F	Sig.
1 Regression	885921.521	2	442960.760	46.756	.000[b]
Residual	5655861.257	597	9473.804		
Total	6541782.778	599			

a. Dependent Variable: Mean_RT
b. Predictors: (Constant), Length, Freq_HAL

Table 7-5. Coefficients Table for the initial multiple regression analysis.

Coefficients[a]							
	Unstandardized Coefficients		Standardized Coefficients			Collinearity Statistics	
Model	B	Std. Error	Beta	t	Sig.	Tolerance	VIF
1 (Constant)	630.076	17.280		36.462	.000		
Freq_HAL	-.017	.003	-.194	-5.096	.000	.996	1.004
Length	17.562	2.061	.325	8.521	.000	.996	1.004

a. Dependent Variable: Mean_RT

Look at Table 7-5. The intercept (constant) is 630.076. That is the predicted reaction time when all of the independent variables are at zero: frequency of 0 and length of 0. Yeah, I know; it's not a very useful number for these data. Now, in simple regression, the unstandardized coefficients tell you the total relationship between that variable and the dependent variable. In the simple regression, where frequency was the only variable, the coefficient for frequency was -61.588.

But now we are dealing with more than one variable in multiple regression; therefore, the unstandardized coefficient (B) gives you the slope of the line, which tells you what the relationship is between a particular variable and the dependent variable when the effect of the other variables is held constant. The effect of word frequency is different now because it is calculated with the influence of word length taken into consideration.

In the simple regression, the slope for word frequency was -61.588, but when it is considered in light of word length, it changes to -.017, meaning that for every additional unit of word frequency, the reaction time changes by -.017, when word length is also figured in the calculations. The slope of 17.562 for length means that for every increase of one letter in the word, reaction time will increase by about 18ms (when the effect of frequency is held constant).

7.2.4 Standardized coefficients

The challenge with looking at the unstandardized coefficient B is that it is given in different units of measure for different independent variables. *Length* is given in number of letters and *word frequency* in number of instances of a word in a corpus. This difference makes it hard to compare them on an equal footing. Fortunately, some warm-hearted statistician came up with a way to put all of the independent variables' coefficients in the same unit so they could be compared on an equal footing. This measurement is called the STANDARDIZED COEFFICIENT, also known as *beta* or β.

Betas show the influence of all the variables on a +1 to -1 scale, like Pearson coefficients in a correlation. So a β close to zero means that that particular variable doesn't affect the dependent variable a heck of a lot. Those variables that are closer to +1 or -1 exert a greater amount of influence. The β for length is .325, indicating a positive relationship with reaction time. The smallest β is the -.194 for frequency, indicating a negative relationship between word frequency and reaction time. Notice that both of these variables are statistically significant (see the significance column in Table 7-5).

7.2.5 Collinearity

One thing you need to watch for, especially when you have a lot of variables, is collinearity. If you think in terms of a Venn diagram, two variables are collinear if they overlap so much with each other that the two can't be distinguished or if one variable is the mirror image of another. It is also possible for combinations of two or more variables to result in collinearity.

The VIF (variance inflation factor) and tolerance scores under the *Collinearity Statistics* column in Figure 7-4 are measurements of collinearity. Look back at Figure 7-4. Here, word length and number of syllables are used to account for the variance in reaction time. Longer words tend to have more syllables, so it is possible that these two variables overlap so much that the contribution of each can't be uniquely measured. The first clue that there is too much collinearity would be a tolerance score lower than .1 or a VIF of 10 or above. In Table 7-6, the VIF and tolerance numbers are fine, so there is nothing to worry about.

The tolerance and VIF numbers are helpful, but when you have a lot of variables, and they indicate collinearity, those numbers don't point you to the two variables that are collinear. You can find the culprits in the Coefficient Correlations table (Table 7-6). Here, each variable is correlated with all of the other variables. A good rule of thumb is that variables that are correlated at .8 or above or at -.8 or below are cause for worry. The correlation between frequency and length is -.063, so no worries here. When the correlation between two variables is high, action must be taken, which often entails choosing to eliminate one variable from consideration in the analysis.

Another way of handling collinearity is to run two different regressions. In the first run, one of the correlated variables is included and the other excluded. In the second run, the variables that are excluded and included are switched. Sometimes two categorical collinear variables can be combined into a single new variable to eliminate collinearity. For instance, gender (Male/Female) and education (no college/college) could be made into a single variable with four values: M College, F College, M No college, F No college.[1]

Continuous variables can sometimes be combined to test for collinearity as well. The score on a foreign language proficiency test could depend on the time spent studying the foreign language as well as the time spent living in the target language country. Since these measures are probably collinear, the ratio of time in the target language country divided by the total time studying the language could be used as an independent variable instead.

Some people suggest that CENTERING VARIABLES can eliminate collinearity, but this suggestion is actually not a solution. Centering variables gives the appearance that collinearity is taken care of, but, in essence, it is still there (Dalal & Zickar 2012). Others present residualizing (the details of which I won't go into) as a cure for collinearity (e.g., Lance 1988), but this technique is equally problematic (Pedhazur 1997; Wurm & Fisicaro 2014). When two variables are collinear, they are collinear, and there is no statistical magic that can undo that.

There are times when you find collinearity but don't need to worry about it (Allison 2012). For example, there may be control variables in the model that are highly correlated with each other. They are included only because we know that they influence the outcome and need to be accounted for. But these variables aren't crucial to the study. If that's the case, don't sweat any correlation between them. There are also times when a new variable is needed that is the square of another variable or is arrived at by multiplying two variables. Obviously, the square or product of the simple variables will be correlated with the simple variables. This correlation won't affect the p values in the model, so you can ignore the collinearity.

Table 7-6. Coefficient Correlations table for the initial multiple regression analysis.

Coefficient Correlations[a]			Length	Freq_HAL
Model				
1	Correlations	Length	1.000	-.063
		Freq_HAL	-.063	1.000
	Covariances	Length	4.247	.000
		Freq_HAL	.000	1.100E-005

a. Dependent Variable: Mean_RT

7.2.6 Using categorical variables in a multiple regression: Dummy coding

Since I've brought up the possibility of using categorical variables in a regression, the obvious question is, "How do you handle categorical data?" To answer this, we'll add a categorical variable to the regression. So if you were trying to determine how parts of speech, specifically nouns versus adjectives versus verbs, influence reaction times, it would be tempting to simply give them numbers so that adjective = 1, noun = 2, and verb = 3 and hope that takes care of the problem. However, this phony numeric coding makes it look like adjectives are somehow closer to nouns than verbs. Statistics isn't quantum physics, so you can't get away with nonsensical stuff. The only exception to this process is if the categorical variable has two values, such as male and female.

When you DUMMY CODE something, you essentially ask a yes or no question. If you had a variable called *female* and the person being coded were female, you'd give it a 1 to mean yes. Males would get zero. Simple enough. The way to handle categorical data with more than two values is to turn them into a series of yes or no variables. More specifically, if you have three possibilities, such as adjective, noun, and verb, you'd code these possibilities with two variables, not with three. I know that's counterintuitive, but you always use one fewer variable than you have categories.

Let me explain. In order to code the values of *adjective, noun,* and *verb*, you could make two different variables, as in Table 7-7. In this table, the number 1 means yes, so the word belongs to that category, and 0 means it does not.

Now, I know you're asking where the flip is *verb* category in all this. The answer is that a noun has a 0 in the *adjective* column and a 1 in the *noun* column. *Adjectives* have 1 in the *adjective* column and 0 in the *noun* column. Now pay attention. This coding with two variables implies that there is a third value that has 0 in both columns. So, the *verb* column has a 0 in both the *adjective* and *noun* columns.

If you fail to heed my warning and include a separate variable for *verb*, SPSS will rightfully send an annoying error message your way, and I will say I told you so. Using the same logic, if you had a variable with four values, you would include only three new variables in the analysis.

Table 7-7. Dummy coding of adjectives, nouns, and verbs.

Test word	Adjective	Noun
green	1	0
sidewalk	0	1
leave	0	0

---

[1] Another advanced method for dealing with collinearity is principal component analysis (Field 2013, Ch. 17).

You are probably wondering what happens to the variable you leave out, the one that is all zeros. Now, pay close attention again because this is important: the value that is coded with zeros in all the columns that are included in the analysis is called the REFERENCE VALUE. Therefore, the coefficient that the regression will calculate for the noun variable indicates how much the reaction times for nouns differ from those of verbs, since *verb* is the reference value. The coefficient for *adjective*, in the same way, shows how much the reaction times for adjectives differ from verbs.

If you wanted to change the reference value and compare adjectives to nouns and verbs to nouns, you would include a *verb* and *adjective* variable and exclude the *noun* variable from the analysis, which would make *noun* the reference value. If you have a control condition in your experiment, that would be the natural choice for the reference value. I hope it is clear that you can use dummy coding to include other categorical variables, such as country of origin, native language, type of phone, and so on.

Now, what happens when we add these two new variables to our regression? (Enter the variables *adjective* and *noun* into the *Independent[s]* box in Figure 7-5 and rerun the analysis.) You can't interpret the betas for a dummy-coded variable in the same way you can for continuous variables. In Table 7-8, the 124.869 for *adjectives* means that adjectives take about 125ms more time to respond to than the reference variable value, which is *verb*. In like manner, nouns take 64.360ms longer on average to respond to than verbs. What if we had coded gender so that female was 1 and male was 0? When you interpret the outcome, you would need to remember that a positive coefficient is related to females, so females are high and males are low.

Think of standardized coefficients in the same way that you think of the *r* in a correlation analysis. A positive coefficient between gender (when 1 means female) and reaction time is that as femininity increases, so does reaction time. A negative coefficient means that as femininity decreases (and masculinity goes up), reaction times increase.

Table 7-8. Coefficients when dummy-coded variables are added to the analysis.

Coefficients[a]							
	Unstandardized Coefficients		Standardized Coefficients			Collinearity Statistics	
Model	B	Std. Error	Beta	t	Sig.	Tolerance	VIF
1 (Constant)	466.887	20.247		23.059	.000		
Freq_HAL	-.012	.003	-.134	-3.915	.000	.974	1.026
Length	29.500	2.059	.546	14.328	.000	.788	1.269
Adjective	124.869	9.833	.564	12.698	.000	.580	1.724
Noun	64.360	9.066	.291	7.099	.000	.682	1.465

a. Dependent Variable: Mean_RT

7.2.7 Centering variables to make the intercept more interpretable

Sometimes we may want to center a variable. To explain why, I'll use a fictitious example: If we wanted to know how TOEFL scores are influenced by the number of years a person has been studying English and the number of months he or she has spent in an English-speaking country, we could get the results in Table 7-9. This table tells us that for each year of study, the TOEFL score increases by about 3.3 points. For every month in the L2 country, the score increases by 4.8 points (when the other variable is held constant). This information is useful, but the intercept of 33.8 gives us kind of an odd prediction: someone who has spent zero years studying English and has never lived in an English-speaking country is predicted to get a 33.8 on the TOEFL. This basically means that if you gave someone an answer sheet to the TOEFL and had him or her randomly fill it out without even looking at the test questions, he or she would score about a 34.

However, we can turn that quasi-useless figure into a helpful one by centering the independent variables. Centering is just a matter of modifying the scores in a systematic way. One common modification is to subtract the mean from each of the scores so that someone whose score is the same as the mean now has a centered score of zero, meaning his or her score doesn't differ from the mean. The new score represents how much each person's score differs from the mean. With centering, the intercept is more interpretable: zero no longer means no experience at all with English but the average number of years the student has studied English (5.94) and the average number of months he or she has spent in the L2 country (4.77).

To really understand what centering does, you need to carefully compare Tables 7-9 and 7-10. As shown in Table 7-10, when you rerun the analysis with centered data, the coefficients for the independent variables stay exactly the same. They are identical to what they were before centering (Table 7-9). The only thing that centering changes is that the intercept moves from 33.8 to 76.6. The intercept of 33.8 was the predicted score for someone with no experience with English who was guessing the answers on the test. After centering the data, the intercept now means something more interpretable, namely that the average student (who has spent 5.94 years studying English and has lived in an English-speaking country for 4.77 months) is predicted to have a TOEFL score of 76.6, which is a heck of a lot more useful to know. In this example, I used centering on the mean. This procedure is common, but you may center on whatever point makes sense to you and your data.

Table 7-9. Regression results for TOEFL test by number of years studying and number of months in L2 country with uncentered values.

Coefficients[a]						
		Unstandardized Coefficients		Standardized Coefficients		
Model		B	Std. Error	Beta	t	Sig.
1	(Constant)	33.872	2.340		14.473	.000
	YearsStudying	3.337	.413	.489	8.075	.000
	MonthsInCountry	4.815	.593	.492	8.119	.000

a. Dependent Variable: TOEFL

7.2.7.1 Using SPSS to center a variable

1. Open *centering.sav*. Click on *Transform > Compute Variable*. In the *Numeric Expression* box, enter the name of the variable to be centered followed by '–' and the mean (e.g., *MonthsInCountry-4.77*).
2. In the *Target Variable* box, enter the new name you will give to this variable (e.g., *MonthsCenter*), then click *OK*. A new column called *MonthsCenter* will be created, which you can now use as the centered independent variable. Repeat using *YearsStudying-5.94* to create new *YearsCenter* variable.
3. To carry out the regression, click on *Analyze > Regression > Linear*. Enter *MonthsInCountry* (or *MonthsCenter*) and *YearsStudying* (or *YearsCenter*) into the *Independent(s)* box and *TOEFL* into the *Dependent* box, then click *OK*.

Table 7-10. Regression results for TOEFL test by number of years studying and number of months in L2 country with centered values.

Coefficients[a]						
		Unstandardized Coefficients		Standardized Coefficients		
Model		B	Std. Error	Beta	t	Sig.
1	(Constant)	76.688	.843		90.985	.000
	YearCenter	3.337	.413	.489	8.075	.000
	MonthsCenter	4.815	.593	.492	8.119	.000

a. Dependent Variable: TOEFL

7.2.8 Assumptions of multiple regression

Let's go back to the results we got using *Length, Freq_HAL, Adjective,* and *Noun* as independent variables and *Mean_RT* as the dependent variable (Table 7-8).

7.2.8.1 Independence, number, and types of variables

One requirement for multiple regression is that the data are independent. What makes the data independent? That no one gives more than one response. Another requirement is that the dependent variable needs to be continuous (but remember that the independent variables can be continuous or categorical if you dummy code them).

How many independent variables can you have? That depends on how extensive your data are. One rule of thumb is that you must have a minimum of about 15–20 observations for every independent variable you test. Can the variables be ordinal? This question has been debated. Some people allow variables to be ordinal, while others feel that using ordinals is a violation. Since there is no easy nonparametric alternative to multiple linear regression, I suggest using ordinal data if that is what you have—but make sure to be clear about that fact. Cite the ordinal data as a possible weakness of the analysis.

7.2.8.2 Normal distribution of the residuals

As with other statistics that we have looked at, we have tested the assumption of normality and homoscedasticity by looking at the distribution of the residuals. With multiple regression, we are dealing with more than one independent variable and must test the assumptions on the residuals that occur when all of the variables are taken into consideration at the same time.

The best way to visualize whether the residuals have a normal distribution is to inspect the histogram of the residuals (Figure 7-7) and the P-P plot of the residuals (Figure 7-8). The histogram indicates some variation from normality because the bars do not fit perfectly within the normal distribution curve. The P-P plot shows this same deviation from normality but in a different way. Perfectly normal residuals would appear as a dark line that is completely straight and diagonal. In this case, what you see is that the dark line departs from a straight diagonal.

Figure 7-7. Histogram of the residuals of the initial multiple regression analysis.

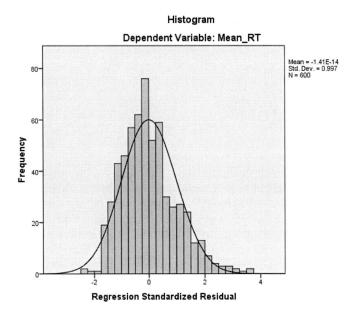

7.2.8.3 Homoscedasticity of the residuals

Homoscedasticity is examined by examining a plot of the standardized residuals (Figure 7-9). The data points of the standardized residuals should be centered on the zero axis and should be about equally distributed along all the ranges of the horizontal axis. A fan or bow-tie shape to the distribution (Figures 7-10 and 7-11) indicates heteroscedasticity. Other odd shapes also indicate that the "scedacity is hetero." With these data, there are a few outliers past three standard deviations, and the vertical distribution is somewhat less spread on the left than on the right. So, there are some indications of mild heteroscedasticity here that I'm not going to get bent out of shape over (pun intended) but that we ought to look at anyway.

Figure 7-8. P-P plot of the residuals of the initial multiple regression analysis.

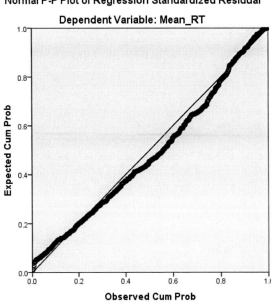

Figure 7-9. Scatter Plot of the standardized residuals of the initial multiple regression analysis.

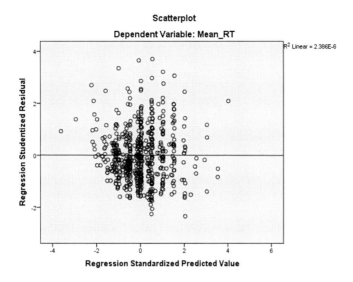

Figure 7-10. Scatter plot of the standardized residuals with a bow-tie shape indicating heteroscedasticity.

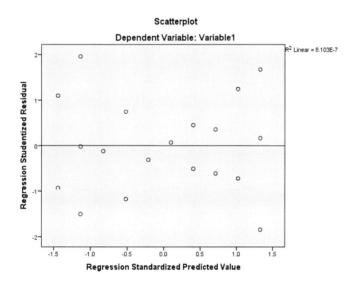

Figure 7-11. Scatter Plot of the standardized residuals with a fan shape indicating heteroscedasticity.

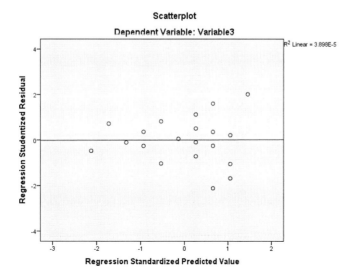

7.2.8.4 Linearity of the data

Because we have more than one variable, when looking for linearity, we need to factor out the influence of the other variables and check the linearity one variable at a time. Doing this results in a PARTIAL REGRESSION PLOT.

The Loess line in the partial regression plot for *length* (Figure 7-12) is fairly straight and has no curvature to worry about. This is also true for the partial regression plots for *adjective* and *noun* (Figures 7-13 and 7-14). However, linearity is clearly out of whack in the partial regression plot for w*ord frequency* (Figure 7-15). The line falls sharply in the densely populated area on the left side of the graph, then straightens out in the less-populated area.

Figure 7-12. Partial Regression Plot of word length and reaction time for the initial multiple regression analysis.

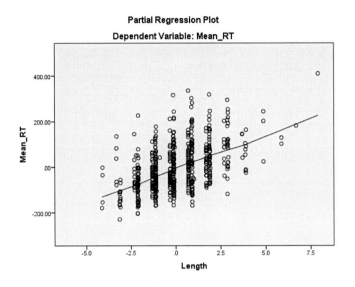

Figure 7-13. Partial Regression Plot of adjective (versus verb) and reaction time for the initial multiple regression analysis.

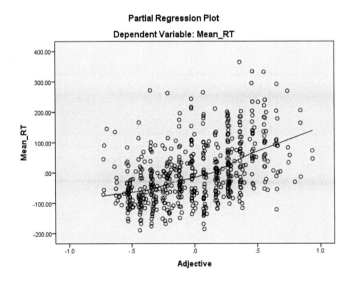

Figure 7-14. Partial Regression Plot of noun (versus verb) and reaction time for the initial multiple regression analysis.

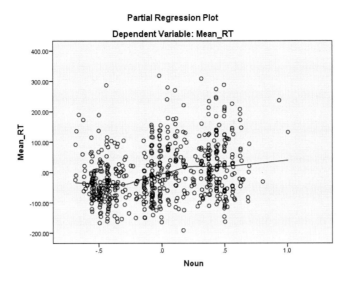

Figure 7-15. Partial Regression Plot of word frequency and reaction time for the initial multiple regression analysis.

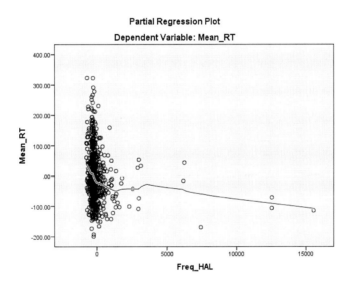

7.2.9 Addressing violations of statistical assumptions

Now that we've run an initial analysis and checked for violations of the assumptions, we must address the following issues before determining the final model:

- The relationship between reaction time and word frequency is not linear.
- The distribution of the standardized residuals is not completely normal.
- There is mild heteroscedasticity.

I was able to deal with the nonlinearity of word frequency by transforming this variable with a natural logarithmic transformation.[2] The new variable is called *LogFreqHAL* (compare Figure 7-16 with Figure 7-15). If you need a refresher on how to perform a transformation, go back to Chapter 3.

If transformations do not achieve linearity, there are other methods you can apply that are not covered in this introductory book, such as adding a polynomial term to the model to account for the curvature (Field 2014, Ch. 20). As a last resort, you could also convert the continuous independent variable that is causing the nonlinear residuals into a categorical variable with two or more values and dummy code it. For example, if *age* were causing the problem, you could collapse it into three groups: 20–39, 40–59, and 60 and older. This change is somewhat controversial since you lose statistical power (Cohen 1983), but pretending a major lack of linearity is not important and running the analysis anyway can result in invalid results, which is the greater of the two evils in my view.

---

[2] The code for this logarithmic transformation in SPSS is *Ln(variable)*.

I eliminated the non-normal distribution of the residuals by transforming the mean reaction time with the formula *1/(Mean_RT*Mean_RT)*. I called the new variable *TransRT*.[3] After this process, I reran the multiple regression analysis to calculate the residuals and to produce the histogram and P-P plot of the residuals. The new P-P plot and histogram both showed a normal distribution. Sometimes removing outliers will help achieve a normal distribution. One of the more advanced methods of dealing with non-normal distributions is bootstrapping, which can also be used with multiple regression.

When there is collinearity, one way of dealing with it is to eliminate one of the variables. It may be best to eliminate the variable that does not add much to the model. You can do this by comparing the r^2 of the model when all of the variables are included in the model except the one whose contribution is being tested. This comparison between the variables gives you a sense of which independent variable has a greater effect on the dependent variable.

When there is heteroscedasticity, you can eliminate it by transforming variables or eliminating outliers in the data. In fact, outliers can sometimes be responsible for the lack of linearity and non-normal distribution among the residuals. Sometimes heteroscedasticity disappears once other violations of assumptions have been addressed. When all else fails, bootstrapping can help, which doesn't have the normality and homoscedasticity requirements.[4] However, that option may not be available in your version of SPSS. There are a number of advanced methods for dealing with heteroscedasticity that you may want to look into if you are having issues, such as using a WEIGHTED LEAST SQUARES LINEAR REGRESSION (Pryce 2002), using an ESTIMATED GENERALIZED LEAST SQUARES REGRESSION (Bickel 2007), or using MAXIMUM LIKELIHOOD ESTIMATION (Smyth 2002).

7.2.9.1 Deleting and winsorizing outliers

I keep mentioning the possibility of addressing the violations of assumptions by removing outliers from an analysis. This solution is tricky because you can't just offhandedly get rid of outliers to make things look nice. There must be a principled reason to do so. In some studies, the outliers may actually be the most interesting results. If that is the case, leave the outliers in. However, the reaction time data we've been considering were chosen quasi-randomly from the ELP database to illustrate how to perform a multiple regression. They aren't the result of an experiment designed to test a particular theory, so I don't see deleting outliers as a problem in this case. I could just have easily chosen a data set that did not contain them.

Figure 7-16. Partial Regression Plot of transformed word frequency and reaction time for the initial multiple regression analysis.

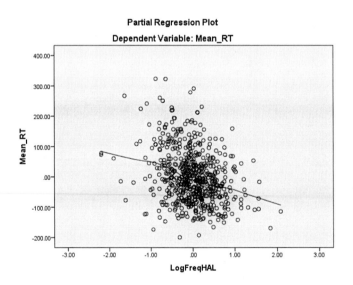

Experiments that involve measurements of reaction times often delete outliers a priori. We generally know what kinds of reaction times to expect, so extreme ones, say those beyond two or three standard deviations, are justifiably oddballs. They are often the result of participants falling asleep at the keyboard or responding before they've even had a chance to actually view and consider the test items. This is the kind of justification that warrants eliminating outliers, but this practice can also introduce other issues into the analysis (Ulrich & Miller 1994).

Instead of eliminating the data, you can WINSORIZE them (sounds fancy, doesn't it?) by converting any data point over three standard deviations (or some other cut-off point) to the highest score below three standard deviations and converting any score below three standard deviations to the lowest score above that cut-off point. For example, if the highest data points were 867, **880, 912,** and **942** (the boldfaced ones are above three standard deviations), you would convert those three data points to 867, resulting in four scores of 867. If the lowest data points were **155, 167,** 178, and

---

[3] I tried quite a few transformations, and this is the one that worked.
[4] When you bootstrap report B, the bias, standard error and the significance of each independent variable.

189 (the boldfaced ones are below three standard deviations), you would convert those data paints to 178, 178, 178, and 189. Don't worry—this practice is kosher.

7.2.9.2 Identifying outliers

On a scatter plot, outliers appear as data points on the periphery, far removed from the bulk of the other data points. In small data sets with fewer than about 80–100 observations, a data point that is more than 2.5 standard deviations above or below the mean should be considered an outlier. In large data sets, with more than 80 or 100 observations, outliers are those data points that go beyond three standard deviations from the mean.

If outliers are responsible for your data not fitting the assumptions of multiple regression, you may consider deleting them if you can justify it and retesting the data to see if doing so has helped them fit into the model criteria.

There are two kinds of outliers: UNIVARIATE OUTLIERS are those continuous observations that are extreme for one variable. For example, a building with 100 floors is a univariate outlier on the variable *number of floors in a building*. MULTIVARIATE OUTLIERS have extreme values for a combination of one or more variables. A building with five floors in Upper Volta (number of floors by country), for example is a multivariate outlier. There are probably few buildings of more than 2 stories in that country.

A number of univariate outliers exist in the data beyond three standard deviations above or below the mean. As far as word length is concerned, *counterespionage* and *compartmentalize* are the only words in the dataset with 16 letters. The rest of the words in the dataset have 13 or fewer. Five words had extremely slow reaction times (over 1,095ms): *cretaceous, moribund, piquant, connubial,* and *counterespionage.* It shouldn't be surprising that participants had to scratch their heads at these words for quite a while before deciding they were real words. The frequency of several words falls beyond the criterion for outliers. *Jocose, jocund, bankbook, frowzy,* and *connubial* have low frequencies, while *transcribe, implemented,* and *formats* have unusually high frequencies. These three words don't seem particularly frequent, but it appears that most of the words I chose from the database of reaction times were on the lower end of the frequency scale.

To test multivariate outliers, I considered combinations of reaction time, length, and log frequency, which identified a number of words as outliers at the $p < .05$ level. When dealing with a combination of so many variables, it is difficult to understand why the words that are identified as outliers are odd.

Simply inspecting the values for each variable for each of the words is useful for univariate outliers or outliers that are combinations of two variables but not so much in these cases. The question that remains is whether we should remove them.

One way to see if the outliers are actually affecting the analysis is to remove them and rerun the analysis to see how much the outcome changes. I did this and found that the outliers that are causing the slight heteroscedasticity were not eliminated, so the final analysis was performed on the entire data set.

7.2.9.3 Using SPSS to identify outliers

Note that only continuous variables can have outliers, not categorical ones.

To identify univariate outliers:
1. Open the file *RTData.sav.* Click on *Analyze > Descriptive Statistics > Descriptives.* Enter *Length, Mean_RT,* and *LogFreqHAL* into the *Variable(s)* box.
2. Check *Save standardized values as variables > OK.* This creates three new columns named *Zlength, Zmean_RT,* and *ZLogFreqHAL.*

Do the following to the newly created *Z* variables one at a time:
1. Click on *Data > Sort cases.* Enter one of the new *Z* variables in the *Sort by* box, then click *OK.*
2. Go to the *Data Editor* spreadsheet and inspect the beginning and end of the new *Z* variable column for outliers. This column shows how much each test item deviates from the mean of the variable in that column by standard deviation.

To identify multivariate outliers:
1. Click on *Analyze > Regression > Linear.* Enter *Mean_RT* into the *Dependent box* and *Length* and *LogFreqHAL* into the *Independent(s)* box. (If you did not want to include the dependent variable in the search for outliers, you could place any of the other independent variables in the *Dependent* box.)
2. Click on *Save* and check *Mahalanobis.* Click *Continue > OK.* This creates a new column in the *Data Editor* spreadsheet called *MAH_1.* These Mahalonobis numbers cannot be interpreted by themselves.

To calculate *p* values for the Mahalanobis numbers:
1. Click on *Transform > Compute variable.* In the *Function* group box, click on *CDF & Noncentral CDF.*
2. In the *Special Functions* box, double-click on *cdf.chisq.* This puts *CDF.CHISQ(?,?)* in the *Numeric Expression* box.

3. Double-click on *Mahalanobis distance [MAH_1]* in the box under the *Type and Label* button. Do not click on the *Type and Label* button. The *Numeric Expression* box now reads *CDF.CHISQ(MAH_1,?)*. Change the question mark to the number of variables being combined and tested for outliers. In this case, the number of variables is five. The *Numeric Expression* box now reads *CDF.CHISQ(MAH_1,5)*.
4. In the *Target Variable* box, type *ProbMAH*, which will create a new column in the spreadsheet with this name. Click *OK*.
5. Go to the *Data Editor* spreadsheet and click on the *Variable View* tab in the bottom-left-hand corner. In the *ProbMAH* row, change the *Decimals* column to 3. Click on the *Data View* tab in the bottom-left-hand corner.
6. Click on *Data > Sort cases*, and enter the variable *ProbMAH* into the *Sort by* box. Click *OK*. Go to the *Data Editor* spreadsheet and inspect the *ProbMAH* column that contains *p* values indicating the probability that a test item is a multivariate outlier.

7.2.10 Reporting the results of a multiple linear regression

Once the data have been modified to deal with violations of the assumptions, the final analysis must be rerun. In this case, it is rerun with the variables that have been modified to address the violations of the assumptions. *TransRT* is the dependent variable, and *LogFreqHAL, Length, Adjective,* and *Noun* are the independent variables. The data that you need to report appear in the Model Summary, ANOVA, and Coefficients tables (Tables 7-11–7-13). These tables can be summarized and reported, as in Table 7-14. Notice the abundance of zeros and the other strange numbers in the tables that are reported in scientific notation. This is due to the fact that the transformation of the dependent variable resulted in a very small number. Whenever a variable is transformed, it makes interpretation of the unstandardized coefficient difficult. In any event, the following is one way to describe the outcome in prose:

In a simultaneous multiple regression, we tested how word frequency, word length, and part of speech influence the reaction times. Our analysis was statistically significant (F (4, 595) = 78.340, $p < .0005$) and accounted for 34% of the variance in the reaction times. As the statistics in Table 7-13 indicate,[5] words that were longer in terms of the number of letters they contain resulted in statistically higher reaction times, while those with higher frequencies were responded to more quickly. When compared to verbs, adjectives and nouns took more time to respond to. We tested the residuals and found that they were normally distributed and that the relationship between the variables and the dependent variable was linear. However, this result was achieved only after the dependent variable and word frequency were transformed. The residuals were largely homoscedastic, with only slight deviations.

Table 7-11. Model Summary of the final regression.

Model Summary[b]			
Model	R	R Square	Adjusted R Square	Std. Error of the Estimate
1	.587[a]	.345	.341	.000000362

a. Predictors: (Constant), LogFreqHAL, Length, Noun, Adjective
b. Dependent Variable: TransRT

Table 7-12. Overall results of the final regression.

ANOVA[a]					
Model	Sum of Squares	df	Mean Square	F	Sig.
1 Regression	.000	4	.000	78.340	.000[b]
Residual	.000	595	.000		
Total	.000	599			

a. Dependent Variable: TransRT
b. Predictors: (Constant), LogFreqHAL, Length, Noun, Adjective

---

[5] Given the difficulty of interpreting the unstandardized coefficient of a dependent variable that has been transformed, the unstandardized coefficients from the analysis using the untransformed reaction time is reported in that column. The betas, however, are those resulting when the transformed reaction time is included.

Table 7-13. Coefficients of the final regression.

Coefficients[a]	Unstandardized Coefficients		Standardized Coefficients			Collinearity Statistics	
Model	B	Std. Error	Beta	t	Sig.	Tolerance	VIF
1 (Constant)	-2.541E-006	.000		-21.971	.000		
Adjective	4.351E-007	.000	.460	10.072	.000	.528	1.894
Noun	1.645E-007	.000	.174	4.034	.000	.592	1.689
Length	1.199E-007	.000	.520	13.829	.000	.780	1.282
LogFreqHAL	-1.898E-007	.000	-.253	-6.979	.000	.837	1.195

a. Dependent Variable: Mean_RT

Table 7-14. Results of the final regression.

	B	β	t	p <
Length	28.060	.520	13.829	.0005
Frequency	-47.541	-.253	-6.979	.0005
Adjective (vs. verb)	105.455	.460	10.072	.0005
Noun (vs. verb)	41.511	.174	4.034	.0005

7.2.11 Types of multiple linear regression

There are a number of different kinds of linear regression.

7.2.11.1 Simultaneous regression

Up to this point, the type of regression we've been looking at is SIMULTANEOUS regression. It is simultaneous because all of the variables are included at the same time. This process factors out the overlap between variables.

Look at Figure 7-17. The variance that the number of syllables accounts for is A. The amount of unique variance that word frequency accounts for is C. The overlap between the two is B and is not reflected in a simultaneous multiple regression.

When using SPSS to perform the regression, there is a button called *Method* under the box where the independent variables are entered (Figure 7-5). When all variables are entered into the *Independent(s)* box and the *Method* button is set to *Enter*, a simultaneous regression is carried out.

Figure 7-17. Venn diagram of overlapping independent variables.

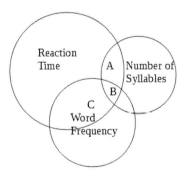

7.2.11.2 Stepwise or stepping up/down regression

Other kinds of regression are specified with this *Method* button. When you click on it, you will see the *Stepwise, Remove, Backward,* and *Forward* options, which refer to a number of procedures in which the computer automatically adds or subtracts variables one at a time in order to come up with the set of those variables that significantly helps explain the variance in the dependent variable.

These methods, which are sometimes called STEPWISE, STEPPING UP, or STEPPING DOWN, have a long history of use in linguistics. However, there is quite a bit of evidence that they are statistically unsound (e.g., Harrell 2001; Huberty 1989; Hurvich & Tsai 1990). In addition, when someone throws a lot of independent variables at the computer and asks it to figure out which are significant without having a hypothesis to guide the procedure it can turn into DATA DREDGING. Data dredging is essentially using the same data both to determine the hypotheses and to test them. For these reasons, I discourage you from using these methods and won't explain how to use them.

7.2.11.3 Hierarchical regression

HIERARCHICAL REGRESSION is used to control for the influence of one or more variables while measuring how much variance one or more additional variables account for. Let's use the same reaction time data as an example. Prior research tells us that reaction times are highly influenced by word length and word frequency. In a hierarchical regression, we don't want to test those independent variables per se. Instead, we want to acknowledge their effect by controlling for them, so our hypothesis is that the number of syllables has an effect above and beyond that of frequency and length.

Look at Figure 7-18. A simultaneous regression would assign the variance in A to word length, C to number of syllables, and E to word frequency. The overlap in B and D is not accounted for, and we can't tell how much more additional variance C actually represents. To find out what the variance of C is, we put length and frequency into the formula as our first model. This process ensures that length is assigned all of the variance in A and B and that frequency is assigned all of the variance in D and E.

In the second model, which is actually a simultaneous regression with all the variables, we add number of syllables to ensure that only the variance represented by C is attributed to this variable, and we see how much more of the variance is accounted for once number of syllables is added. With length and frequency in Model 1, the r^2 is .226 (see Table 7-15). When number of syllables is added in Model 2, it increases to .269.

This increase is statistically significant, as the data in the Model 2 row under *Change Statistics* indicate. What this tells us is that the number of syllables explains about 4% more of the variance (.269–.226) than length and frequency do by themselves. Just a word of caution: when running a series of models, variables that are significant in one model can become insignificant (or vice versa) when another variable is included.

Figure 7-18. Venn diagram of overlapping independent variables.

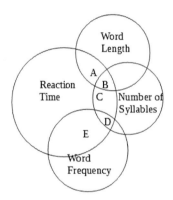

Table 7-15. Model Summary of hierarchical regression.

Model Summary[c]									
				Std. Error of the Estimate	Change Statistics				
Model	R	R Square	Adjusted R Square		R Square Change	F Change	df1	df2	Sig. F Change
1	.475[a]	.226	.223	3.93E-7	.226	86.965	2	597[a]	.000
2	.519[b]	.269	.266	3.82E-7	.044	35.782	1	596[b]	.000

a. Predictors: (Constant), LogFreqHAL, Length
b. Predictors: (Constant), LogFreqHAL, Length, NSyll
c. Dependent Variable: TransRT

7.2.12 Using SPSS to perform a hierarchical multiple linear regression

To produce Table 7-14:

1. Open the file *RTData.sav*. Click on *Analyze > Regression > Linear*. Enter *TransRT*[6] into the *Dependent* box and *Length* and *LogFreqHAL* into the *Independent* box. This specifies the first model. Make sure *Method* says *Enter*, and click on *Next*. Enter *NSyll* in the *Independent(s)* box. This specifies the second model.
2. Click on *Statistics* and check *Model fit, R square change*, and *Collinearity diagnostics > Continue*.
3. Click on *Plots* and check *Histogram, Produce all partial plots*, and *Normal probability plot*. Move *SRESID* to the *Y* box and *ZPRED* to the *X* box, then click *Continue > OK*.

---

[6] This is the reaction time data after it has been transformed with –1 (meanRT*meanRT).

7.2.13 Finding the most parsimonious regression model

Many researchers will take the necessary steps to eliminate or transform problematic variables and then report that analysis as their final results. However, in many cases, those results will include variables that are significant and other results that are not. In the reaction time data, all of the independent variables were significant, but if there were some that were not, many other researchers would suggest taking the analysis a step further in search of the most PARSIMONIOUS MODEL. The most parsimonious model is the one that best describes the data with the fewest number of variables. This model should only contain significant variables. How is this done? It entails finding the least significant variable by inspecting the *p* values and eliminating that least significant variable, then rerunning the analysis. The next variable that is found to be the least significant is then eliminated, and the analysis is rerun again. This procedure is repeated until all insignificant variables are eliminated. The results that make up the final analysis are reported.

Two questions may arise: Why go through this whole cycle, and why not just simplify the whole freaking thing by eliminating all of the insignificant variables in one fell swoop? You'll recall that the influence of each variable is calculated after holding the influence of all the others constant. In some cases, eliminating a variable doesn't change the standardized coefficients of the others much. In other cases, eliminating a variable may result in a formerly significant variable becoming insignificant or vice versa. You don't know what will happen until you try removing the least-significant variables one at a time.

Of course, once you have arrived at your most parsimonious model, you need to make sure the assumptions are still met. One thing to watch out for is when you have both a main effect and interaction of that main effect with another independent variable. Say you find that gender is not significant but that the interaction of gender and age is significant. Of course, you would leave in gender by age, but you may be tempted to remove gender. The rule is that any variable that makes up an interaction must be included in the model as a separate variable as well.

7.2.14 Contrast coding and coding interactions

Given the introductory nature of this book, it is impossible to cover all aspects of multiple regression, some of which have been the topic of book-length treatises themselves. I have shown how to dummy code categorical variables, which forces one of the values to act as the reference value against which the other values are compared.

There are many other ways to code categorical variables that are covered under the topic of CONTRAST CODING. For example, one type of contrast coding allows you to obtain coefficients that show how much each value differs from the mean of all the values. Another type of contrast coding lets you see how much nouns affect reaction times in contrast to verbs and adjectives taken together. A number of introductions to this topic are available (see Serlin & Levin 1985, and Wendorf 2004).

In this chapter, I have included only simple variables. At times it is important to consider interactions between variables. This is done by combining two variables into a new interaction variable. For example, the possibility exists that reaction times may be affected differently by words with one or two morphemes but not by words with three or four morphemes. This would constitute an interaction. Interactions may occur between two continuous variables or between categorical and continuous variables. Encoding such interaction variables requires different methods (see West, Aiken, & Krull 1996).

7.2.15 Multiple regression with several categorical variables

I've shown you how to dummy code categorical variables with more than two values by creating a series of variables. Wouldn't it be nice if you didn't have to do all that coding by hand? Well, I've forced you to do it by hand to this point so you can see how dummy coding works. However, SPSS can do all of the coding for you if you run the regression in a different way. The process has positive and negative aspects. The positive aspect is that you don't have to create multiple variables, which can be a pain if they have lots of values.

Look back at *RTData.sav*. Here, we dummy coded the values of *Part of Speech* (adjective, noun, verb) with three different columns. To choose the reference variable, we just left out one of the columns, and the value that that column encoded became the reference value.

Notice that in that same data set, there is another variable called *POS* that simply names the different parts of speech as a single variable in a single column. You were probably wondering what that variable was all about. If we run the regression a different way, we can have SPSS do all of the work for us.

There is a downside, however. You have to remember that SPSS is just a dumb program that has no idea which value you want to be your reference value. It just blindly chooses the value that falls last alphabetically or that is the highest number. It would choose *verb* as the reference category because it comes later in the alphabetized card catalog than *noun* and *adjective*. In order to beat SPSS at its own game, say if you wanted adjective to be the reference category, you could call it *Zadjective* to make sure it is the last one alphabetically. Sneaky, huh?

Another negative aspect? For some reason, when you run a regression this alternative way, you don't have the option to get the tests and outputs that you see on the *Linear Regression Statistics* dialog box in Figure 7-5. You can't directly plot the residuals and predicted values to test the assumptions. However, you can save them and graph the values later. Some of these options and statistics are pretty important, which is why I explain the other method first. In any event, complete the following steps to carry out a multiple regression in this manner:

1. Click on *Analyze > General Linear Model > Univariate*. Enter the dependent variable into the aptly named box, any categorical variables into the *Fixed Factor(s)* box, and any continuous variables into the *Covariate(s)* box.
2. If you want to test interactions between variables, you can make them by clicking on the *Model* button. Use the *Save* button to save the residuals and predicted values. Choose the *Options* button, and click on *Parameter estimates* to see the table with the coefficients. In this same box, you can choose which categorical variables you want estimated means and pairwise comparisons for.

7.2.16 Using SPSS to carry out a bootstrapped multiple regression

In the final analysis of the reaction time data, I was able to eliminate heteroscedasticity by transforming reaction time. If your version of SPSS supports bootstrapping, you can stop worrying about all those assumptions that have to do with the residuals. Bootstrap instead. We'll use the untransformed reaction times here. To bootstrap, follow the instructions for carrying out a regression but add the following steps:

1. Look for the *Bootstrap* button on the *Main Regression* dialog box (see Figure 7-19).
2. Click on the dialog box, then check *Perform bootstrapping*. Make sure that the *Number of samples* is 1,000, then click *Continue*.
3. The coefficients table for the bootstrapped reaction time data appears in Table 7-16. Compare this data to the results without bootstrapping (see Table 7-13).

When comparing the data of both tables, you'll see that the numbers change a bit but that all of the same independent variables remain significant. What this information tells you is that whether or not you transform the data to address the violations of assumptions or if you use bootstrapping, which doesn't care about the assumptions, both methods give you about the same results.

Figure 7-19. Regression dialog box with *Bootstrap* button.

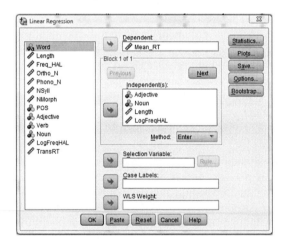

Table 7-16. Bootstrapped results of the reaction time data.

Bootstrap for Coefficients						
		Bootstrap[a]			95% Confidence Interval	
Model	B	Bias	Std. Error	Sig. (2-tailed)	Lower	Upper
(Constant)	595.954	-1.498	25.932	.001	544.994	645.518
Adjective	105.455	.552	10.058	.001	86.456	125.533
Noun	41.511	.135	9.183	.001	23.715	59.856
Length	28.060	.141	2.036	.001	24.385	32.236
LogFreqHAL	-47.541	.106	6.795	.001	-60.888	-34.471

a. Unless otherwise noted, bootstrap results are based on 1,000 bootstrapped samples.

7.2.17 Recipe for a multiple regression

1. Dummy code any categorical variables. Choose the most meaningful reference value.
2. Center the variables if it makes interpretation of the intercept clearer.
3. Run a regression with all variables included.
4. Check variables for issues with collinearity, normality, linearity, and homoscedasticity.
5. Make the necessary changes to address those issues (e.g., transform variables, deal with outliers, bootstrap).
6. Eliminate insignificant independent variables one at a time to find the most parsimonious model. (Optional.)
7. Rerun the analysis with only significant variables. (Optional.)
8. Retest the assumptions, and make changes to address any violations of assumptions.
9. Rerun the analysis
10. Report the results.

7.2.18 Hands-on exercises for multiple linear regression

Answers are available at http://linguistics.byu.edu/faculty/eddingtond/Data_Sets/answers.pdf

7.2.18.1 Reaction time

This exercise is similar to the one used as an example in this chapter. Open the file *RT_Homework.sav*. The research question is, "What is the effect of word length (*length*), word frequency (*FreqHAL*), number of orthographic neighbors (*Ortho_N*), number of phonological neighbors (*Phono_N*), and part of speech on reaction time (*Mean_RT*)?" Orthographic and phonological neighbors are words that are similar to the test word based on either spelling or phonemic make-up.

1. What variable will you need to change in order to use it in the regression? Use the right recodes. What is the reference value for part of speech?
2. Run an initial simultaneous regression with all of the variables, and check for normality, linearity, homoscedasticity, and collinearity. What problems do you find?
3. How can you address the problems?
4. Make necessary adjustments and rerun the analysis. Check for collinearity, normality, linearity, and homoscedasticity. If you find additional problems, take care of them and rerun until they are solved. How did you resolve the problems?
5. Hone your results to determine the most parsimonious model, and rerun the final analysis. Present the results of your analysis in the standard format. Include both the statistical results and a prose description of the results. Include a brief synopsis of how well the assumptions were met.

7.2.18.2 Mental calculation

Dewaele (2007) wanted to know what factors relate to how often a person does mental calculations in his or her second language. The frequency of mental calculation in the second language was measured on a scale that ranged from 1 (*rarely*) to 5 (*all the time*). The independent variables were age of acquisition, writing ability (on a scale that ranged from 1 [*least proficient*] to 5 [*maximally proficient*], frequency that second language was used (on a five-point scale that ranged from 1 [*never*] to 5 [*all day*], and the context the second language was learned in (1 = classroom, 2 = classroom and natural setting, and 3 = natural setting only). The file with the data is *DewaeleMentalCalculation.sav*.

1. What possible issues are there with the kind of data used as variables?
2. How do you handle the variable that encodes the context the second language was learned in?
3. Do an initial run and evaluate the assumptions of homoscedasticity, normality, and linearity. Look at collinearity as well. What problems are there? Which of these can bootstrapping handle?
4. Rerun the analysis to deal with the problems. Give the results of your final analysis in the standard format. Include both statistical results and a prose description. Include a brief synopsis of how well the assumptions were met.

CHAPTER EIGHT

MIXED-EFFECTS MODELS:
ANALYSIS OF REPEATED (AND OTHER NESTED) MEASURES

Dependent variable: Continuous.
Independent variables: Continuous or categorical.

Mixed-effects models (also known as multilevel models, hierarchical models, or random coefficient models) can answer questions such as

- How does the gender of the speaker, the gender of the addressee, and the social relationship between the interlocutors affect the pitch of the speaker? The data come from recordings of conversations, and the pitch of the speakers in the study is taken from measurements of many different utterances produced by each speaker.
- Test participants listen to recordings of nonnative speakers and judge their level of fluency. How do the listener's language, age, gender, and speaker's proficiency level influence those judgments? The participants make multiple ratings of speakers of all languages, ages, genders, and proficiency levels.
- Stroke victims with language impairment have their language abilities tested at various points in time. Some are enrolled in speech therapy while others are not. How are the victims' language abilities influenced by their age, the time since the stroke, and whether they had therapy or not?

At first glance, those kinds of data look like the type that would be amenable to a t-test or an ANOVA, both of which use a continuous dependent variable and a categorical independent. For that matter, it doesn't look much different from a multiple linear regression model that allows both continuous and categorical independent variables. The key difference is that independent t-tests, ANOVAs, and multiple linear regression all assume that the data are independent. This means that participants can't give responses to different experimental groups within a categorical independent variable, nor can they contribute more than one score or observation to any one group. Paired t-tests, on the other hand, are specifically designed to accommodate data that are dependent. Paired t-tests and mixed-effects models are similar because they allow repeated measures.

One common type of repeated measures study are studies that compare pretest and posttest scores given by the same participants. Another type involves longitudinal studies, in which people (or test items) are measured at several different points in time. If you think about it, a person's score on a pretest is probably not independent of his or her score on the posttest. A person with a relatively high score on the pretest most likely will have a high posttest score as well, and this needs to be taken into consideration.

Psycholinguistic experiments often place each participant into every experimental condition, which also entails repeated measures. For example, consider an experiment designed to test different relationships between words: (1) regular inflection (*sing/singing*); (2) derivation (*wash/washer*); and (3) irregular inflection (*bring/brought*). Participants carry out a lexical decision task in which they see words and nonwords on a computer screen and decide whether what they see is a word or not and press the corresponding key, which records their response time. How is reaction time influenced by seeing *sing* right before seeing a regular inflection *singing* or by seeing *wash* before *washer*? In this kind of study, the participants see words with all three kinds of relationships, so each person belongs to all three of the experimental conditions. It is also common in studies like these for participants to provide reaction times for a number of different words in each experimental condition, which produces even more repeated measures.

One way to think of repeated measures is that they entail clustering. When participants give multiple responses, their responses are clustered within the individual that provides them. We expect that an individual's responses are correlated. For example, in a reaction time experiment, some people may be fast responders and others slower than average. Often, all of a fast responder's responses will be quicker than average, which gives rise to the correlation between the respondent and his or her responses.

Besides multiple responses clustered by participant, there are other kinds of clustered data. For example, members of the same family are probably similar enough that their responses on some sort of measure would be more similar than those of respondents who don't belong to the family. In like manner, students in the same classroom should be grouped together since they have the same teacher and have been taught by the same method. For this reason, the statistical analysis needs to somehow account for the correlations that may arise when participants come from the same cluster. Test items that belong to the same subgroup or block may also create correlated responses that need to be dealt with as well. When fieldwork is carried out by a number of different researchers, the data gathered by each researcher are clustered together by researcher. This allows us to account for the possibility that people may respond differently depending on who is interviewing them or applying the survey. We need to account for any such possible correlations, and mixed-effects models are the way to do it.

8.1 Fixed Variables and Random Factors

A few definitions are in order at this point. Mixed-effects analysis gets its name from the fact that two kinds of variables are used. The kind of independent variables we've looked at so far in this book have all been fixed variables.[1] Imagine an experiment that has nonnative speakers judging sentences in their L2 for degree of correctness. The participants vary in terms of their gender, country of origin, and age at L2 acquisition, and the test sentences vary according to the kind of errors they contain. These are all fixed variables, and we are extremely interested in how all of these variables influence the judgments of correctness, which is why we include them as independent variables in the first place. Now, what if you redid the study with new participants and new test sentences? The kinds of errors used in the sentences and the gender, country of origin, and age of acquisition of the participants would not change because those things are precisely what you want to experiment with in the first place. They are called fixed variables because they would not change if the study were replicated.

What could change if you replicated the experiment? Well, the particular people who participate and the particular sentences chosen to be included as test items do. So, test item and participant are the most common RANDOM FACTORS in linguistic studies. They would or could change if the study were replicated. They are random in the sense that the test items and participants are random members of the entire set of possible sentences and entire set of possible participants. They are variables in the sense that they could possibly influence the outcome of the study, but their effect is not of primary interest to us. We don't really care which particular participant might tend to give lower ratings to the sentences or to particular types of sentences. In the same vein, we don't really care which particular test item might elicit higher or lower scores than the others in its category. I mentioned other nesting relationships, such as students in classrooms and members of families, as well as data gathered by different researchers. These are also random factors if the purpose of the study is not to see what differences there are between classes, families, and the like.

In an experiment, it is possible that particular test items or participants may be quirky and cause outliers. For example, one male participant may have had one too many lattes before the test and thus has reaction times much faster than all the other males. If he gave only one response, he's not likely to overly influence the outcome, but if he provided a number of responses, because the study includes repeated measures, he may overly influence the results. If the mean reaction times for men are lower than for women, we would want to make sure that that effect is truly above and beyond the effects introduced by the one caffeine-hyped male participant.

In a similar way, when data are gathered naturalistically, it is completely expected that some people will provide more data than others. If a particular participant is especially talkative, that sets up the possibility that he or she may overly influence the results of the study if we don't account for that fact. Test items may also have idiosyncrasies that need to be accounted for, so by factoring these random effects out, the chances are higher that we would get the same results regardless of the particular people or test items that were included.

You'll recall that residuals measure how much of the variance we are not accounting for in our model. Some of that residual error is due to the properties of the participants and test items themselves, so including random effects helps reduce the residuals in the model and lets us account for more of the variance. In short, whenever a study entails repeated measures or other clustered or nested data, we need to control for the fact that the responses could be correlated, or else the true effect of the fixed effects may be obscured. When we include random factors, we also are able to account for a larger degree of the variance in the data. At the same time, when random factors are included, the results arc considered more generalizable to other members of the random factors (other people and other test items) that we haven't actually tested.

8.2 Random Intercept

I hope that I've thoroughly convinced you that repeated measures need to be accounted for, so we are ready to look at the three things we can do to account for them: add a RANDOM INTERCEPT, add a RANDOM SLOPE, and account for the residuals with a REPEATED EFFECT or use a combination of the three. Before going any further, I'd like to suggest that an integral part of understanding the material in this chapter is a careful scrutiny of the tables and figures alongside the written description of their contents. The contents of one table often say more than many pages of my finest prose.

Let's look at how the use of *EndUpVerbing* expressions (e.g., *end up hating, end up spending*) has changed across time. In Figure 8-1, you can see that these expressions have become more frequent,[2] as evidenced in four different corpora: Google Books: American English (hereafter GoogleUS), Google Books: British English (hereafter GoogleUK), *Time* Magazine Corpus of American English (hereafter *Time*), and the Corpus of Historical American English (hereafter COHA). (By the way, these corpora are all freely available online thanks to the corpus linguistic

---

[1] I use this term to include categorical variables that are fixed factors and continuous variables that are fixed covariates.
[2] The raw data are not linear, so I linearized them for the purposes of the discussion by applying the cube root transformation (see Chapter 3).

wizardry of Mark Davies.[3]) The residuals for GoogleUS are marked in Figure 8-1. There, the repeated measures are not measurements of the same participants but of the same corpora over time. The research question involves the effect of time on frequency of usage. The data happen to come from four different corpora, but the effect of a particular corpus is not an independent variable we are interested in. It is not a fixed variable. Instead, corpus is a random factor. This is so because we could do the same study and test the effect of time but use different corpora instead.

Up to this point, I've been talking about how the observations from the same corpus, or same person, are correlated. In actuality, it is not the correlation between the observations themselves but the correlations between the residuals of the observations that we are interested in. Those residual correlations are very obvious in Figure 8-1. For example, all of the residuals for the *Time* data and COHA data are higher than the predicted values indicated by the regression line. This is true across all decades. All of the data points for the other two corpora, on the other hand, always fall below the line and have negative residuals. If they weren't correlated, they would be more randomly distributed above and below the line. The second thing we see is that the data points for each corpus stay mostly in relative order to each other across the decades. Google UK is usually dead last, followed closely by Google US. *Time* magazine and COHA are usually neck and neck for having the highest number of *EndUpVerbing* constructions in each decade. This is what is meant by correlation between the residuals.

One thing we can do to eliminate this correlation is add a random intercept for each corpus. Look at the regression line in Figure 8-1. If we consider the 1930s to be the zero point, the line intercepts the vertical axis at about .25. This is the overall intercept. In order to add a random intercept for a corpus, we calculate how much the corpus in question deviates on average from the overall intercept. For example, COHA is about .25 higher than the overall intercept, so we make a regression line for COHA that starts at .5 that is parallel to the overall regression line (Figure 8-2). The same thing is done for the rest of the corpora, and in this way, we allow each corpus to have its own intercept.

Figure 8-1. Cube root frequency of *EndUpVerbing* in four corpora from the 1930s to 2000s.

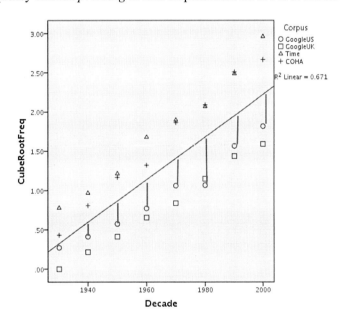

Here's the cool thing: once we've added a random intercept for each corpus, we no longer measure the residuals as the distance between the data points and the regression line of the overall intercept. Instead, the residuals are calculated as the distance between a data point and the regression line defined by its individual intercept. Look at the circle icons in Figure 8-1, which represent the data from GoogleUS. Where the icon doesn't fall right on the line, the residuals for GoogleUS are marked. Without a random intercept, all of the residuals fall below the overall line. They are all negative, which is why they are correlated. However, when measured to their individual regression line (Figure 8-2), some fall below and others above. What this means is that the correlation is eliminated. What's more, the hierarchy in the values of the residuals was *Time* > COHA > GoogleUS > GoogleUK in most decades when all were calculated from the overall regression line. However, that hierarchy falls apart when each corpus is allowed to have its own intercept and you calculate the residuals to each corpora's individual regression line. So allowing participants (corpora in this case) or test items to have their own intercept is often all that needs to be done to eliminate the correlation between their repeated measures.

[3] See http://corpus.byu.edu.

Figure 8-2. Random intercepts for the *EndUpVerbing* data where time is continuous.

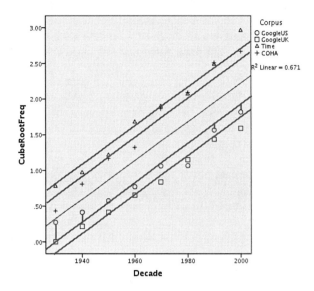

These corpus data give us nice, straight regression lines because time is a continuous variable and we are fitting a line with a particular slope to it. For categorical data, such as treatment type or experimental condition, we aren't going to fit a line. That doesn't make sense. Instead, we just calculate a mean for each condition. Consider an experimental design in which there are four conditions and all of the participants give multiple responses in each one. The random intercept in this case is the mean amount each participant varies from the overall mean. When we connect each participant's mean in each of the four conditions with a line (Figure 8-3), the particular zigzag of the lines represents each subject's intercept from the overall mean. In this case, the lowest scores are obtained in condition 3 and the highest in condition 4.

8.3 Random Slope

If we really want to reduce the residuals and alter the correlation between them, we can sometimes get the individual lines even closer to the residuals by allowing the lines to vary in slope. That is, we can not only allow each one to vary in their intercept, depending on what their average distance from the overall regression line is, but let each one have its own slope or trajectory. In other words, we allow the individual lines to not be parallel. This is illustrated in Figure 8-4. It should be obvious that the residuals are even smaller with random slopes. Smaller residuals mean that the model fits the data better. We also hope that the residuals from a random slope will be less correlated.

Figure 8-3. Possible random intercepts for categorical data.

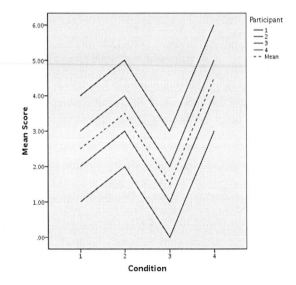

In the corpus data, the independent variable of time is continuous, and we can allow each corpus to have a random slope. Categorical independent variables, such as test conditions, may also be allowed a random slope. Now, when there is a random intercept the average amount each participant (or test item) varies from the overall mean is calculated and used to determine the residuals. That is why the lines drawn between those means are all parallel. A random slope for categorical data means that each subject's mean is not equally distant from the overall mean in each experimental condition but can vary from condition to condition. This could look something like Figure 8-5, in which the means are connected with a line. Random slopes in a study that uses different experimental conditions make sense when participants give several responses in each condition. If they only give one response per condition, the mean would equal the response in that condition, and the statistics wouldn't be happy with that. It should be clear that it's possible to fit a random intercept by itself. In the same way, it's probably a good idea to conceive of random slopes as always having an accompanying random intercept since slopes without intercepts are rare.

Figure 8-4. Random slopes for the *EndUpVerbing* data where time is continuous.

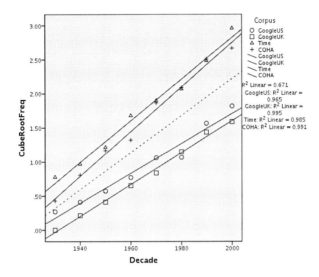

Figure 8-5. Possible random slopes for categorical data.

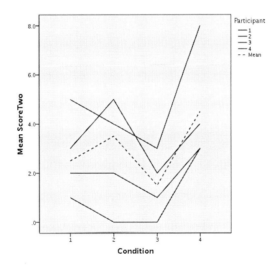

8.4 Covariance Structures and the G Matrix in a Random Effects Model

When running a mixed-effects analysis, you will need to specify some information about the slope and intercept as well as what the relationship between them is. This is done by specifying a COVARIANCE STRUCTURE. The covariance structure of a random effect is specified in what is known in statistical parlance as the G (OR D) MATRIX. When the model includes a random intercept, the G matrix doesn't contain much information, just an estimate of how spread out the individual intercepts are from the overall intercept when having low numbers means the individual intercepts don't depart much from the overall intercept. When the model only has a random intercept, there's only one covariance structure that you use. It is the default in SPSS and is called VARIANCE COMPONENTS (VC).

Now, when you have a random slope as well, the G matrix contains estimates of three things. The first is how spread out the random intercepts are from the overall intercept (the variance of the intercepts). It also has a measure of how much the random slopes vary. If they are all pretty parallel to the overall slope, that number will be small. It will be large if their trajectories are far from parallel. The third thing in the G matrix is an estimate of how much the intercept and slope are related. This is known as their COVARIANCE. This has to do with the relationship between the residuals themselves at each point of measurement. You can call this relationship a correlation, but that is not technically correct. Remember that a correlation is always expressed as a value ranging between −1 and +1, regardless of the scale it is being measured in (milliseconds, hertz, intensity). Its actual value has been standardized. An unstandardized correlation that is expressed in the original units of measure is called the covariance.

Now, exactly what a slope-by-intercept relationship means isn't easy to grasp. As an example of one type of relationship, consider an experiment involving reaction times. As the experiment goes on, people get the hang of it, and by the end, they all have gotten faster. Consider the six participants in Figure 8-6, all of whom show a downward slope, indicative of responding more quickly at the end of the study. Participants 1, 2, and 3 are the slowpokes. They start slower and end slower than participants 4, 5, and 6.

HINT
- A MIXED-EFFECTS MODEL contains random intercepts, random slopes, or both. It may also include a repeated effect.
- A MARGINAL MODEL only includes a repeated effect, never a random intercept or slope.

However, the slopes for these slowpokes is much steeper than for the quick draws. The slow pokes improve more, so the correlation between intercept and slope in this case is that people with initially higher intercepts (slower reaction times) have steeper negative slopes. People with the fastest reaction times at the beginning of the experiment have flatter slopes. Of course, there are many other kinds of relationships that may exist, but this should give you an idea of how an intercept and slope can be correlated. But never fear: it isn't something you have to figure out yourself. SPSS does it for you.

Figure 8-6. Example of a correlation between a slope and an intercept.

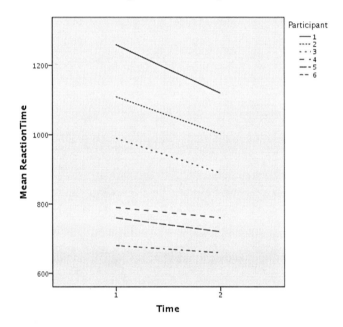

In a random slope model, there are two covariance structures that we generally consider. The first is UNSTRUCTURED (UN). When you choose this structure, the G matrix contains a unique estimate of the variance of the intercept, slope, and covariance between the intercept and slope at each point it is measured (e.g., each point in time or each experimental condition). The other covariance structure is VARIANCE COMPONENTS (VC), which gives a unique estimate for the intercept and slope but assumes that there is no covariance between the two. How do you know which one to use? Choose the one that fits your data best. I'll explain how in a minute.

8.5 Repeated Effect

The third way of accounting for repeated measures is to use a model with a repeated effect. Unlike random intercepts and random slopes, a repeated effect is not a random factor. It has nothing to do with trying to fit the closest line (or mean) to the individual data points in order to reduce and change the values of the residuals. In fact, if you only include a repeated effect and it isn't coupled with a random intercept or random slope, you are actually running not a mixed-effects model but a MARGINAL MODEL.

A repeated effect model takes the residuals that exist and controls for any correlation between them by telling the statistical model how they are related to each other. In a marginal model, where you only have a repeated effect, you give information about the residuals that are derived by measuring the distance of each data point to the *overall intercept or mean*. Now, in a true mixed-effects model, where you have a random intercept or slope, you can also include a repeated effect. When a repeated effect is included with a random intercept or slope, it still specifies information about the residuals, but those residuals are now calculated by measuring how far each data point is from the individual subject's intercept or mean instead of from the overall intercept or mean.

When you include a repeated effect, you need to give the model two pieces of data, or parameters, that the residuals can vary on. The first is their variance, or how spread out they are from the regression line at each point of measurement. (The point of measurement could be time, experimental condition, trial, etc.) The variance can stay roughly the same at each point, increase equally across time, increase, decrease, or be completely different at each point as time goes on.

The second parameter is the covariance, which is the relationship between the residuals themselves at each point of measurement. Is it equal? Does it steadily increase or decrease? Is there no relationship at all? The pattern of values of these two parameters for all the residuals across all the points of measurement is what is estimated, and that estimate appears in the covariance structure for the repeated effect.

8.5.1 Covariance structures and the R matrix in a repeated effects model

I know what you are thinking. Didn't we just see that covariance structures are used to specify the variances of the intercept, slope, and covariance between the intercept and slope in a random slope model? Yes, that is true. That information appears in the G matrix, which has to do with the random effects. What we are looking at now is the information that appears in a different matrix. The R MATRIX contains information about the structure of the residuals, and so when we talk about covariance structures in a repeated effects model, they specify the structure of the residuals. Some of the same covariance structures can be used to specify the contents of both the G and R matrices. I know it's a bit confusing to use covariance structures to mean different things, but think of the covariance structures as patterns. So, just as a shirt or jacket can have a plaid or paisley pattern, a G or an R matrix can have an Unstructured or Variance Components covariance pattern.

> **HINT**
> Covariance structures:
> - A random intercept model contains an estimate of the variance of the individual intercepts (or means) from the overall intercept (or mean). This estimate is in the G matrix.
> - In a random slope model, the covariance structure specifies an estimate of the variance of the individual intercepts (or means), an estimate of the variance of the individual slopes, and an estimate of the covariance between the intercepts and slopes. These estimates are in the G matrix.
> - In a model with repeated effects, the covariance structure specifies an estimate of the variance of the residuals from the overall intercept (or mean) at each point of measurement and an estimate of the covariances that occur when the residuals at each point of measurement are compared to each other. These estimates are in the R matrix.

8.5.2 The variance and covariance of the residuals in a model with a repeated effect

This should make more sense if we consider the *EndUpVerbing* data again. You'll recall that each decade has four different measurements taken from the four corpora. If you compare the residuals of those four frequency measurements in each decade against the residuals of those four measurements in every other decade and report the covariances rather than the correlation coefficients, you get the data in Table 8-1. Remember that the correlation of one set of numbers against itself will always be 1. The same is not true for covariances. Instead, the covariance of the numbers in one decade against themselves is the variance for that decade. Isn't stats cool? So, the variances appear along the diagonal and are boldfaced. For these data, the variance goes up with time. It starts at .11 and moves progressively to .43. You can see this graphically when you look back at Figure 8-4. The scores in the earlier decades are slightly closer to the overall intercept than they are in more recent decades, so the residuals become a bit more disperse from the line over time. The covariances between the frequency scores for each decade appear off of the diagonal. They range from about .11 to .37, and they show a trend of getting larger in more recent decades.

Table 8-1. Variances and covariances of the *EndUpVerbing* data.

	1930s	1940s	1950s	1960s	1970s	1980s	1990s	2000s
1930s	**.11**	.11	.12	.15	.16	.15	.16	.20
1940s		**.12**	.14	.16	.19	.18	.20	.23
1950s			**.17**	.19	.22	.22	.24	.27
1960s				**.23**	.25	.25	.26	.31
1970s					**.30**	.30	.31	.36
1980s						**.32**	.32	.36
1990s							**.33**	.37
2000s								**.43**

8.5.3 More on covariance structures of the residuals in a model with a repeated effect

The idea of covariance structures for the residuals may seem like a novel concept, but we've had to deal with it already. For example, when you run an ANOVA or a regression, you don't specify the covariance structures directly because they are already built into the assumptions of the analysis itself. One of these assumptions is that the residuals are independent of each other. That is, there should be no relationship (or covariance) between the residuals resulting from measurements taken under different conditions or at different times. You've heard that before, right? When we include a repeated effect, we can loosen up this strict requirement by explicitly specifying the kind of relationship that exists among the residuals instead of assuming there is none. This is done by choosing a covariance structure that estimates how much covariance there is among the repeated measures.

We have also implicitly assumed that the variances of the residuals are equal across time or experimental condition (aka homoscedasticity) and that we have done everything in our power to make them be equal if they are not. However, by using a repeated effect, we are now freed from that sometimes hard-to-achieve requirement as long as we choose a covariance structure that gives a good estimate of what the variance is actually like among the residuals. There are a bunch of covariance structures, and following time-honored statistics tradition, they go by funky names that make them sound overly technical. In fact, it is advisable to avoid using these names with someone you're attracted to or you may not get many dates (except with statisto-geeks). Some of the most common appear in Table 8-2.[4]

Table 8-2. Common covariance structures for repeated effects.

Covariance Structure	Variance across repeated measures	Covariance across repeated measures	Acronym
Unstructured	Different	Unique	UN
Scaled Identity	Constant	None	ID
Diagonal	Different	None	DIAG
Compound Symmetry	Constant	Constant	CS
Heterogeneous Compound Symmetry	Different	Constant	CSH
Autoregressive	Constant	Measurements closer in time have higher covariances than more distant measurements.	AR1
Heterogeneous Autoregressive	Different	Measurements closer in time have higher covariances than more distant measurements.	ARH
Toeplitz	Constant	Adjacent measurements have the same covariance, but the covariance is different for nonadjacent measurements.	TP
Heterogeneous Toeplitz	Different	Adjacent measurements have the same covariance, but the covariance is different for nonadjacent measurements.	TPH
Variance Components	Is the same thing as Diagonal in a repeated effect.		VC

---

[4] These are the names and parameters of the structures that SPSS uses. They differ between statistic packages.

HINT

Suggested rules for choosing a covariance structure in a repeated effects model:

- Since UN is the most general, try it first.
- If your study is longitudinal because your dependent variable involves time (or another measure in which closer points of measurement may be more correlated than distant ones), it makes sense to try UN, AR1, ARH, TP, TPH, CS, or CSH.
- If your study is not longitudinal, try UN, CS, or CSH. The structures AR1, ARH, TP, and TPH don't make sense with nonlongitudinal studies.
- Use VC (DIAG) or ID in a repeated effect only when there is also a random effect in the model. Don't use VC (DIAG) or ID by themselves in a marginal model.

8.5.4 Testing the fit of different covariance structures with a likelihood ratio test

In Table 8-2 and the rules in the hint box, I've given some general guidelines about what covariance structure to use in particular situations. However, it's often not clear what the right covariance structure is for the residuals, and people generally don't construct an actual covariance table like I did to examine it (Table 8-1). Even there, it isn't clear which covariance structure fits the pattern among the covariances. The best way to determine which one most closely fits is to try several and then compare their fits statistically using a LIKELIHOOD RATIO TEST and also by comparing the information criteria.

As far as the *EndUpVerbing* expressions are concerned, the question is what the effect of time is on their frequency, and the random factor is the corpora the data come from. We'll run a marginal model by including only a repeated effect. This specifies information about the variance of the residuals across time as well as how related they are across all of the decades (with decades as a continuous variable). However, remember that a marginal model does not fit a random intercept or slope. If it did, it would be a mixed-effects model.

What we are looking for is the consumer model, in which you want to get the most for the least amount of money, but sometimes you're willing to pay more for something of better quality. In our situation, you're looking for the best-fitting model with the fewest number of parameters. Let's look at the Autoregressive covariance structure, which results in a model with four parameters, as can be seen at the bottom of the *# of Parameters* column in Table 8-3.

Table 8-3. Model data for the *EndUpVerbing* data.

Model Dimension[a]		# of levels	Covariance structure	# of parameters	Subject variables	# of subjects
Fixed effects	Intercept	1		1		
	DecadeNUM	1		1		
Repeated effects	DecadeNUM	8	First-order Autoregressive	2	Corpus	4
Total		10		4		

a. Dependent variable: CubeRootFreq.

One thing to look at is the R matrix that SPSS estimates for the data. Table 8-4 contains just a part of the matrix since the whole matrix is too big to fit on the page. Autoregressive assumes equal variances, and as you can see, the boldface variances along the diagonal are all estimated to be about .265. Autoregressive also assumes that measurements taken in closer decades will have higher covariances than those taken between more distant decades. For example, the covariance between decades 0 and 1 is .257, and this lowers to .248 between decades 0 and 2 and then to .241 between decades 0 and 3.

Table 8-4. R matrix for the Autoregressive covariance structure (truncated).

	[DecadeNUM = 0]	[DecadeNUM = 1]	[DecadeNUM = 2]	[DecadeNUM = 3]
[DecadeNUM = 0]	**.265440**	.257073	.248969	.241121
[DecadeNUM = 1]	.257073	**.265440**	.257073	.248969
[DecadeNUM = 2]	.248969	.257073	**.265440**	.257073
[DecadeNUM = 3]	.241121	.248969	.257073	**.265440**

The information criteria for this model are given in Table 8-5. One way these criteria are used is to compare models that have different covariance structures or different random effects. These numbers really don't mean anything by themselves. The idea is that the *lower* these measures are, the smaller the residuals are, which means that the model fits the data better. The nice thing about the −2 Restricted Log-Likelihood (−2RLL) is that you can use it to compare the fit of the residuals of two different models, and better-fitting residuals are an indirect measure of a better-fitting model. What's more, you can determine whether the difference between them is statistically significant. Unfortunately, you can't test significance with the other information criteria. However, the −2RLL does not take the number of parameters into consideration like the other information criteria measures, which penalize a model with more parameters, do, so it's a good idea to consider using both of them.

Table 8-5. Information criteria for the *EndUpVerbing* data with an Autoregressive covariance structure.

Information Criteria[a]	
−2 Restricted Log-Likelihood	−24.806
Akaike's Information Criterion (AIC)	−20.806
Hurvich and Tsai's Criterion (AICC)	−20.362
Bozdogan's Criterion (CAIC)	−16.004
Schwarz's Bayesian Criterion (BIC)	−18.004

The information criteria are displayed in smaller-is-better forms.
a. Dependent variable: CubeRootFreq.

A word of caution: you can only use the −2RLL to compare models if those models are nested. A model is nested in another model if it is a subset of that model, so Models X and Y are nested if X contains parameters A, B, and C and if Y contains A and B (or A and C, or B and C, or just one of the three variables). Models X and Y are not nested if X contains A, B, and C and if Y contains A, B, and D. Two models that only vary in the random effects or the covariance structure they use are also nested. The nesting requirement holds for comparisons using −2RLL, but the other information criteria can be used to compare unnested models as well.

Table 8-6 contains the results for a number of different covariance structures.[5] How do you choose which one fits the best? Remember that we want the lowest information criteria and the fewest parameters. So, Toeplitz has the lowest −2RLL (−33.149), but Autoregressive has the lowest BIC (−18.004) and the fewest parameters. However, based on Table 8-1, Heterogeneous Autoregressive and Heterogeneous Compound Symmetry may work well because they take into consideration the fact that the variance changes over time, so let's consider them as well. The question we first need to answer is whether the −2RLL for each of these is truly different. If they aren't different, we shouldn't put so much weight on the fact that one is a bit lower or higher than another. We'll compare them with a likelihood ratio test.

Table 8-6. Comparison of five covariance structures on the *EndUpVerbing* data.

	# of parameters	−2 Restricted Log-Likelihood	Schwarz's Bayesian Criterion (BIC)	p of Decade
Compound Symmetry	4	−9.839	−3.037	.0005
Heterogeneous Compound Symmetry	11	−30.438	0.172	.0005
Autoregressive	4	−24.806	−18.004	.0005
Heterogeneous Autoregressive	11	−31.833	−1.222	.0005
Toeplitz	10	−33.149	−5.940	.004

If you look up the difference between the −2RLLs (Figure 8-6) by the difference in the number of parameters in the chi-square table (Table 8-7), you'll see that none of the differences are significant. For example, the difference of 7.027 between ARH and AR1 at 7 *df* (or parameters) is smaller than the value in the chi-square table of 14.07, which appears under the .05 level of significance. If the difference were 14.07 or larger, we could assert a difference, but no cigar here.

---

[5] There were too few data points to use UN, and ID and VC/DIAG don't make sense in a marginal model.

Figure 8-6. Difference between the −2 Restricted-Log Likelihood by the difference in the Number of Parameters.

	−2RLL	df		−2RLL	df		−2RLL	df
	ARH −31.833	11	ARH	−31.833	11	TP	−33.149	10
	AR1 −24.806	4	TP	−33.149	10	AR1	−24.806	4
Difference	7.027	7		1.316	1		8.343	6
	−2RLL	df		−2RLL	df		−2RLL	df
	CSH −30.438	11	CSH	−30.438	11	CSH	−30.438	11
	AR1 −24.806	4	TP	−33.149	10	ARH	−24.806	4
Difference	5.632	7		2.711	1		5.632	7

Table 8-7. Chi-square table.[6]

df	p = 0.05	p = 0.01	p = 0.001	df	p = 0.05	p = 0.01	p = 0.001
1	3.84	6.64	10.83	10	18.31	23.21	29.59
2	5.99	9.21	13.82	11	19.68	24.73	31.26
3	7.82	11.35	16.27	12	21.03	26.22	32.91
4	9.49	13.28	18.47	13	22.36	27.69	34.53
5	11.07	15.09	20.52	14	23.69	29.14	36.12
6	12.59	16.81	22.46	15	25.00	30.58	37.70
7	14.07	18.48	24.32	16	26.30	32.00	39.25
8	15.51	20.09	26.13	17	27.59	33.41	40.79
9	16.92	21.67	27.88	18	28.87	34.81	42.31

Since the −2RLL values don't differ significantly from each other, we can consider two other things. The first is that Autoregressive has the lowest BIC. The second is that when we look at the actual variances of the residuals (Table 8-1), they go up across time, which fits the definition of a Heterogeneous Autoregressive (and Heterogeneous Compound Symmetry) structure. The numbers tell us that the best deal is Autoregressive, but in order to get a better intuitive fit, we may want to "spend" seven more parameters and choose Heterogeneous Autoregressive. It's a judgment call you'd have to make, but lest you get bent out of shape about that, notice in Table 8-6 that the significance of Decade doesn't change regardless of which one you decide on, and it is precisely the effect of time on the use of *EndUpVerbing* that we are testing in the first place.

Up to this point, I've shown how to use a likelihood ratio test and information criteria tests to find the best-fitting covariance structure in a marginal model that contains only a repeated effect. However, these same tests can be used to determine whether including a random intercept or random slope improves the model fit, as we will see.

8.5.5 Using SPSS to run a marginal model

1. Load the file corpus *data.sav.*
2. Click on *Analyze > Mixed Models > Linear.*
3. In this case, the *Corpus* variable indicates what the subjects are. Repeated responses are made to *DecadeNUM.* Place these variables in the appropriate box. The covariance type is also chosen in this dialog box in the *Repeated Covariance Type* drop-down menu (Figure 8-8).
4. Choose *AR1: Heterogeneous > Continue.*
5. In the *Linear Mixed Models* dialog box (Figure 8-9), *CubeRootFrequency* is the dependent variable. All random effects variables and independent variables are also chosen here. Categorical variables such as *Corpus* go in the *Factor(s)* box, and continuous variables such as *DecadeNUM* go in the *Covariate(s)* box (Figure 8-9).
6. Click on *Fixed* and move the independent variable *DecadeNUM* to the *Model* box by highlighting it > *Add > Continue.*
7. Click on the *Statistics* button and check *Parameter estimates* and *Covariances of residuals > Continue > OK.* Among other things, this will produce Tables 8-3, 8-4, and 8-5.

---

[6] If you need to go beyond 9 *df*, google "chi-square table" and you'll find dozens of tables.

Figure 8-8. Running a marginal model.

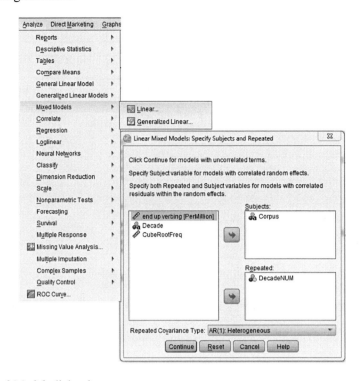

Figure 8-9. *Linear Mixed Models* dialog box.

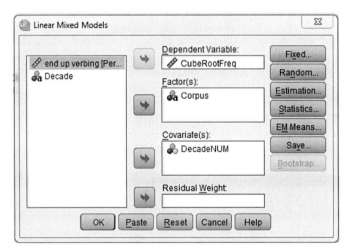

8.6 Simple Example of a Mixed-Effects Model

Now that we've seen how to use a marginal model to account for repeated measures, let's see how we can carry out a mixed-effects model to account for the repeated measures in the *EndUpVerbing* data. The dependent variable is frequency (which has been transformed by the cube-root transformation to make it linear), and the independent variable is time as measured in decades. Here, Decade is treated as a continuous variable, so, to make the decades evenly spaced, 1930s is coded as 0, 1940s is 1, and so on until 2000s, which is 7. The random effect is Corpus since the data are repeated measures from four different corpora.

Following West et al. (2007:39–40), I am going to describe how to use a top-down strategy, in which you begin with a model that contains all independent variables and random effects. The first step is to find the best fit among the random effects. Models 1 and 2 (Table 8-8) fit a random slope so that each corpus is allowed to have its own intercept and trajectory slope (see Figure 8-4). Those two models differ in the covariance structure that is applied. Model 3 fits a random intercept that allows only the intercepts to vary, not the trajectories. It should be clear by the lower −2RLL and BIC numbers that allowing random slopes provides a better fit than just allowing a random intercept does.

Table 8-8. Results of a number of models of the *EndUpVerbing* data.

Model #		# Par.	−2RLL	BIC	*p* of Decade
Random effects					
1	Random slope for Corpus by Decade UN	6	−32.974	−19.370	.002
2	Random slope for Corpus by Decade VC	5	−29.449	−19.245	.002
3	Random intercept for Corpus VC	4	−9.839	−3.037	.0005
Random and repeated effects					
4	Random slope for Corpus by Decade UN Repeated Corpus by Decade UN	Model cannot be fitted because number of observations is less than or equal to number of model parameters.			
5	Random slope for Corpus by Decade UN Repeated Corpus by decade VC	Hessian matrix not positive definite.			
6	Random slope for Corpus by Decade UN Repeated Corpus by Decade CSH, ARH, TP, TPH, CS	No convergence.			
7	Random slope for Corpus by decade UN Repeated Corpus by Decade ID	6	−32.974	−19.370	.002
8	Random slope for Corpus by Decade UN Repeated Corpus by Decade AR1	7	−33.251	−16.245	.002
Marginal model					
9	Repeated Corpus by Decade AR1	4	−24.806	−18.004	.0005

So, once you've found the best-fitting random effects, the next step is to see if you can further improve the fit by controlling for any additional correlation among those residuals with a repeated effect. Models 4–8 take the best random effects model (Model 1) and add a repeated effect to it with different covariance structures. Of the two models that don't result in errors, Model 8 is not a better fit or a worse fit than Model 1 or 7 (do a likelihood ratio test and you will see). Model 7 produces an identical fit to Model 1 but has one fewer parameter than Model 8, so Models 1 and 7 are preferred over 8. Since Models 1 and 7 have identical outcomes, which is better? I'd go with Model 1 because it is simpler; it has only a random effect, not a random and a repeated effect like Model 7. For comparison's sake, I included Model 9, which is the numerically superior marginal model from Table 8-6 and which is no better than Model 1 either. So my humble opinion would be to go with Model 1.

Many of the above models with a repeated effect give the dreaded NO CONVERGENCE and HESSIAN MATRIX not positive definite errors. When you get one of these errors, it generally means that there are too many parameters in the model, that the algorithm can't find a good fit, or both. Often this is because it's trying to model variation where there isn't much to model. There are a number of ways to handle this (West et al. 2007:32–33):

- Use a different covariance structure. Unstructured is often the culprit for such errors.
- If you have a numeric variable that is large, try converting it to a smaller number by changing the unit. For example, convert milliseconds to seconds so that a score of 2000 milliseconds is reduced to 2 seconds, which results in smaller numbers for the algorithm to work with. Try to keep the ranges of your continuous variables similar.
- Use a marginal model with a repeated effect rather than a random-effect model to capture the repeated measures.
- Eliminate some variables or random effects.

When there are nested data, such as individuals within a family or students within a class, one way to avoid lack of convergence is to restructure the data (Heck et al. 2012). For instance, if you had 90 students (numbered 1–90) in 10 classes (numbered 1–10) and your data don't converge, renumber the 90 students, starting from 1 in each class. So if class 1 has 12 students, renumber the students 1–12. If class 2 has 9 students, renumber them 1–9, and so on. This is okay to do because student 1 from class 1 is not going to be confused with student 1 from class 2—student and class are nested and their nesting relationship is specified.

HINT
When you get a model that hasn't converged or has a nonpositive Hessian matrix, under no circumstances can you use the results of that model. Those numbers may look good, but they aren't accurate.

This is a good time to point out something else. Notice that in the marginal model, the best fit numerically (according to BIC) was obtained with AR1 in the repeated statement (Table 8-5). However, of the models with both random and repeated effects, the best fit for the repeated effect is arguably ID (Model 7 in Table 8-8). How can that be? Shouldn't the same covariance structure give the best fit regardless? No, not at all. The difference is that in a marginal model, we are modeling the residuals that result when each data point is measured to the overall regression line. When a random effect is added alongside a repeated effect, each corpus gets its own intercept, and the residuals are measured to the individual corpus line rather than the overall regression line. In short, the residuals are very different beasts in each kind of model, and you can't compare them.

At this point you may ask, Why is it so important to find the best-fitting model if in most cases the significance of the independent variable Decade doesn't change? Isn't that a lot of work for nothing? It's true that in many cases, but not all, the significance of the independent variables changes little regardless of the way the random effects are modeled. However, you need to be honest about the existence of repeated measures in your data and carry out a thorough analysis that accounts for them. Only when you've factored out any influence that repeated measures may exert can you be confident that the effect of the independent variables on your dependent variable is not influenced by the correlations among the data caused by the repeated measures.

Finally, sometimes as the last step in carrying out a mixed-effects model you will need to find the most parsimonious model by factoring out any insignificant independent variables. However, if your hypothesis includes a particular variable that turns out to be insignificant, you may want to leave it in. In the case of the *EndUpVerbing* data, there is only one independent variable, and it's significant, so we can stop here.

8.7 A Closer Look at the R and G Matrices

Up to this point, I've emphasized how to compare models with different random and repeated effects and different covariance structures. This involves considering the number of parameters in the model (Table 8-3) and the information criteria (Table 8-5). However, we haven't even looked at a single G matrix yet and have only seen one example of an R matrix (Table 8-4). Let's use the G and R matrices from Model 7 in Table 8-8 as examples. That model has a random slope for Corpus over Decade with an Unstructured (UN) covariance structure. In addition, it contains a repeated effect of Corpus over Decade with a Scaled Identity (ID) covariance structure.

A portion of the R matrix appears in Table 8-9. Scaled Identity estimates that the variance of the residuals is constant across Decades. Here, it is .007867. The zeros off the diagonal indicate that by using ID, we are assuming that there is no covariance between the residuals. In Model 8, on the other hand, we assumed an Autoregressive structure (AR1) for the residuals rather than ID. AR1 also assumes the same variance across all Decades, but the difference between ID and AR1 is that the latter assumes that the residuals covary across Decades, and it estimates those covariances. When you look at the covariances, though, you see that they are very small (Table 8-10). Is there really much difference between having no covariance and having tiny covariances? Well, if you look at the Information Criteria for Models 7 and 8 in Table 8-8, you'll see that they fit about equally well, so the difference is negligible.

Table 8-9. The R matrix for Model 7 with ID (truncated).

	[DecadeNUM = 0]	[DecadeNUM = 1]	[DecadeNUM = 2]	[DecadeNUM = 3]
[DecadeNUM = 0]	.007867	0	0	0
[DecadeNUM = 1]	0	.007867	0	0
[DecadeNUM = 2]	0	0	.007867	0
[DecadeNUM = 3]	0	0	0	.007867

My guess is that some readers at this point have looked back at the residuals in Tables 8-1 and 8-4 and are wondering why they are so different from the estimates in Tables 8-9 and 8-10. Just a quick reminder: The residuals reported in Tables 8-1 and 8-4 come from a marginal model and represent the distance between each data point and the overall regression line. Tables 8-9 and 8-10 come from a model with a random slope for each corpus. This means that the residuals are defined as the distance between the data points for a particular corpus and the regression line for that corpus.

Table 8-10. The R matrix for Model 8 with AR1 (truncated).

	[DecadeNUM = 0]	[DecadeNUM = 1]	[DecadeNUM = 2]	[DecadeNUM = 3]
[DecadeNUM = 0]	.008785	.001495	.000255	.000043
[DecadeNUM = 1]	.001495	.008785	.001495	.000255
[DecadeNUM = 2]	.000255	.001495	.008785	.001495
[DecadeNUM = 3]	.000043	.000255	.001495	.008785

Now let's move on to the G matrix for Model 7, which has an Unstructured covariance structure. SPSS provides two tables with this information: 8-11 and 8-12. I've modified Table 8-11 a little to specify how it relates to Table 8-12. When there is a random slope, the G matrix contains an estimate of the variance of the intercepts—in other words, how spread out the intercepts for each of the four corpora are from the overall intercept. For these data, the variance is .096, and this figure, minus a few decimal places, appears in Table 8-11 in column 1 row 1. This corresponds to *UN (1, 1)* in Table 8-12.

Table 8-11. G matrix for Model 7 with UN.

		1	2
		Intercept | Corpus	DecadeNUM | Corpus
1	Intercept | Corpus	.096409	.014404
2	DecadeNUM | Corpus	.014404	.002636

Table 8-12. Covariance parameters for Model 7 with UN.

Estimates of covariance parameters[a]		Estimate	Std. error
Parameter		Estimate	Std. error
Repeated measures	Variance	.007867	.002271
Intercept + DecadeNUM [subject = Corpus]	UN (1,1)	.096409	.081400
	UN (2,1)	.014404	.012524
	UN (2,2)	.002636	.002306

a. Dependent variable: CubeRootFreq.

The G matrix also contains an estimate of how much the slopes vary. If the regression lines for each corpus were completely parallel to the overall regression line, this number would be zero. The variance in slopes appears in column 2 row 2 in Table 8-11 and in the row labeled *UN (2, 2)* in Table 8-12. Here, the variance is .002, which says there's not much variation. Go back and compare the lines in Figure 8-4 and you will see that their trajectories don't vary much from the overall regression line. However, the question is whether they vary enough to make a better-fitting model when compared to the random intercept model in which the individual regression lines for each corpus are parallel. Models 1, 2, and 7 allow random slopes, while Model 3 allows only a random intercept. It should be clear by the Information Criteria in Table 8-8 that models that allow random slopes provide a better fit.

The last thing the G matrix contains is an estimate of the covariance between the intercepts and slopes, which is .014. The positive number means that higher intercepts have steeper slopes and lower intercepts have flatter slopes. In Figure 8-4, the corpora with higher intercepts are *Time* and *COHA*. Their slopes are a bit steeper than those of *GoogleUK* and *GoogleUS*, which explains the positive covariance. If this figure were negative, it would indicate a situation in which higher intercepts have flatter slopes and lower intercepts have steeper ones.

When a model includes a random slope, you may try a VC covariance structure rather than a UN one. There are times when using a UN covariance structure will cause the model to not converge, and sometimes, VC provides a better model fit. In any event, when Model 7 is run with VC as the covariance structure for the random slope, the G structure contains only two bits of information (Table 8-13). The first is an estimate of the variance of the intercepts (.102673). The second is an estimate of the variance of the slopes (.002814). These numbers differ very little from the estimates under UN. The major difference between UN and VC is that the G matrix does not contain an estimate of the covariance between intercept and slope when VC is used. This is because VC assumes that there is no covariance.

Table 8-13. Covariance parameters with G matrix figures for Model 7 using VC.

Estimates of covariance parameters[a]		Estimate	Std. error
Parameter		Estimate	Std. error
Repeated measures	Variance	.007809	.002238
Intercept [subject = Corpus]	Variance	.102673	.086534
DecadeNUM [subject = Corpus]	Variance	.002814	.002450

a. Dependent variable: CubeRootFreq.

8.8 Using SPSS to Run a Mixed-Effects Model with a Random Slope and a Repeated Effect

To run Model 7 in Table 8-8:

1. Click on *Analyze > Mixed Models > Linear* and place *Corpus* in the *Subjects* box and *DecadeNUM* in the *Repeated* box > *Continue*. Choose *Scaled Identity* in the *Repeated Covariance Type* drop-down menu. This delineates the repeated effect and its covariance type.
2. In the *Linear Mixed Models* dialog box place *CubeRootFrequency* in the *Dependent Variable* box. All random effect variables and independent variables are also chosen here. Categorical variables such as *Corpus* go in the *Factor(s)* box, and continuous variables such as *DecadeNUM* in the *Covariate(s)* box.

3. Click on *Fixed* and move the independent variable *DecadeNUM* to the *Model* box by highlighting it > *Add* > *Continue.*
4. Click on the *Statistics* button and check *Parameter estimates*, *Covariances of random effects*, and *Covariances of residuals* > *Continue* > *OK.*

8.9 Example of a Mixed-Effects Model with Random Effects for Subject and Item

Let's look at an analysis that is a bit more complex and has characteristics that are fairly common in linguistic studies. Winter and Bergen (2012) contend that language comprehension does not uniquely involve language mechanisms but involves perceptual systems as well. They hypothesize that when someone processes a sentence that describes an object, that act produces a mental image of the object that can affect the perception of that object. In their study, the subjects read sentences that described objects that were either near (e.g., "you're staring at the Frisbee in your hand") or far away (e.g., "you're staring at the Frisbee in the sky"). Afterward, subjects were shown a picture and asked to respond *yes* if it matched the preceding sentence or *no* if it didn't. (i.e., "Was there a Frisbee in the picture or not?") When there was a match, there were actually two kinds of matching pictures: one showed the object close up and the other far away.

In other words, the difference was in the size of the object in the picture since large objects are perceived to be closer than small objects. When subjects read a sentence about a Frisbee, they should answer *yes* to a picture of a Frisbee regardless of whether the Frisbee is depicted as being close or far away. However, the authors hypothesized that the subjects would respond more quickly when the distance in the sentence matched the distance in the picture and more slowly when there was a mismatch (e.g., a picture of the object up close and a sentence describing the object in the distance).

This experiment involves repeated measures because each subject responded to different test items in each of the four conditions: far sentence, small object; far sentence, large object; close sentence, small object; close sentence, large object. There were eight unique trials in each of the four conditions that each subject responded to as well. In addition to the independent variables of *Sentence Distance* and *Picture Size*, they included another independent variable—*Distance Marker*. Half of the test sentences indicated distance with an adverbial expression (protagonist-based; e.g., *in the distance, close to you*) while others marked it with a landmark of some sort (landmark-based; e.g., *in the sky, in your hand*). This could also possibly influence the subjects' reaction times, which is why it was included.

8.9.1 Running a mixed-effects analysis with random effects for subject and test item

So, the dependent variable is *Reaction Time*[7] and the independents are *Sentence Distance* (e.g., near vs. far), *Picture Size* (e.g., large vs. small), and *Distance Marker* (how distance was marked in the test sentences; e.g., protagonist-based vs. landmark-based). Most importantly, the authors hypothesized that *Sentence Distance* and *Picture Size* would interact, so that interaction was also included as a variable. Just for the sake of exposition, I threw in all other possible interactions (*Sentence Distance by Distance Marker and Picture Size by Distance Marker*).

What are the possible random effects for a study like this? The best guideline I have found is this (Barr et al. 2013:262):

> The general principle is that a by-subject (or by-item) random intercept is needed whenever there is more than one observation per subject (or item or subject-item combination), and a random slope is needed for any effect where there is more than one observation of each unique combination of subject and treatment level (or item and treatment level).

In this study, the subjects gave multiple responses, so a random intercept for subject needs to be explored. This gives all subjects their own individual intercept according to how much they vary from the overall intercept. In this way, each subject's mean varies equally from the overall mean across all of the experimental conditions. However, the subjects also responded to several different test items in each of the *Sentence Distance* and *Picture Size* conditions. This could warrant a random slope of subject by *Sentence Distance* or *Subject by Picture Size* to account for the possibility that some people were inordinately faster (or slower) in one or more of the particular *Sentence Distance* or *Picture Size* conditions. It is also possible that the subjects responded differently to each combination of *Sentence Distance* and *Picture Size*, which would call for a random slope for this interaction. Subjects may also have responded differently to type of *Distance Marker* (protagonist-based vs. landmark-based), but I already know it doesn't help the model much, so I'll leave it out to keep the description as simple as possible.

One reason for giving subjects a random intercept or slope is to control for their possible personal eccentricities so that the repeated measures are accounted for. Clark (1973) and Baayen et al. (2007) contend that like subjects, test items may also have idiosyncrasies that should be controlled for and that test items should also be allowed to have random intercepts, and possibly slopes as well. This is especially important in experiments such as this one, in which every subject responds to every test item. For this reason, a random intercept for test item is also something to consider. In summary, the possible random effects are:

---

[7] The data were winsorized (see section 7.2.9.1).

1. Random intercept for *Test Item*
2. Random intercept for *Subject*
3. Random slope for *Subject by Sentence Distance*
4. Random slope for *Subject by Picture Size*
5. Random slope for *Subject by Picture Size*Sentence Distance*

At this point, you may be wondering, why are you so freaking worried about messing with those residuals again? First of all, by fitting lines that are closer to the data points, you reduce the residuals. Since residuals represent what the model is not accounting for, smaller residuals mean a better statistical model. Second, the data contain repeated measures, so they are probably correlated, and you need to eliminate or account for the correlation to make the statistics happy. Changing the regression line that is used to measure the residuals often eliminates the correlation between the residuals. Third, subjects gave several responses, and test items were responded to several times. These factors could possibly allow a quirky person or an odd test item to skew the results. Adjusting the residuals helps take care of any such oddities.

Now, it may be tempting to fit a random slope for each subject by test item, but in this experimental design, the subjects gave only one response per individual test item so that a subject's mean reaction time to a test item would be the same thing as the one actual response they gave to that particular test item, and that won't work. In other studies where subjects respond to the same test item more than once (repeated trials), a subject slope by test item would make sense.

So, the first step is to begin with a model that contains all independent variables (fixed variables) and random factors. In this step, the goal is to find the best fit for the random effects. The models in Table 8-14 contain all of the fixed effects. To save space, it doesn't report the significance of the kind of *Distance Marker* or the other interactions, which are never significant anyways. Models 1-5 have random effects for both subject and item. Model 1 fits an intercept for Item and Subject. Models 2 fits a slope for *Subject* across *Picture Size*, and Model 3 fits a slope for *Subject across Sentence Distance*. Model 4 includes slopes for both random effects, while Model 5 includes a slope for the interaction between Sentence Distance and *Picture Size*. When you compare the −2RLL and BIC figures, it should be clear that none of the more complicated models (2–5) fit any better than Model 1.[8]

Table 8-14. Results of a number of models of the Winter and Bergen data.

Model	# Par.	-2RLL	BIC	p of Distance	p of Size	p of Distance by Size
1 Intercept for Subject VC Intercept for Item VC	10	9784.048	9803.601	.601	.682	.007
2 Slope for Subject by Size VC Intercept for Item VC	11	9782.738	9808.809	.565	.718	.007
3 Slope for Subject by Distance VC Intercept for Item VC	11	9784.009	9810.080	.620	.678	.007
4 Slope for Subject by Size VC Slope for Subject by Distance VC Intercept for Item VC	12	9792.659	9815.247	.591	.714	.007
5 Slope for Subject by Size*Distance VC Intercept for Item VC	11	9783.927	9809.998	.610	.685	.011
6 Intercept for Subject VC Intercept for Item VC Repeated subject over Distance*Size*Trial VC, DIAG	41	9418.307	9639.908	.091	.471	.338
7 Intercept for Subject VC Intercept for Item VC Repeated Subject over Distance*Size*Trial UN, CS, CSH	No convergence.					
8 Intercept for Subject VC Intercept for Item VC Repeated Subject over Distance*Size*Trial ID	10	9784.048	9803.601	.601	.682	.007

---

[8] Model 5 has a smaller −2RLL than Model 1, but the difference is not significant and its BIC is higher. It also has one more parameter than Model 1.

As far as the covariance structures that were used in each model are concerned, Variance Components (VC), which is the default in SPSS, is the only one that fits a random intercept. You can try other covariance structures, but SPSS will kick you back into the default if you do. When a random slope is involved, it is fairly standard procedure to try both Unstructured (UN) and Variance Components (VC) in the random slopes. I tried an Unstructured covariance structure in all the random slopes in Table 8-14, but none of them converged, so I didn't bother to include them in the table.

Now that we know that the best fit for the random effects is Model 1, the second step is to see if adding a repeated effect can produce an even better fit by defining the relationship among the remaining residuals. For these data, each person gave eight responses in each of the four conditions (*Picture Size* by *Sentence Distance*),[9] so that produces a repeated effect of *Subject* by *Condition*. It is tempting to define the repeated effect as *Subject over PictureSize*SentenceDistance*, but if you do, you'll get a semicryptic error message: "The levels of the repeated effect are not different for each observation within a repeated subject." What this is telling you is that there are data that you haven't specified in the repeated effect. Repeated effects need to include everything. Each subject responded to eight test items in each *Size by Distance* combination, but SPSS doesn't know about those eight trials unless you include them in the repeated effect as well. The repeated effect needs to specify subject across *Picture Size* by *Sentence Distance* by *Trial* in order to include all of the data. That is, each subject responded to all four conditions (Picture Size by Sentence Distance), and the conditions all had eight trials.

Models 6–8 add a repeated effect to the best random effect from Model 1, and Model 6 results in much lower information criteria figures; but at the same time, it has 41 parameters compared to Model 1's 10. Are the 31 extra parameters worth it? Well, the difference between the two −2RLLs is well over 300. At 31 degrees of freedom,[10] in order for Model 6 to be a significantly better fit than Model 1, the difference needs to be about 45 or larger, which more than fits the bill in this case, so we choose Model 6 as the best fit.

Alright, back to the task at hand. Now that we've found the best fit for the random effects and repeated effects, in the third step, we turn to the fixed effects.[11] Winter and Bergen had a pretty clear idea about what outcome they expected. Their hypothesis was that *Sentence Distance* and *Picture Size* would interact. They included type of *Distance Marker* to be thorough, and they were rightly content to report the results of those variables. However, sometimes when you have a lot of independent variables and you are not sure how they will affect the dependent because your study is more exploratory, you may want to take the last step and weed out the insignificant variables in search of the most parsimonious model. The possibility always exists that once an insignificant variable is removed, another variable may become significant.

For expository purposes, I'd like to start with a model that contains all of the fixed variables along with the random and repeated effects that we found provided the best fit and then eliminate insignificant independent variables. The best fit of the random effects is Model 6 in Table 8-8, which I've renamed Model 1 in Table 8-15.

Table 8-15. Results of some models that vary in fixed variables.

Model	# Par.	−2RLL	BIC	A	B	C	D	E	F
1	All fixed variables (REML)	41	9418.307	9639.908	.091	.471	.115	.338	.639	.569
2	All fixed variables (ML)	41	9476.427	9744.119	.086	.463	.104	.366	.561	.616
3	Less Picture Size by Distance Marker	40	9476.770	9737.888	.086	.337	.090	.338	.711	—
4	Less Sentence Distance by Distance Marker; Picture Size by Distance Marker	39	9476.889	9731.480	.062	.349	.089	.292	—	—
5	Less Sentence Distance by Distance Marker; Picture Size by Distance Marker; Distance Marker	38	9479.830	9555.830	.077	.412	—	.236	—	—
6	Same as 5 with REML	38	9448.114	9669.865	.081	.422	—	.228	—	—

A = *p* of Sentence Distance
B = *p* of Picture Size
C = *p* of Distance Marker
D = *p* of Sentence Distance by Picture Size
E = *p* of Sentence Distance by Distance Marker
F = *p* of Picture Size by Distance Marker

---

[9] The data set has a Condition variable that is merely the combination of Sentence Distance and Picture Size.
[10] I found this on an online chi-square chart.
[11] When comparing models with different fixed effects, we use maximum likelihood estimation (ML) rather than REML.

There are two different algorithms that SPSS uses when calculating mixed-effects models: restricted maximum likelihood (REML) and maximum likelihood (ML). When comparing models that differ in random or repeated effects or both, the correct estimating method is REML; however, when comparing models that differ in fixed effects, we switch to ML, so the only difference between Models 1 and 2 is the estimation method. In Model 1, we were comparing models with different random effects, and Model 2 will be our starting point for comparing the fixed effects. The first fixed effects to remove are the ones that are most complex, which in this case are the interactions between two variables. We start with the effects that are least significant. In Model 3, we remove *Picture Size* by *Distance Marker* first because it is the least significant ($p = .616$). Of the remaining interactions, Sentence Distance *by Distance Marker* is removed in Model 4. Notice that the BIC goes down as we remove insignificant variables. That shows we are fitting the data better by excluding them.

HINT
Use the REML method when comparing models that differ in their random or repeated effects or both. Use ML when comparing models that differ only in their fixed effects. Also, use REML on your final model.

It would be tempting to remove *Picture Size* next because of its large *p* value (.349), but we can't. The hypothesis is that *Picture Size* and *Sentence Distance* interact, and we need to see if that interaction is significant, so we leave it in. Now, when you leave in an interaction, either because it is significant or of interest to the study, and one or more of the variables it is made up of is not significant, you have to leave any of the variables that make up the interaction in the model even if they are insignificant themselves. *Sentence Distance* and *Picture Size* both appear in an interaction of interest, so we must leave them in. This leaves *Distance Marker* as the only insignificant variable to remove (Model 5). Now that we have the random and fixed effects of the most parsimonious model, we rerun the whole thing using REML and report those results (Model 6).

HINT
If an interaction between two or more variables is significant but one or more of the simple variables the interaction is composed of is not, you must always leave those simple variables in the model.

8.9.2 Using SPSS to carry out a mixed-effects analysis

It is an unfortunate truth about mixed-effects analysis that using the SPSS menu interface, all by itself, has been known to drive the most chaste mouthed ascetic to fits of vulgar profanity. In order to spare you that fate, I will describe the menu system enough that it will put most of what you need into the *Syntax Editor*. From there, running other models is most easily accomplished by modifying the code in the *Syntax Editor* itself rather than by returning to the hellish labyrinth of menus.

1. Open. *Analyze > Mixed Models > Linear*.
2. Move *Subjects* and *Item* into the into the *Subjects* box > *Continue* (Figure 8-10). These two things will be used as random effects. If you also put a variable into the *Repeated* box, SPSS will create a repeated effect between the variables in the *Repeated* and *Subjects* boxes. We won't do that now.
3. Place the dependent variable *ReactionTime* into the *Dependent Variable* box. Place all categorical independent variables and random factors in the *Factor(s)* box (Figure 8-11). Any continuous independent variables would go into the *Covariate(s)* box. We don't have any here.
4. Click on *Fixed*. This is where you specify the actual independent variables. Move *SentenceDistance*, *PictureSize*, and *DistanceMarker* into the *Model* box by clicking on each name, followed by the *Add* button.
5. Make the interaction variable *SentenceDistance*PictureSize* by checking *Build nested terms*. Click on *SentenceDistance* > "down arrow" > *BY** > *PictureSize* > "down arrow" > *Add*. Make sure *Include intercept* is checked.
6. Follow the same strategy to make the other interaction variables (*SentenceDistance*DistanceMarker*; *PictureSize*DistanceMarker*) > *Continue* (Figure 8-12).
7. Another way to do the interactions is to highlight *SentenceDistance*, *PictureSize*, and *DistanceMarker* in the *Factors and Covariates* box, select *All 2-way* in the drop-down menu between the *Factors and Covariates* box and the *Model* box, then click *Add*.
8. To create a random intercept for *Item*, move *Item* into the *Combinations* box, check *Include intercept* > *Continue*.
9. Click on the *Statistics* button and check *Parameter estimates* > *Continue*.
10. Click on *EM means* and move *SentenceDistance*, *PictureSize*, and *DistanceMarker* along with all the variables made of the interactions between variables into the *Display means for* box by highlighting them and clicking on the arrow between the boxes. This sets up the post hoc analysis for categorical variables. Check *Compare main effects* and choose *Bonferroni* in the *Confidence Interval Adjustment* drop-down menu *Continue > Paste*.

11. *Paste* puts all of the commands you just gave SPSS via the menus into the *Syntax Editor* (Figure 8-14).
12. Click on *Random*. This is where you specify the random effects. To create a random slope of *Subject* by *PictureSize*, move *PictureSize* into the *Model* box by highlighting it and pressing *Add*, then move *Subject* into the *Combinations* box using the arrow button (Figure 8-13). Check *Include intercept > Next*.

Figure 8-10. The mixed models *Specify Subjects* and *Repeated* dialog box.

Figure 8-11. *Variable specification* dialog box.

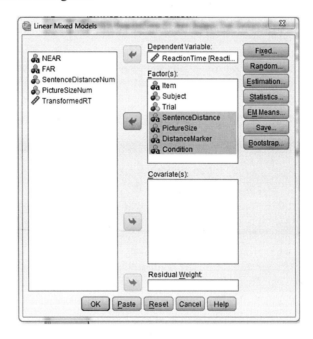

Figure 8-12. *Fixed effects* dialog box.

Figure 8-13. *Random Effect* dialog box with random slope.

Figure 8-14. The *Syntax Editor* window.

8.9.3 Introduction to the *Syntax Editor*

Once you have gone through the menus to get to this point, I highly suggest abandoning the menus and making all of your changes directly in the *Syntax Editor* window. The code we've derived by following the steps above gives us the syntax for Model 2 in Table 8-8. This gives us a good example to use to explain what the syntax in Figure 8-14 means. Now, don't get blown away by this code. It really isn't that bad, and you only have to deal with a small portion of it anyway. Let's go through it a step at a time.

Table 8-16. Step-by-step discussion of *Syntax Editor* code.

Term	Meaning
`MIXED`	means you are running a mixed-effects model.
`ReactionTime`	is the dependent variable.
`BY`	specifies any categorical variables to be used as fixed, random, or repeated effects.

`Item`
`Subject`
`Trial`
`SentenceDistance`
`PictureSize`
`DistanceMarker`
`Condition`
	are the categorical variables that you can choose your independent variables and random factors from.

`WITH`	would precede continuous variables that you put in the *Covariate(s)* box, but there are none here, so you don't see it in the code above.
`/CRITERIA . . . ABSOLUTE)`	contains instructions for the program that you don't have to worry about.
`/FIXED=`	precedes the independent variables.

`SentenceDistance, PictureSize, and`
`    DistanceMarker.`
`SentenceDistance*`
`    PictureSize`
`SentenceDistance*`
`    DistanceMarker`
`PictureSize*`
`    DistanceMarker`
	are the independent variables.

`| SSTYPE(3)`	tells the program to use a type 3 sum of squares. Leave it alone.
`/METHOD=REML`	tells the program to use REML estimation. When you are trying different models of random and repeated effects, this is the correct setting. When you are trying models containing different independent variables, set this to `/METHOD=ML`.
`/PRINT=SOLUTION`	asks for the parameter estimates of fixed effects to be displayed. If you'd like to see the G and R matrices as well, change it so that it reads: `/PRINT=SOLUTION G R`.
`/RANDOM=INTERCEPT PictureSize |` `    SUBJECT(Subject) COVTYPE(VC)`	specifies the random slope of subject (the subject in parentheses) over *PictureSize* with a covariance structure of VC.
`/RANDOM=INTERCEPT	SUBJECT(Item)` ` COVTYPE(VC)`	specifies a random intercept for *Item* with a covariance structure of VC.

`/EMMEANS=TABLES`
`    (SentenceDistance) COMPARE`
`    ADJ(BONFERRONI)`
`/EMMEANS=TABLES`
`    (PictureSize) COMPARE`
`    ADJ(BONFERRONI)`
`/EMMEANS=TABLES`
`    (DistanceMarker) COMPARE`
`    ADJ(BONFERRONI)`
	asks for group means for *SentenceDistance*, *PictureSize*, and *DistanceMarker*. A Bonferroni post hoc test is also done to compare the groups. This is useful for categorical but not continuous variables.

`/EMMEANS=TABLES`
`    (SentenceDistance*PictureSize)`
`/EMMEANS=TABLES`
`    (SentenceDistance*DistanceMarker`
`    )`
`/EMMEANS=TABLES`
`    (PictureSize*`
`    DistanceMarker).`
	These last three lines ask for means for all of the interactions between variables. For example, *SentenceDistance*PictureSize* will give you means for *big/near*, *big/far*, *small/near*, and *small/far*.

To run an analysis from the *Syntax Editor*, press the green triangular arrow at the top middle part of the *Syntax Editor* window. Often you may have several lines of code representing different models in the *Syntax Editor* at once. Be sure that the last line in a sequence of lines of code that represent one model ends in a period. To run a particular model, make sure that the cursor is somewhere in the code you want to run or make sure to highlight the entire block of code you want to run and then press the green arrow. I'll include some other information about the *Syntax Editor* later. For now, let's get back to the analysis of the reaction-time data.

8.9.4 Results of the Winter and Bergen study

We've decided that Model 6 (Table 8-15) is the best-fitting model. It looks like this in the *Syntax Editor*:

```
MIXED ReactionTime BY Item Subject Trial SentenceDistance PictureSize DistanceMarker
    Condition
/CRITERIA=CIN(95)    MXITER(100)    MXSTEP(10)    SCORING(1)    SINGULAR(0.000000000001)
    HCONVERGE(0, ABSOLUTE) LCONVERGE(0, ABSOLUTE) PCONVERGE(0.000001, ABSOLUTE)
/FIXED=SentenceDistance PictureSize SentenceDistance*PictureSize
 | SSTYPE(3)
/METHOD=REML
/PRINT=SOLUTION
/RANDOM= Subject Item | COVTYPE(VC)
/REPEATED=SentenceDistance*PictureSize*Trial | SUBJECT(Subject) COVTYPE(VC)
/EMMEANS=TABLES(SentenceDistance) COMPARE ADJ(BONFERRONI)
/EMMEANS=TABLES(PictureSize) COMPARE ADJ(BONFERRONI)
/EMMEANS=TABLES(SentenceDistance*PictureSize).
```

You can modify the syntax you got in Figure 8-14 so that it matches the above syntax. That way, you will get the same output described in the tables below for Model 6. For example, the Model Dimensions (Table 8-17) tells you what the fixed, random, and repeated effects are in Model 6 as well as what covariance structure is used and the number of parameters. The Information Criteria (Table 8-18) contains the −2RLL, BIC, and other measures that are used to compare models. The results of the analysis as far as the independent variables are concerned appear in Table 8-19. The estimates of the fixed effects are found in Table 8-20, and the post hoc analyses appear in Table 8-21, and the estimated (not actual) means of the interactions in 8.21. One important post hoc analysis is not specified by the syntax above. In order to produce a post hoc analysis that compares the means of each variable value in the *SentenceDistance* by *PictureSize* interaction to the other (Table 8-23), a final line on the syntax needs to be added that reads

```
/EMMEANS=TABLES(SentenceDistance*PictureSize)COMPARE(SentenceDistance) ADJ(BONFERRONI).
```

There is no way to specify this with the menus. Sorry. In fact, the random and repeated effects as they appear here need to be modified by hand. You can't get them with menus.

Table 8-17. Model dimension Table.

Model dimension[a]		# of levels	Covariance structure	# of parameters	Subject variables	# of subjects
Fixed effects	Intercept	1		1		
	SentenceDistance	2		1		
	PictureSize	2		1		
	SentenceDistance*PictureSize	4		1		
Random effects	Subject + Item[b]	54	Variance Components	2		
Repeated effects	SentenceDistance*PictureSize*Trial	32	Diagonal[c]	32	Subject	22
Total		95		38		

a. Dependent variable: ReactionTime.
b. As of version 11.5, the syntax rules for the RANDOM subcommand have changed. Your command syntax may yield results that differ from those produced by prior versions. If you are using version 11 syntax, please consult the current syntax reference guide for more information.
c. The Variance Component (VC) structure is no longer used on the REPEATED subcommand. The keyword DIAG, for diagonal structure, should be used instead.

Table 8-18. Information criteria table.

Information Criteria[a]	
−2 Restricted Log Likelihood	9448.114
Akaike's Information Criterion (AIC)	9516.114
Hurvich and Tsai's Criterion (AICC)	9519.804
Bozdogan's Criterion (CAIC)	9703.865
Schwarz's Bayesian Criterion (BIC)	9669.865

The information criteria are displayed in smaller-is-better forms.
a. Dependent variable: ReactionTime.

Table 8-19. Results of the mixed-effects analysis.

Type III Tests of Fixed Effects[a]				
Source	Numerator df	Denominator df	F	Sig.
Intercept	1	37.285	514.412	.000
SentenceDistance	1	266.782	3.065	.081
PictureSize	1	253.706	.647	.422
SentenceDistance*PictureSize	1	300.862	1.457	.228

a. Dependent variable: ReactionTime.

Table 8-20. Estimates of fixed effects of the mixed-effects analysis.

Estimates of Fixed Effects					
Parameter	Estimate	Std. Error	df	t	Sig.
Intercept	671.136498	33.830957	67.142	19.838	.000
[SentenceDistance =FAR]	-46.016277	23.992608	130.089	-1.918	.057
[SentenceDistance =NEAR]	0[b]	0	.	.	.
[PictureSize=BIG]	-31.392716	24.054541	153.902	-1.305	.194
[PictureSize =SMALL]	0[b]	0	.	.	.
[SentenceDistance =FAR] * [PictureSize =BIG]	38.040084	31.513487	300.862	1.207	.228
[SentenceDistance =FAR] * [PictureSize =SMALL]	0[b]	0	.	.	.
[SentenceDistance =NEAR] * [PictureSize=BIG]	0[b]	0	.	.	.
[SentenceDistance =NEAR] * [PictureSize =SMALL]	0[b]	0	.	.	.

Table 8-21. Post hoc analyses.

Pairwise comparisons[a]							
Sentence distance (I)	Sentence distance (J)	Mean difference (I − J)	Std. error	df	Sig.	95% CI for difference Lower bound	Upper bound
Far	Near	−26.996	15.421	266.782	.081	−57.359	3.366
Near	Far	26.996	15.421	266.782	.081	−3.366	57.359
Picture Size (I)	Picture Size (J)						
Big	Small	−12.373	15.380	253.706	.422	−42.662	17.916
Small	Big	12.373	15.380	253.706	.422	−17.916	42.662

CI = Confidence interval

Table 8-22. Estimated means of the interaction of the variables.

Estimates						
Sentence distance	Picture size	Mean	Std. error	df	95% CI Lower bound	Upper bound
Far	Big	631.768	30.612	49.170	570.256	693.279
	Small	625.120	30.542	48.820	563.738	686.503
Near	Big	639.744	30.208	47.185	578.979	700.509
	Small	671.136	33.831	67.142	603.612	738.661

Table 8-23. Post hoc analysis of the interaction.

Pairwise comparisons								
							95% CI for difference	
PictureSize	Sentence distance (I)	Sentence distance (J)	Mean difference (I – J)	Std. error	df	Sig.	Lower bound	Upper bound
BIG	FAR	NEAR	−7.976	19.913	212.188	.689	−47.229	31.277
	NEAR	FAR	7.976	19.913	212.188	.689	−31.277	47.229
SMALL	FAR	NEAR	−46.016	23.993	130.089	.057	−93.482	1.450
	NEAR	FAR	46.016	23.993	130.089	.057	−1.450	93.482

CI = Confidence interval

8.9.5 Reporting the results of a mixed-effects model

The fact that mixed-effects models have only recently become widely available is probably the reason why there is no standard way of reporting them. I suggest reporting the results as you do with an ANOVA and then stating how the repeated measures were accounted for, something along these lines:

> A mixed-effects analysis of the data was carried out. The effect of Sentence Distance was not significant (F (1, 266.783) = 3.065, p = .081), nor was Picture Size (F (1, 253.706) = .647, p = .422), nor was the interaction between these two variables (F (1, 300.862) = 1.457, p = .228).

If there were significant differences, you would cite which combinations of variables were significant in the post hoc analysis. For example,

> The post hoc analysis indicates that significantly faster reaction times resulted with pictures in which the object was small when the sentences indicated that the object was far away in comparison to pictures in which the object was small when the sentences that indicated that the object was near. However, pairings of big objects with sentences that indicated that the object was either far or near did not produce significantly different reaction times.

It is also important to explain what random or repeated effects, or both, produced the best model fit:

> In order to account for the repeated measures in the study, each subject and test item were allowed a random intercept, and the resulting residuals were specified with a repeated effect of subject over the interaction of picture size by sentence distance with a Variance Components covariance structure.

If there were a random slope or repeated effect, you'd also need to say what they were along with the covariance structure used in each. This gives your readers enough information to replicate the study themselves, which is what's important.

8.10 Testing the Assumptions of a Mixed-Effects Model

Once you have the analysis whittled it down to your final model, you need to make sure that it fits the assumptions of a mixed-effects analysis. For this analysis, there are so many violations that the results just described can't be trusted or reported. The first assumption is that the residuals of the model are normally distributed. We are out of luck since our residuals do not fit a normal distribution very well, as you can see in Figures 8-15 and 8-16.

Second, not only must the residuals be normally distributed, they must be homoscedastic. We are out of luck again because the final analysis we've been looking at has pretty dang heteroscedastic residuals (Figure 8-17). What we'd like to see is a nice bird's nest, with the residuals centered around zero on the horizontal axis and no fan, bow tie, or other funky shape to them. Here, the residuals have a definite fan shape with more variation at the higher levels and less spread at the lower levels.

The third assumption of mixed-effects models is that the relationship between a continuous independent variable and the residuals must be linear. In the present data, all the variables we've been looking at are categorical, so this assumption does not apply. However, when you have continuous data, you can test linearity by graphing a scatter plot of the values of the continuous independent variable against the residuals and then overlay a Loess line on them to evaluate their linearity. A thorough evaluation of the assumptions underlying a mixed-effects analysis would also test the random coefficients for normal distribution and homoscedasticity. It is unfortunate that the most current version of SPSS (21) is unable to perform these evaluations.[12]

---

[12] However, West et al. (2007:76–77) describe how they can be calculated in SPSS for a random intercept but not for a random slope.

Figure 8-15. Histogram of the residuals of the final model.

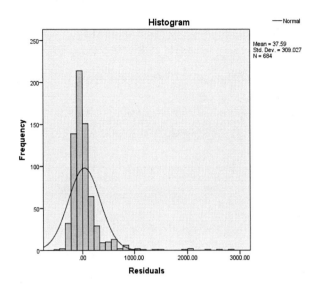

Although it is not an assumption of mixed-effect models, collinearity among the independent variables needs to be checked by correlating all of the continuous independent variables with each other. This is not an issue for the present analysis since all the variables are categorical. Refer back to Chapter 7 for instructions on carrying this out and how to handle cases of collinearity.

In any event, in the present data, we've got some issues to deal with. When the residuals are heteroscedastic and non-normal, we can check a number of things. Sometimes it is helpful to look at a scatter plot of the residuals against each individual variable to determine which one may be causing the problem. In Figures 8-18 and 8-19, the spread of the residuals of *Near* and *Far* doesn't differ a great deal and neither does that of *Small* and *Big*, so we're not getting any hints there. The next thing to check is the dependent variable, and as you can see in Figure 8-20, the reaction times are pretty skewed, as it is the nature of reaction times to be. It's possible that by transforming the reaction times, the distribution of the residuals will normalize. Lo and behold, the power of transformations. Look at Figures 8-21 and 8-22. Those are the residuals after a transformation was applied to the reaction times (i.e., 1 / (Reaction Time / 1000)). Admire the nice bell curve in the histogram and the bird's nest distribution of the residuals in the scatter plot.

Figure 8-16. Q-Q plot of the residuals of the final model.

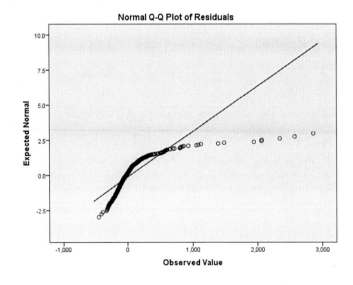

Figure 8-17. Scatter plot of the residuals of the final model.

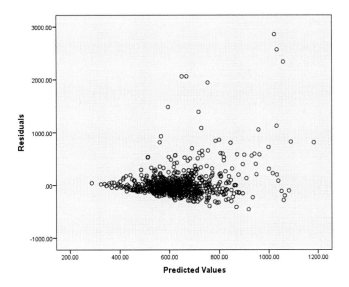

Figure 8-18. Residuals of the final model plotted against *SentenceDistance.*

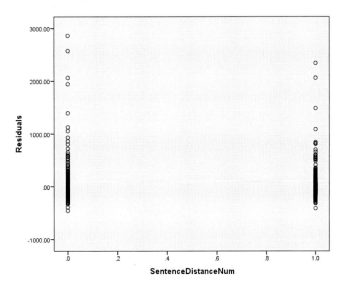

Figure 8-19. Residuals of the final model plotted against *PictureSize.*

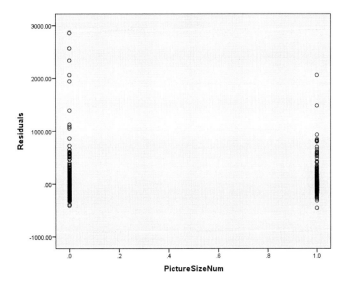

Figure 8-20. Distribution of the reaction time.

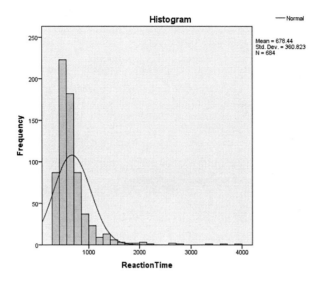

Figure 8-21. Distribution of the residuals of the final model with transformed reaction times.

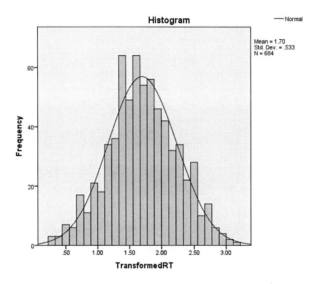

Figure 8-22. Residuals of the final model with transformed reaction times plotted against the predicted values.

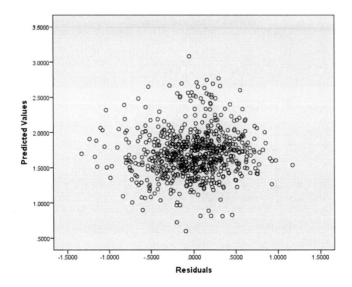

Another way to handle violations of assumptions is to bootstrap the analysis. This option is only available in more recent versions of SPSS. Notice the bootstrap button in Figure 8-11. One limitation to using bootstrapping is that it appears that it's not possible when the model contains a random slope. Another downside to SPSS bootstrapping is that it only provides the estimates of the fixed effects (Table 8-20) and not the tests of fixed effects (Table 8-19) nor the post hoc tests (Tables 8-21, 8-23) which makes interpretation of the results a bit trickier.

8.10.1 Using SPSS to test the assumptions of mixed-effects models

Add the following line of code to the syntax of the best model (in this case Model 6 in Table 8-15) and rerun the analysis. Be sure that the last line of the code ends in a period.

```
/SAVE=PRED RESID
```

This code adds two new columns of data to your spreadsheet. PRED (more specifically PRED_1 or PRED_2, depending on how many times you've asked SPSS to calculate them) contains the predicted values and RESID, the residuals of the model.

To evaluate the degree of normality of the residuals:
1. Click on *Analyze > Descriptive Statistics > Explore*. Move *RESID* to the *Dependent List.*
2. Click on *Plots* and check *Histogram* and *Normality plots with tests > Continue > OK*. This produces Figures 8-15 and 8-16.

To evaluate the residuals for homoscedasticity:
1. Click on *Graphs > Legacy Dialogs > Scatter/Dot*. Choose *Simple Scatter > Define*. Place *RESID* in *Y Axis* and *PRED* in *X Axis > OK*. This produces Figure 8-18.

To evaluate a particular independent variable, such as Sentence Distance, against the residuals for homoscedasticity:
1. Click on *Graphs > Legacy Dialogs > Scatter/Dot*. Choose *Simple Scatter > Define*. Place *RESID* in *Y Axis* and *SentenceDistanceNum* in *X Axis > OK*. This produces Figure 8-18.

Notice that graphs can't be made with variables that are specified as strings. Categorical data must be converted into numeric data for this purpose, which explains using the *SentenceDistanceNum* variables rather than *SentenceDistance.*

To test a continuous independent variable for linearity:
1. Click on *Graphs > Legacy Dialogs > Scatter/Dot*. Choose *Simple Scatter > Define*.
2. Place *RESID* in *Y Axis* and *[a continuous variable]* in *X Axis > OK*.
3. Double-click on the resulting scatter plot. Click on *Elements > Fit line at total >* check *Loess > Apply > Close.*

8.11 More about Using the *Syntax Editor*

It is a fairly straightforward thing to modify the commands in the *Syntax Editor* rather than via the menus. For example, the random slope of *Subject* over *PictureSize*

```
/RANDOM=INTERCEPT PictureSize | SUBJECT(Subject) COVTYPE(VC)
```

can be converted to a random intercept for each subject by deleting *PictureSize* and making it read

```
/RANDOM=INTERCEPT | SUBJECT(Subject) COVTYPE(VC)
```

In like manner, the covariance structure of the random effect can be changed from Variance Components to Unstructured by changing COVTYPE(VC) to COVTYPE(UN). An additional random intercept can be included by adding another line of code:

```
/RANDOM=INTERCEPT | SUBJECT(Subject) COVTYPE(VC)
/RANDOM=INTERCEPT | SUBJECT(Item) COVTYPE(VC)
```

A variant syntax for the above two random intercepts is

```
/RANDOM=Subject Item | COVTYPE(VC)
```

There are times when this syntax will work with another random or repeated effect when the former two-line variant will not. For instance, Model 6 in Table 8-8 must be

```
/RANDOM=Subject Item | COVTYPE(VC)
/REPEATED=SentenceDistance*PictureSize*Trial | SUBJECT(Subject) COVTYPE(VC)
```

The following will not run even though it should have the identical meaning:

```
/RANDOM=INTERCEPT | SUBJECT(Subject) COVTYPE(VC)
/RANDOM=INTERCEPT | SUBJECT(Item) COVTYPE(VC)
/REPEATED=SentenceDistance*PictureSize*Trial | SUBJECT(Subject) COVTYPE(VC)
```

In like manner, two random slopes can be written either as

```
/RANDOM=INTERCEPT PictureSize | SUBJECT(Subject) COVTYPE(VC)
/RANDOM=INTERCEPT SentenceDistance | SUBJECT(Subject) COVTYPE(VC)
```

or

```
/RANDOM=INTERCEPT SentenceDistance PictureSize | SUBJECT(Subject) COVTYPE(VC)
```

For example, Model 4 in Table 8-8 must be specified in this manner:

```
/RANDOM=INTERCEPT SentenceDistance PictureSize | SUBJECT(Subject) COVTYPE(VC)
/RANDOM=INTERCEPT | SUBJECT(Item) COVTYPE(VC)
```

Although the syntax above is supposed to be identical to this,

```
/RANDOM=INTERCEPT PictureSize | SUBJECT(Subject) COVTYPE(VC)
/RANDOM=INTERCEPT SentenceDistance | SUBJECT(Subject) COVTYPE(VC)
/RANDOM=INTERCEPT | SUBJECT(Item) COVTYPE(VC)
```

the latter will produce an error message.

To give some examples, which are always helpful, the code for the random slope and random intercept in Model 3 from Table 8-8 is

```
/RANDOM=INTERCEPT SentenceDistance | SUBJECT(Subject) COVTYPE(VC)
/RANDOM=INTERCEPT | SUBJECT(Item) COVTYPE(VC)
```

The marginal models used the syntax below but varied the covariance structure:

```
/REPEATED=SentenceDistance*PictureSize*Trial | SUBJECT(Subject) COVTYPE(VC)
```

For data that doesn't have repeated measures but other kinds of nested data such as students of the same teacher, members of a family, or participants interviewed by a particular researcher, you would include a variable to encode different teachers, families, or researchers and would then include them in a random effect along these lines:

```
/RANDOM=INTERCEPT | SUBJECT(student*teacher) COVTYPE(VC)
/RANDOM=INTERCEPT | SUBJECT(subject*family) COVTYPE(VC)
/RANDOM=INTERCEPT | SUBJECT(subject*researcher) COVTYPE(VC)
```

If students of the same teacher were measured at different points in time, the following could be investigated by including a random slope

```
/RANDOM=INTERCEPT time | SUBJECT(student*teacher) COVTYPE(VC)
```

or by specifying the covariance structure of the residuals

```
/REPEATED=time | SUBJECT(student*teacher) COVTYPE(VC)
```

or both.

I've tried to give a sampling of syntax for the most common kinds of analyses, but deciding exactly which is appropriate with a particular data set or experimental design is probably the most difficult part of carrying out a mixed-effects analysis.

8.12 Recipe for a Mixed-Effects Model

1. Try a model that includes all possible independent variables, their interactions, and all relevant random effects. Use REML.
2. Compare and test the fit of models containing different random effects using −2RLL along with the other information criteria. Test the significance between models by doing a likelihood ratio test on the difference between the two −2RLLs and their parameters.
3. Once you've found the best random effects, try adding a repeated effect to see if that improves the model fit. If you can't get models with random effects to run without errors, try a marginal model instead.
4. When you've found the model with the best-fitting repeated and random effects, eliminate any insignificant independent variables one at a time (if you want to eliminate insignificant variables). Use ML.
5. Rerun the final model using REML.
6. Test the assumptions. If they are not met, deal with any issues that arise with transformations, eliminating variables, and so on. Follow all of the steps from the beginning until the assumptions have been met.
7. Report the final model.

8.13 Hands-On Exercises for Mixed-Effects Models

Answers are available at http://linguistics.byu.edu/faculty/eddingtond/Data_Sets/answers.pdf

8.13.1 Grammaticality judgments

Dąbrowska (2010) wanted to see how linguists' intuitions compared to those of nonlinguists. She had both groups judge 16 sentences (Item) on how grammatical they were on a scale of 1 to 5, where 5 meant *fine* and 1 meant *very bad* (Score). The participants responded to a number of sentences that were clearly grammatically incorrect and a number that were correct. In this analysis, the ratings of the sentences are the dependent variable, and the independent variables are Linguist or Nonlinguist (Group) and Sentence Type (GramUngram). Consider the interaction of Grammaticality and Group also. The data are found in *Dabrowska 2010.sav*.

1. In order to account for the repeated measures, run a marginal model that contains the fixed factors Group, GramUngram, and the interaction between the two. Consider a repeated effect of Participant over GramUngram. Remember that each participant responded to several test items that were grammatical and several that were ungrammatical. The repeated statement needs to include this information about items also:

```
/REPEATED=GramUngram*Item | SUBJECT(Participant) COVTYPE(CS).
```

   Try the covariance structures for the repeated effect that make sense for the data (i.e., UN, CS, CSH). Compare the resulting −2RLL and BIC to determine which produces the best-fitting model. Does the significance of the independent variables change depending on the covariance structure used in the repeated effect? Which covariance structure gives the best fitting model?

2. Now run a mixed-effects model to account for the repeated measures. Keep the same dependent and independent variables as before, but account for the repeated measures by trying the following random effects. This time, don't include a repeated effect:

   Model 1: Random slope for participant by GramUngram (try both UN and VC) and random intercept for Item:

```
/RANDOM=INTERCEPT GramUngram | SUBJECT(Participant) COVTYPE(VC)
/RANDOM=INTERCEPT | SUBJECT(Item) COVTYPE(VC).
```

   Model 2: Random slope for participant by GramUngram (try both UN and VC):

```
/RANDOM=INTERCEPT GramUngram | SUBJECT(Participant) COVTYPE(VC).
```

   Model 3: Random intercept for participant and random intercept for Item:

```
/RANDOM=INTERCEPT | SUBJECT(Participant) COVTYPE(VC)
/RANDOM=INTERCEPT | SUBJECT(Item) COVTYPE(VC).
```

3. What is the best fit you can find among the random effects? Does the significance of the independent variables change depending on which random effects are included?
4. Now that you have found the best-fitting random effects, can you add a repeated effect to it to account for the repeated measures even better? If not, explain why not. If not, what is the best-fitting repeated effect that can be added to the best-fitting random effects?

5. Don't worry about eliminating insignificant independent variables. Once you have determined the best-fitting random and repeated effects, check the residuals of the resulting model to make sure they meet the assumptions of a mixed-effects model. How well are they met? Can they be bettered by transforming the dependent variable?

6. Now that you have the best-fitting model, what are the results of the experiment? How do you interpret them given the significant interaction? Look at the group means to aid your interpretation. How would you report these results

8.13.2 Formality in pitch

Winter and Grawunder (2012; *Winter & Grawunder2012.sav*) tested the idea that Koreans mark register by altering their pitch. More specifically, higher pitch is associated with informal polite, subservient speech and lower pitch with formality and social dominance. So the dependent variable they looked at was Median Pitch, and the independent variable was Level of Formality. They also considered the influence of Gender by including it as an independent variable.

In the study, participants performed two tasks. In one, they were given a situation such as asking for a letter of recommendation, and were asked to initiate a roleplay based on it. There were five different roleplays (Scenarios 1–5), and each one was done in a polite and informal setting. In the second task, they had to convey information as if they were leaving a voice mail message. They conveyed two different voice mails (Scenarios 6–7), and each of the two messages were given in a polite and an informal situation as well; so in total, the participants responded to 7 different scenarios. The research question is what the effect of Formality and Gender (and the interaction of Formality and Gender) was on the participants' Mean Pitch level in the scenarios.

1. Run a marginal model to account for the fact that each subject gave formal and informal responses in each of the seven scenarios. Your repeated statement must include this fact:

```
/REPEATED=item*formality | SUBJECT(subject) COVTYPE(CS).
```

Try UN, CS, and CSH. Which covariance structure gives the best fit?

2. Now run a mixed-effects model that includes a random intercept for subject and one for test item (Model 1). Model 1: Random intercepts for subject and scenario:

```
/RANDOM=subject item | COVTYPE(VC).
```

3. The possibility also exists that subjects may vary according to Scenario, Task, Formality, or a combination of the three, so we should test all possible combinations by considering each in a random slope. Try random slopes for subject by Scenario, subject by Task, and subject by Formality (Model 2). The following code includes a random slope for all three:

```
/RANDOM=INTERCEPT scenario task formality | SUBJECT(subject) COVTYPE(VC).
```

4. Model 3: Try random slopes for subject by Scenario and subject by Task with both UN and VC.
5. Model 4: Try random slopes for subject by Scenario and subject by Formality with both UN and VC.
6. Model 5: Try random slopes for subject by Formality and subject by Task with both UN and VC.
7. Model 6: Try a random slope for subject by scenario with both UN and VC.
8. Which of the 6 models provides the best fit?
9. Once you have determined the best-fitting random and repeated effects, test the assumptions and report the results of the study as far as the fixed effects are concerned. How does it relate to the author's hypothesis?

CHAPTER NINE

MIXED-EFFECTS LOGISTIC REGRESSION

Dependent variable: Categorical with two or more values.
Independent variables: Continuous or categorical.

You have probably noticed that most of the statistics we've looked at involve a numeric dependent variable of some sort. There are many linguistic studies that measure numeric things like voice-onset time, word frequency, language aptitude, reaction time, number of words spoken per utterance, and so on. (Remember that *and so on.* means you've run out of examples.) However, there are many other cases where what you are interested in measuring is categorical: inflected verb versus uninflected verb, deleted consonant versus retained consonant, [b] versus [p], periphrastic versus inflectional tense marking, *has* versus *has got, Bob's car* versus *the car of Bob*, and the like. Data like these are handled by logistic regression. Binomial logistic regression is used when the dependent variable has two values (e.g., *will Verb* versus *going to Verb*), and multinomial when the independent variable has three or more values (e.g., [t] versus [ʔ] versus [ɾ]). Logistic regression helps us figure out what it is that favors the appearance of one of the values of the dependent variable, For example,

- Possession is expressed with *have, have got,* and *got*. What favors the use of each one? Could it be the animacy of the possessor? The animacy of the thing possessed? The socioeconomic status of the speaker? The frequency of the noun that follows?
- Word-final /t/ and /d/ in words such as *went* and *field* are sometimes pronounced and other times deleted. What is the role of the following consonant, the preceding vowel, the frequency of the word, the ethnicity of the speaker, and the age of the speaker in deletion or retention of these consonants?

The principles behind mixed-effects logistic regression are very similar to those explained in Chapter 8, so please be sure you are familiar with that information before moving on to this chapter. Also note that the procedures described in this chapter may only be carried out with SPSS version 19 or newer.

9.1. Binomial Logistic Regression

Let's look at an example from sociolinguistics to illustrate logistic regression. Words like *kitten* and *mountain* are generally pronounced with a glottal stop followed by a syllabic nasal in colloquial American English (i.e., *kitten* [kʰɪʔn̩] and *mountain* [mawʔn̩]). In these variants the glottal stop is released nasally. An alternate pronunciation involves an oral release after the glottal stop: [kʰɪʔən] and [mawʔən]. Although oral releasing in these words has been documented across the United States, it has been stigmatized in the state of Utah. A colleague and I wanted to know what social factors are related to the use of the stigmatized oral release variety, so our independent variables were the speaker's age and gender and the proportion of his or her life lived in Utah (Eddington & Savage 2012).

To carry this study out, we asked people who had lived in Utah for varying amounts of time to read a passage containing 25 words whose medial glottal stop could be released orally or glottally. We observed whether the pronunciation of each word contained a glottal stop followed by a nasal release ([kʰɪʔn̩]), a glottal stop followed by an oral release ([kʰɪʔən]), or had no glottal stop at all ([kʰɪtən]). Since each person read the same passage, each person saw the test words in the same order, so it's possible that his or her pronunciation could change toward the end of the reading, which is why we added the *Word_order* variable. Because each speaker gave us 25 responses, we accounted for those repeated measures by allowing each speaker to have a random intercept. The test words were also allowed a random intercept.

In the first analysis we'll do a binomial regression, which gets its name from the fact that there are two nominal (categorical) outcomes in the dependent variable. We were interested in which variables favor the use of the oral release variant. We combined the other two kinds of responses—those with nasal releases and those without a glottal stop—into one value of the dependent variable called *ZOther* to achieve binarity (or possibly achieve binariness—but definitely not achieve nirvana).

9.1.1 Results of the binary mixed-effects logistic regression

For most of the other statistics, SPSS gives you the results of an analysis in the output window as a bunch of drab tables and figures. It looks like SPSS has tried to jazz up those black-and-white tables in generalized models like mixed-effects logistic regression by making the results colorful and more graphically pleasing. The downside to the graphic dazzle is that you have to open up a boatload of different windows to see what your results are. You start this click-happy journey in the *Output* window by double-clicking on the graphic in SPSS depicted in Figure 9-1 once you've run your analysis. This opens up the *Model Viewer* window. From there, you open the individual windows along the left-hand side by double-clicking on each one to see the rest of the results. It's almost as good as a video game.

Figure 9-1. The *Model Viewer* window with the *Model Summary*.

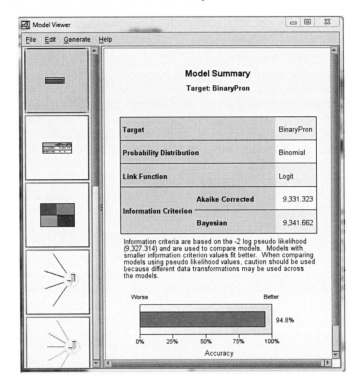

9.1.1.1 Basic model information

The *Model Summary* window tells you that you are carrying out a binary logistic regression with *BinaryPron* as the dependent variable (where the values are *glottal_oral* and *ZOther*). It also gives you the overall accuracy rate of the model, along with a number of information criteria that in theory can be used to compare different models. However, those numbers are coupled with a dire warning that they are not based on real −2LL values but on pseudo −2LL values and that you shouldn't trust them. In other words, you really can't compare different pseudo −2LL values from different models to determine which fits best. (Since this is the case, I wonder why SPSS bothers to give them to you at all.) In any event, the *Data Structure* window (Table 9-1) shows you what variables the random effects are based on, how many of each there are (25 words and 56 participants), and what the dependent variable is. It also shows you what the data for the first line of data for the first subject in the spreadsheet are.

9.1.1.2 Calculating the accuracy rate

The classification window (Table 9-2) contains a confusion matrix (I just had to use that term) that indicates how well the model did at predicting each of the values of the dependent variable. This is good stuff to know because it lets us calculate exactly how accurate the model is. What we want to know is whether the model is doing a better job of predicting the outcome than what you'd get by chance. What I mean by chance is that even if the dependent variables didn't exert any influence on the outcome, you'd expect to get some correct classifications by chance. Another way of looking at it is that even if you always predicted the same outcome for everything, you'd get many classifications right. What is the possibility of that happening? In this model we've got 144 cases of *glottal_oral* and 1166 of *ZOther* for a total 3,010 cases. The by-chance accuracy rate is calculated in this manner (Bayaga 2010):

$$144 \ / \ 1310 = .110 \qquad .110^2 = .012$$
$$1166 \ / \ 1310 = .890 \qquad .890^2 = \underline{.792}$$
$$.804 \ \text{by-chance accuracy rate is the sum}$$

So, how is the model doing when compared to this .804 accuracy rate? Well, it got 1,136 of the 1,166 *ZOther* responses right (1166 × .974 = 1136; see Table 9-2), and 106 of the 144 *glottal_oral* responses right (144 × .736 = 106) so the overall accuracy rate is .948 (1136 + 106 / 1310), which is 14.4% better than you'd get by chance (.948 − .804).

If there wasn't much difference between the predicted and actual accuracy rate, that would indicate that the variables in the model aren't very useful predictors of the dependent variable, and we ought to try others instead or recognize that we really can't predict when oral releases versus other pronunciations occur.

9.1.1.3 Significance of the random effects in the model

Now that we've done an initial run, the next step is to look at the random effects to see if they are significant. There are two random effects: a random intercept for each subject and a random intercept for each test word. The *Covariance Parameters* window (Table 9-3) gives information about the number of parameters and the significance of the random effects according to the Wald statistic.[1] Click on *Effect > Block 1* at the bottom of the *Covariance Parameters* window to see the results for the random intercept for participants. This tells you that there is a significant degree of variability (.002) between the intercepts for each participant, so that random intercept ought to be included in the model. The significance of the random intercept for test words appears in Figure 9-4. The variability among the intercepts for the 25 test words also reaches significance, so it should arguably be left in the model as well. Finally, there are no random slopes or repeated effects that would make sense for these data, so we may move on to the fixed effects.

Table 9-1. The *Data Structure* window.

Data Structure

Target: BinaryPron

	Subjects		Target
	Participant	Word	BinaryPron
Data For First Subject	42	beaten	glottal_oral
Total Number of Levels	56	25	

Table 9-2. The *Classification* window.

Classification

Target:BinaryPron

Overall Percent Correct =94.8%

Observed	Predicted		Row Percent
	glottal_oral	ZOther	■ 100.00
glottal_oral	73.6%	26.4%	■ 80.00
			■ 60.00
			■ 40.00
ZOther	2.6%	97.4%	20.00
			0.00

---

[1] Among others, Fears, Benichou, and Gail (1996) show that the Wald statistic is not always reliable, which is why some researchers are hesitant to depend on it. Since we can't judge fit using −2LL, the Wald statistic is the best way available for determining whether there is enough variability in the random and repeated effects that they should be included in the model (Hox 2010:120).

Table 9-3. Number of parameters and significance of the random intercept for participants.

Covariance Parameters

Target:BinaryPron

Covariance Parameters	Residual Effect	0
	Random Effects	2
Design Matrix Columns	Fixed Effects	6
	Random Effects	81[a]
Common Subjects		1

Common subjects are based on the subject specifications for the residual and random effects and are used to chunk the data for better performance.

[a] This is the number of columns per common subject.

Random Effect Block 1	Estimate	Std.Error	Z	Sig.	95% Confidence Interval	
					Lower	Upper
Var(Intercept)	3.763	1.201	3.134	.002	2.013	7.034

Covariance Structure:Variance components
Subject Specification:Participant

Table 9-4. Significance of the random intercept for test words.

Random Effect Block 2	Estimate	Std.Error	Z	Sig.	95% Confidence Interval	
					Lower	Upper
Var(Intercept)	0.610	0.309	1.970	.049	0.225	1.649

Covariance Structure:Variance components
Subject Specification:Word

9.1.1.4 Result for the fixed effects

The default view of the *Fixed Effects* window (Figure 9-2) is this infelicitous octopus diagram that I won't bother trying to explain. Go to the numeric data that the octopus is based on by choosing *Table* in the *Style* drop-down menu at the bottom left of the figure. You'll have to look hard for this menu, it's almost microscopic. Once you do locate it and choose *Table* you'll get Table 9-5, where you can see that *Age, Gender,* and *Percent_in_UT* are significant while *Word_order* is not.

Figure 9-2. The *Fixed Effects* window diagram style.

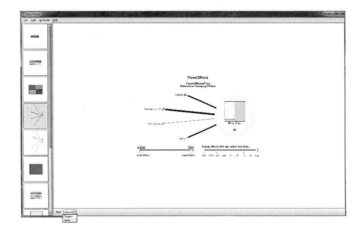

Table 9-5. The *Fixed Effects* window table style.

Fixed Effects

Target:BinaryPron
Reference Category:ZOther

Source	F	df1	df2	Sig.
Corrected Model ▼	6.322	4	1,305	.000
Gender	8.232	1	1,305	.004
Percent_in_UT	12.359	1	1,305	.000
Word_order	1.437	1	1,305	.231
Age	9.669	1	1,305	.002

Probability distribution:Binomial
Link function:Logit

```
Gender                                                    Age

First Effect                                          Last Effect
Display effects with sig. values less than...

  .0001  .0005  .001  .005  .01  .05  .10  .20  1.00
```

The statistics in Table 9-5 just indicate what's significant but don't tell you the strength of each effect or the direction of the effect. To view those numeric results you have to once again get past another octopus diagram (Figure 9-3) by choosing *Table* in the *Style* drop-down menu depicted at the bottom of that figure. Doing that displays Table 9-6 where the meat of the analysis resides. Be sure to click on the *Exponential* button at the bottom of the table to expose the exponential coefficient column. Also click on the *Coefficient* button in the table itself to reveal the standard errors and confidence intervals.

Figure 9-3. *Fixed Coefficients* window diagram style.

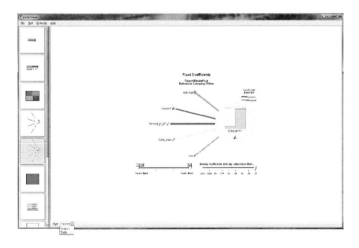

Table 9-6. *Fixed Coefficients* window table style.

Fixed Coefficients

Target:BinaryPron
Reference Category:ZOther

Model Term	Coefficient ▼	Std.Error	t	Sig.	Exp(Coefficient)	95% Confidence Interval for Exp (Coefficient)	
						Lower	Upper
Intercept	-6.013	1.568	-3.836	.000	0.002	0.000	0.053
Gender=f	2.408	0.839	2.869	.004	11.116	2.142	57.699
Gender=m	0[a]						
Percent_in_UT	0.052	0.015	3.516	.000	1.053	1.023	1.084
Word_order	-0.035	0.029	-1.199	.231	0.965	0.911	1.023
Age	-0.092	0.030	-3.109	.002	0.912	0.860	0.967

Probability distribution:Binomial
Link function:Logit

[a] This coefficient is set to zero because it is redundant.

Gender ⌐   ⌐ Age
First Effect   Last Effect
Display coefficients with sig. values less than...

.0001   .0005   .001   .005   .01   .05   .10   .20   1.00

9.1.1.5 Interpreting the coefficients and effect size

The first thing to note in Table 9-6 is that the reference category is *ZOther*. Now pay attention, because this is kind of tricky. This means that the coefficients in the table refer *not* to *ZOther*, but to the *glottal_oral* pronunciation as they contrast with *ZOther*. So, as far as gender is concerned, male is the reference category. The positive coefficient of 2.408 in the female row indicates that in comparison to males, females are more likely than males to use the *glottal_oral* pronunciation (e.g., [kʰɪʔən]) over another pronunciations (e.g., [kʰɪʔn̩] or [kʰɪtən]). The exponentiated value of 11.116 (more commonly known as the *odds ratio*, which is what I'll call it from now on) is nice to have because it is a good indication of effect size. Odds ratios larger than one mean that as the level of the independent variable increases, so do the odds of getting the outcome. In this case the odds ratio means that the odds of a female using the *glottal_oral* pronunciation is about 11 times higher than for males. Of course, this is accurate when the effects of the other independent variables are held constant.

A teeny bit of math is in order here. The relationship between the coefficient b and the odds ratio is always calculated as 2.718 raised to the power of b, or 2.718^b. So $2.718^{2.408} = 11.11$. If you have a lame calculator that doesn't do this kind of thing, search the web for an exponential-power calculator and use 2.718 as the base and the coefficient as the exponent.

The participant's age and the percent of his or her life spent in Utah are continuous variables and have a different interpretation. The positive coefficient of 0.052 for *Percent_in_UT* indicates that the more time someone has lived in Utah, the greater the odds that he or she will use the *glottal_oral* variety. In this case, the odds ratio (1.053) tells us that the odds of saying [kʰɪʔən] is increased by a factor of 1.053 for every 1% increase in the percent of one's life spent in Utah. (Another way of looking at it is that the odds increase by 5.3%. If the odds ratio were 1.72, that would be a 72% increase in odds.) What if we wanted to know what the odds of using the oral release are for someone who has lived 70% of his or her life in Utah (when compared with someone who has not lived in Utah at all)? To figure this out we'd first multiply the coefficient of 0.052 by 70 and then exponentiate it (i.e., $70 \times .052 = 3.64$, $2.718^{3.64} = 38.077$). This means that the odds are 38 times higher for a 70 percenter Utahn to orally release than a never-lived-there kinda person. Wow. Another nice thing about the odds ratio is that it is a measure of effect size. However, you can't directly compare odds ratios of continuous and categorical variables, nor can you compare the odds ratios of continuous variables that are measured on different scales.[2]

Age is also a significant variable. The negative coefficient of −0.092 says that the older someone is, the lower the odds that he or she releases the glottal stop orally. The odds ratio of .912 can be interpreted in this way: As age increases by one year, the odds of using *glottal_oral* are multiplied by .912. Since .912 is smaller than one, this means that the odds go down. For this reason, odds ratios that are smaller than one are a bit counterintuitive to interpret. An odds ratio smaller than one means that as the as the independent variable goes up, the odds of getting the outcome go down, so sometimes it's helpful to take the reciprocal of the odds ratio, which is easier to wrap your head around. You get this by subtracting the odds ratio from one, so $1 - .912 = .088$. This number means that for every year older, the odds of using *glottal_oral* decrease by 8.8%. What would a difference of 10 years do, say between 20-year-olds and 30-year-olds? Just plug the 10-year difference into the formula and you get the odds ratio of .399 ($10 \times 0.092 = -0.92$, $2.718^{-0.92} = .399$). The reciprocal of .399 is .601 ($1 - .399$), so the use of the glottal release is predicted to decrease by

---

[2] If there were a number of continuous variables that you needed to compare on equal footing you'd need to convert those variables into z-scores and rerun the analysis (see Field 2013:179).

60% between a 20-year-old and a 30-year-old (or between a 30-year-old and a 40-year-old). Of course, these figures are valid when the effect of the other variables is taken into consideration as well.

Now that we have determined that the random intercepts are significant and have seen which fixed variables are significant, we may want to systematically eliminate insignificant variables (such as word order), rerun the analysis, and report the model that contains only significant variables. In this case word order is not crucial to the hypothesis being tested so it could be removed. However, you wouldn't want to remove a variable that is an integral part of the hypothesis that you are testing, even if it is insignificant.

9.1.1.6 Comparing variable values with different contrast types

The default way of handling categorical variables, like gender, is to take one value, such as *male* in Table 9-6, as the reference and compare the other value(s) to it. This is called TREATMENT CODING. When you've only got two values (e.g., male versus female), it doesn't really matter which one you set as the reference; the outcome will tell you the same story. Sometimes this kind of coding makes sense even when there are more than two values. For example, many studies compare two groups that receive different treatments with a third control group that receives no treatment. The control group is the ideal candidate to be the reference value, and the results would tell us how the two treatments compare to no treatment at all.

There are other designs where no particular value makes sense as the reference. If you were interested in *–ing* versus *–in'* rates among four different high school social groups (e.g., nerds, jocks, drama people, and band geeks) with treatment coding you are forced to choose one value and compare the other three to that one. You run up against the same problem if one of your variables has phonological values, such as voiced stop, voiceless stop, nasal, or fricative. In both these cases, what you really want to do is compare each value to each of the other values (PAIRWISE CODING).

Another useful type of coding is DEVIATION CODING, which like just about everything else in statistics, goes by several different names (e.g., *sum coding* and *effects coding*). Instead of comparing all the other values to the reference value, deviation coding uses the mean of all the values and calculates how much each of the values deviates from the mean.[3] As far as *–in'* rates are concerned, deviation coding could tell you that jocks do it significantly more than average—that is, they favor *–in'*. On the other hand, the nerds may use significantly fewer instances of *–in'* than average. In other words, they disfavor it. If the rates of drama people and band geeks turn out to be insignificant, that says that they don't differ much from the mean rate.

So what would the outcome look like for the gender variable using deviation coding? Figure 9-4 shows that females on average score higher than the mean, and males lower. It's important to see the data the graph is based on in table format (Table 9-7). Females score about .015 above the mean and males about .015 below. Notice that these differences are not significant. I can already hear you saying, "Wait, in Table 9-6 gender was significant. Why isn't it significant here?" The results in Table 9-6 are done with treatment coding and the scores for males are compared to the scores for females. In Table 9-7 the insignificance is a result of the fact that the two genders aren't compared to each other, but to their mean score. It should be clear that in this case, treatment coding probably makes more sense than deviation coding.

One thing to keep in mind is that the means are not necessarily the actual means. They are the estimated means that SPSS calculates when it takes all of the other independent variables in the model into account. In other words, the results in Table 9-7 may change when different variables are included or excluded from the model.

---

[3] While treatment coding is the default in SPSS, some logistic regression programs specifically designed for the sociolinguist (i.e., Varbrul, Goldvarb, and Rbrul) have deviance coding as the default.

Figure 9-4. Graph of how females' and males' scores differ from the mean score.

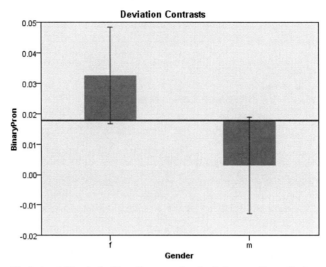

The horizontal line is the BinaryPron overall estimated mean. The vertical bars are the deviation contrasts (BinaryPron at each level of Gender minus BinaryPron overall).

Significant contrasts are shaded gold. The least significant difference adjusted significance level is .05.

Table 9-7. Table of how females' and males' scores differ from the mean score.

Deviation Contrasts

Gender Deviation Contrasts	Contrast Estimate ▼	Std. Error	t	df	Adj. Sig.	95% Confidence Interval	
						Lower	Upper
f - Mean	0.015	0.008	1.829	1,305	0.068	-0.001	0.031
m - Mean	-0.015	0.008	-1.829	1,305	0.068	-0.031	0.001

Significant contrasts are shaded gold. The least significant difference adjusted significance level is .05.

9.1.2 Carrying out a binomial mixed-effects logistic regression in SPSS

One way of doing a mixed-effects logistic regression is to start with a model that includes all fixed, random, and repeated effects, then to find which random and repeated effects are significant. Those that are insignificant are eliminated. Once the significant random and repeated effects are identified, move on to the fixed effects and find which are significant.

1. To begin the analysis, open the file *Eddington&Savage2012.sav*.
2. Click on *Analyze > Mixed Models > Generalized Linear*. This brings up the dialog box in Figure 9-5 with the *Data Structure* tab selected. This is where you specify which variable to create a random effect for. (Repeated effects are also specified here when you also include a variable under *Repeated Measures*.)
3. Move *Participant* and *Word* to the position under the *Subject* bar.

Figure 9-5. *Data Structure* tab.

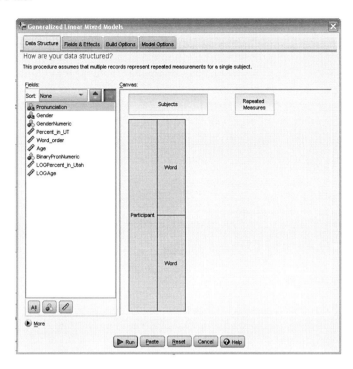

The fact that the *Word* bar is divided into two shows that *Word* is nested under *Participant*. We actually want two separate random intercepts rather than a nesting between them. Alas, SPSS won't let us specify that here, so we'll have to modify that later. However, if you wanted to consider nestings such as students in a classroom, or test items in a block, this would be an appropriate way to specify the nesting.

4. Click on the *Fields & Effect*s tab, which brings up the dialog box in Figure 9-6. Highlight *Target* under *Select an item. Target* is the dependent variable, which in this case is *BinaryPron,* which needs to be selected in the *Target* drop-down menu.

Figure 9-6. *Fields & Effects* tab with *Target.*

We also need to choose which value of *BinaryPron* is going to be the reference value against which the other value will be compared. We want to see what favors the use of oral releases over other pronunciations, so *ZOther* is the reference value. The coefficients will be calculated for oral release (*glottal_oral*) in this case.

5. Click on the triangle next to *More*, check *Customize reference category*, and type in *ZOther* in the *Reference value* box. Choose *Binary logistic regression* as the type of analysis to carry out on the data.

The independent variables are entered by choosing *Fixed Effects* under the *Select an item* window (Figure 9-7).

6. Drag *Gender, Percent_in_UT, Age,* and *Word_order* from the *Fields* window to the *Effect builder* window under *Main.* If you wanted to include interactions, you would highlight the variables to use in the interaction in the *Fields* window and drag them to the *Effect builder* window under *2-way* or *3-way.*
7. Make sure that *Include intercept* is checked. There are a number of icons to the top right of the *Effect builder* window. Variables can be deleted from the *Effect builder* window by clicking on the red *X*, or reordered using the up and down arrows there. The pencil icon opens a window that allows you to create interactions or to nest variables by hand.

Figure 9-7. *Fields & Effects* tab with *Fixed Effects.*

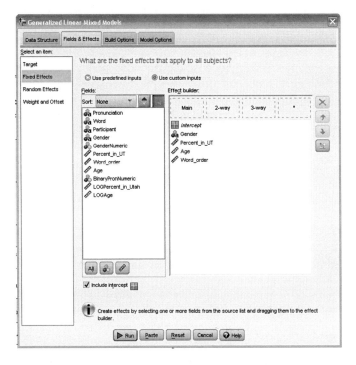

Random intercepts and random slopes are specified by choosing *Random Effects* in the *Select an item* window (Figure 9-8). We'll set up two random intercepts.

8. Click on *Add Block* and the two variables entered on the *Data Structure* tab (Figure 9-4) appear under the *Subject combination* drop-down menu, namely *Participant* and *Participant*Word.*
9. Choose *Participant* (if it has not been done automatically for you), check *Include intercept > OK.* Click on *Add Block*, choose *Participant*Word* under the *Subject combination* drop-down menu, check *Include intercept > OK* (Figure 9-9).

Participant*Word is a nested variable at this point, which we don't want. We'll change it to a simple random intercept for *Word* later.

10. There are a number of things that can be done on the *Build Options* tab (Figure 9-10). SPSS will alphanumerically choose either the first or last value of a variable as the reference value. In Figure 9-5 we hand-picked what value of *BinaryPron* was the reference value so we don't have to sweat anything here.

Figure 9-8. *Fields & Effects* tab with *Random Effects,* random intercept for *Participant.*

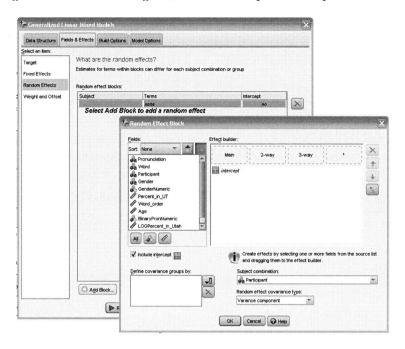

Figure 9-9. *Fields & Effects* tab with *Random Effects,* random intercept for *Participant*Word.*

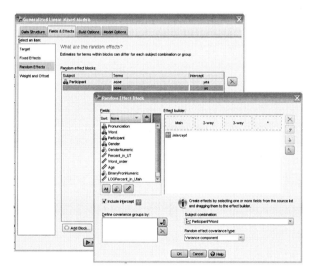

Figure 9-10. *Build Options* tab.

But, if you didn't select a value to be the reference you can specify the *Sorting order for categorical targets* here. There are two values: *glottal_oral* and *ZOther*. I specifically put the *Z* there so that *ZOther* would fall last alphabetically. When *Sorting order for categorical predictors* is set to *Descending*, the last value (*ZOther*) is set as the reference. When it is set to *Ascending*, the first value (*glottal_oral*) is chosen as the reference value. The same holds for the values of any categorical independent variables. For instance, *Gender* has two values: *f* and *m*. When *Sorting order for categorical predictors* is set to *Descending, m* is the reference value. When set to *Ascending, f* becomes the reference value. Set both of these sorting orders to *Ascending*.

The *Degrees of freedom* box has two settings: *Fixed for all tests* and *Varied across tests.* As the menu explains, the second option is preferable with small data sets and unbalanced data sets (e.g., where one value of an independent variable is much more frequent than another), and when using an Unstructured covariance structure. In the *Tests of fixed effects and coefficients* box there is an option called *Use robust estimation to handle violations of model assumptions.* This option tells SPSS to use the Huber-White sandwich estimator to calculate robust standard errors. It is supposed to be used when certain assumptions are violated, such as when there are repeated measures or other nested data (Heck et al. 2012:112). I know what you are thinking. If this option exists to account for repeated measures, why not just choose it and forget about running a mixed-effects model at all? My understanding is that this option is kind of a quick-and-dirty way to deal with repeated measures but that running a true mixed-effects model is much better (UCLA Statistical Consulting Group 2014). What is interesting is that you can choose this option even when you are running a mixed-effects model. I guess you'd be doubly sure you were taking care of the repeated measures in that case.

The *Model Options* tab is helpful if you want to estimate what the mean of a categorical variable would be at different levels of any continuous variables in the model. It also allows you to choose different kinds of codings to apply. In Figure 9-11, *Gender* is checked. Under *Contrast Type* the default is *None,* which means that no contrast will be calculated. If you would like to see how each value varies from the mean, choose *Deviation,* as shown in Figure 9-11. This produces the graph in Figure 9-4. In the *Style* drop-down menu on the bottom left of that screen you can switch from *Diagram* to *Table* to see the same results in table format (Table 9-7). Be sure to click on *Contrast Estimate* to display the entire table. Another useful option under *Contrast Type* is *Pairwise,* which compares each value of a variable to every other value.

In the *Fields* box you can estimate the outcome given different values of the independent variable. The default is the mean. To make estimates at other values you can click the triangle in the *Constant* column and choose *Value,* then put the value of that variable you want to estimate at in the *Value* column.

Figure 9-11. *Model Options tab.*

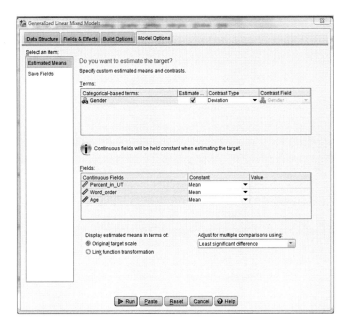

At this point you can run the analysis by pressing the *Run* button at the bottom of the window, as depicted in Figure 9-11. As we saw in Chapter 8, the menu system can be quite a pain to use, especially when you are comparing a number of different models. My suggestion is to follow the steps I've outlined to use the menus, then hit the *Paste* button to put all the code into the *Syntax Editor* (Figure 9-12) where it can be modified more easily at your leisure. To run the analysis from the *Syntax Editor,* press the green triangular arrow at the top center of the *Syntax Editor* window. For some reason that I am at a loss to explain, the syntax SPSS uses for generalized linear mixed models is not identical to what SPSS uses for linear mixed models, so let me explain what it means line by line.

Figure 9-12. *The Syntax Editor window.*

Table 9-8. Step-by-step discussion of *Syntax Editor* code.

Term	Meaning
`GENLINMIXED`	means that a generalized linear mixed-effects model is being performed.
`/DATA_STRUCTURE SUBJECTS=Participant* Word`	shows that the random effects deal with the variables *Participant* and *Word*.
`/FIELDS TARGET=BinaryPron`	specifies *BinaryPron* as the dependent variable.
`TRIALS=NONE OFFSET=NONE`	refer to options not discussed.
`/TARGET_OPTIONS REFERENCE='ZOther'`	shows that *ZOther* is the reference value of the dependent variable.
`DISTRIBUTION=BINOMIAL LINK=LOGIT`	indicates that the logistic regression is being carried out on a dependent variable with two values.
`/FIXED EFFECTS=Gender Percent_in_UT Age Word_order USE_INTERCEPT=TRUE`	enumerates what the independent variables are.
`/RANDOM USE_INTERCEPT=TRUE SUBJECTS=Participant COVARIANCE_TYPE= VARIANCE_COMPONENTS`	specifies a random intercept for each participant.
`/RANDOM USE_INTERCEPT=TRUE SUBJECTS=Participant* Word COVARIANCE_TYPE= VARIANCE_COMPONENTS.`	should specify a random intercept for word. The first thing to notice is that in order to do this you have to delete *Participant**. This is something you can't do via menu mania.
`/BUILD_OPTIONS TARGET_CATEGORY_ ORDER=ASCENDING INPUTS_CATEGORY_ ORDER=ASCENDING MAX_ITERATIONS=100 CONFIDENCE_LEVEL=95`	contains information the computer needs to do its magic.
`DF_METHOD=RESIDUAL`	identifies the method of calculating degrees of freedom. Change this to *SATTERTHWAITE* if the data set is small or unbalanced or the covariance structure is Unstructured.
`COVB=MODEL`	is the default setting for estimation method. Change this to *ROBUST* if you want to use the Huber-White estimator.
`/EMMEANS TABLES=Gender COMPARE=Gender CONTRAST=DEVIATION`	applies deviation coding to gender so that each value of gender is compared to the mean.
`/EMMEANS_OPTIONS SCALE=ORIGINAL PADJUST=LSD.`	are the settings for estimating the outcome using particular values of the independent variables.

9.2 Assumptions of Logistic Regression

Since logistic regression doesn't have a continuous dependent variable, it doesn't have the assumptions that other kinds of statistics require—but don't be too relieved. It has its own set of requirements and things you need to consider. For instance, although it's not an assumption, in order to get accurate results from a logistic regression, you need to have about 20 observations for each independent variable you include. That is a very rough figure. Another thing to keep an eye on is the standard error for each independent variable. A large standard error[4] often indicates problems with the data that would make the results inaccurate (Hosmer & Lemeshow 2000), although this doesn't apply to the

---

[4] Some researchers suggest anything over two is problematic (Costea 2006:66, and Naderi et al. 2009:33), but I haven't seen that figure in a statistics text.

standard error of the intercept. Large standard errors could indicate collinearity in the data, too few observations for the model to make a good estimate from, or that an important independent variable hasn't been included. It may indicate COMPLETE SEPARATION[5] which occurs when an independent variable or some combination of values of independent variables completely predicts the outcome. One example of this in the data we are considering would be if all cases of oral release were produced by women, and no cases by men.

9.2.1 Collinearity

One possible issue with the data that should be familiar to you is collinearity. Too much overlap between independent variables may make it impossible to distinguish the effect of one variable from the effect of the other. Luckily, SPSS calculates two tests of collinearity that we've seen already in Chapter 7: VIF and Tolerance. A Tolerance under .1 or a VIF over 10 indicates collinearity, so we are okay here (Table 9-9). If there were indications of collinearity, to see which variables are responsible for it, all of the independent variables can be correlated with each other (Table 9-10). Pearson correlations at .8 or higher are reason for concern.

Table 9-9. Collinearity statistics.

Coefficients[a]		Collinearity statistics	
Model		Tolerance	VIF
1	Percent_in_UT	.981	1.019
	Word_order	1.000	1.000
	Age	.982	1.018
	GenderNUM	.997	1.003

a. Dependent variable: BinaryPronNUM

Table 9-10. Correlations between the independent variables.

Correlations		Percent in_UT	Word _order	Age	Gender NUM
Percent_in_ UT	Correlation	1	−.004	.130	−.045
	Sig.		.871	.000	.106
	N	1310	1310	1310	1310
Word _order	Correlation	−.004	1	−.002	.001
	Sig.	.871		.950	.962
	N	1310	1310	1310	1310
Age	Correlation	.130	−.002	1	.021
	Sig.	.000	.950		.440
	N	1310	1310	1310	1310
GenderNU M	Correlation	−.045	.001	.021	1
	Sig.	.106	.962	.440	
	N	1310	1310	1310	1310

9.2.2 Linearity of the logit

The linearity of the logit is different from the kind of linearity we've had to deal with before. You only need to test it on continuous variables such as percent of life in Utah, and age. It entails calculating the natural logarithm of each continuous variable, then making an interaction variable between the variable and its natural logarithm,[6] and finally, determining whether that interaction is significant. If it is *not* significant, you've met the assumption. If the interaction is significant, the logit isn't linear. As you can see in Table 9-11, none of the interactions are significant, so there are no violations of the assumption of the linearity of the logit. (Note: Don't use the results of the analysis with these interactions in the final analysis of the data. They are included as a diagnostic of the linearity of the logit and aren't true variables that are important in the analysis of the fixed effects.)

---

[5] In sociolinguistics this is often referred to as a *knockout*.
[6] This is called the *Box-Tidwell test*.

Table 9-11. Tests of the linearity of the logit.

Fixed Coefficients

Target:BinaryPron
Reference Category:ZOther

Model Term	Coefficient ▼	Std.Error	t	Sig.	Exp(Coefficient)	95% Confidence Interval for Exp (Coefficient) Lower	Upper
Intercept	-3.852	5.737	-0.671	.502	0.021	0.000	1,640.962
Gender=f	2.429	0.876	2.773	.006	11.346	2.035	63.259
Gender=m	0ᵃ						
Percent_in_UT	-0.377	0.286	-1.317	.188	0.686	0.391	1.203
Word_order	-0.616	0.313	-1.965	.050	0.540	0.292	0.999
Age	0.420	0.732	0.574	.566	1.522	0.362	6.390
LogPercent_in_UT*Percent_in_UT	0.086	0.057	1.504	.133	1.090	0.974	1.219
LogWord_order*Word_order	0.171	0.092	1.860	.063	1.186	0.991	1.420
LogAge*Age	-0.117	0.166	-0.702	.483	0.890	0.642	1.233

Probability distribution:Binomial
Link function:Logit

If there were violations, then the problem would be that leaving the lack of linearity in the model ups the chances of getting Type II errors, which make the results inaccurate. One way of dealing with linearity problems is to exclude the offending variable if you can justifiably do so. For example, if word order were problematic, I wouldn't be opposed to excluding it since it's not a significant predictor anyways. Another way to deal with lack of linearity is to transform the continuous variable until you make it linear (see Chapter 3). If that doesn't work, an act of final desperation is to convert the continuous variable into a categorical one with several values, although this is frowned upon statistically (Cohen 1983).

9.2.3 Using SPSS to check the assumptions of a logistic regression

To get the collinearity diagnostics, run a linear regression analysis on the data. Linear regression doesn't handle categorical variables, so you'll need to use the numeric variables for gender and pronunciation instead (*GenderNUM* and *BinaryPronNUM*).

1. Click on *Analyze > Regression > Linear*. Place *BinaryPronNUM* in the *Dependent* box and *Percent_in_UT, Word_order, GenderNUM*, and *Age* in the *Independent(s)* box.
2. Click on the *Statistics* button and check *Collinearity diagnostics > Continue > OK*. This produces Table 9-9.

To check the correlations between variables,

1. Click on *Analyze > Correlate > Bivariate*. Place *Percent_in_UT, Word_order, GenderNUM*, and *Age* in the *Variables* box.
2. Make sure *Pearson* is checked > *OK*. This produces Table 9-10.

To determine whether the logit is linear, you must first calculate the natural logarithm of every continuous variable. Chapter 3 gives instructions similar to those below, but it includes screenshots of the SPSS windows, so you may want to go back and refer to those figures

1. Click on *Transform > Compute Variable*. In the *Function* group box click *Arithmetic*. In the *Functions and Special Variables* box double-click on *Ln* (natural logarithm) to move it to the *Numeric Expression* box, where it appears as *LN(?)*.
2. Highlight the continuous variable you want to transform and then click on the arrow button to move the variable into the formula in the *Numeric Expression* box. If the *Age* variable were chosen, the formula would now read *LN(Age)*.
3. Give the new variable a name in the *Target Variable* box such as *LogAge > OK*. The natural logarithm of *Age* now appears in the *Data Editor* in a new column called *LogAge*. Repeat the steps to calculate the natural logarithm of all the continuous variables.

Next, include the interaction of the variables in the model.

1. If you still have the model in the *Syntax Editor* (Figure 9-12), modify the line that specifies the fixed effects so that it reads

```
/FIXED  EFFECTS=Gender  Percent_in_UT  Word_order  Age  LogPercent_in_UT*Percent_in_UT
    LogWord_order*Word_order LogAge*Age USE_INTERCEPT=TRUE
```

2. Press the green triangle in the *Syntax Editor* to run the analysis with the interactions.
3. If you don't have the model in the *Syntax Editor*, which you can edit by changing the above line of syntax, follow the instructions above for carrying out a binary logistic regression with the menus, and when you get to the instructions relating to Figure 9-6, add the interaction effects (*LogPercent_in_UT*Percent_in_UT LogWord_order*Word_order LogAge*Age*) along with the main effects (*Gender Percent_in_UT Word_order Age*), and follow the rest of those instructions.

9.3 Reporting the Results of a Mixed-Effects Logistic Regression

There is a lot of data to report in a logistic regression, and I'd suggest putting it in table form. In fact, most of the data in Table 9-6 is relevant, and your table could include all of that—perhaps minus the column containing the *t* score and the *male* row. In addition, you would need to explain that you accounted for the repeated measures by including a random intercept for each test word and participant. Explain that both of these random effects were significant (Tables 9-3 and 9-4). If you removed independent variables from the final model, mention which ones don't appear in the table because they were not significant.

9.4 Multinomial Logistic Regression

In the previous example we looked at a categorical outcome with two values: *glottal_oral* ([kʰɪtən]), and *ZOther,* which actually combines the *glottal_nasal* outcome ([kʰɪʔn̩]) and the *non-glottal* outcome ([kʰɪtən]). The question that binomial logistic regression asks in this case is what factors influence a *glottal_oral* outcome over any other possible outcomes. There may be times, however, when the research question asks what variables influence three or more possible outcomes. We can easily convert the present data into a multinomial logistic regression by considering all three outcomes: *glottal_oral, glottal_nasal,* and *non-glottal.* As usual, we need to choose one of these to be the reference value. Let's take the most common pronunciation, the *glottal_nasal* variety as the reference and ask what variables favor a *non-glottal* over a *glottal_nasal,* and what variables favor a *glottal_oral* over a *glottal_nasal.*

The *Classification table* (Table 9-12) gives us the information we need to see how well the model does when compared to chance. There is only an 11.6% probability of getting the results by chance, while the actual accuracy rate is much higher, at 84.4%.

glottal_oral   144 / 3010 = .110 $.110^2$ = .012
glottal_nasal 951 / 3010 = .315 $.315^2$ = .099
No-glottal   215 / 3010 = .071 $.071^2$ = .005
                                              .116 by-chance
                                                    accuracy rate

Table 9-12. *Classification* table.

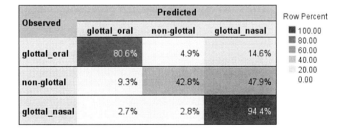

Table 9-13. The *Fixed Effects* window table style.

Fixed Effects

Target:Pronunciation
Reference Category:glottal_nasal

Source	F	df1	df2	Sig.
Corrected Model ▼	4.744	8	1,300	.000
Gender	4.153	2	1,300	.016
Percent_in_UT	9.483	2	1,300	.000
Word_order	0.686	2	1,300	.504
Age	8.076	2	1,300	.000

Table 9-13 lets us know that *Gender, Percent_in_Utah*, and *Age* are significant variables, but once again we need to turn to the *Fixed Effects* table (9-14) to interpret how each independent variable influences the dependent variable, as well as the size of the effect that each one exerts. This table is where you will see the major difference between binomial and multinomial analyses. Remember that to see this table you need to choose *Table* from the *Style* drop-down menu (Table 9-14 bottom) on the bottom left of the *Fixed Coefficients* octopus diagram. Next, click on the *Exponential* button on the bottom of the screen to display the odds ratios. Also click on the *Coefficient* button on the top row of the table itself to display the coefficients.

Table 9-14. *Fixed Coefficients* window table style for *glottal_oral* (options at the bottom of the screen are included).

Fixed Coefficients

Target:Pronunciation
Reference Category:glottal_nasal

Model Term	Coefficient ▼	Std.Error	t	Sig.	Exp(Coefficient)	95% Confidence Interval for Exp (Coefficient) Lower	Upper
Intercept	-5.717	1.668	-3.428	.001	0.003	0.000	0.087
Gender=f	2.372	0.903	2.626	.009	10.719	1.823	63.040
Gender=m	0ᵃ						
Percent_in_UT	0.056	0.016	3.550	.000	1.057	1.025	1.090
Word_order	-0.032	0.030	-1.066	.287	0.968	0.912	1.028
Age	-0.104	0.032	-3.203	.001	0.901	0.846	0.960

Probability distribution:Multinomial
Link function:Generalized logit

Style:	Table ▼	Multinomial	glottal_oral ▼	Exponential

Notice that the *Reference Category* is *glottal_nasal* and that at the bottom of the screen in the *Multinomial* drop-down menu you can decide which value to compare to this reference value, either *glottal_oral* or *non-glottal*. Whatever value is chosen in this drop-down menu is what the coefficients and other numbers in the table refer to. As far as gender is concerned, the positive coefficient and small *p* value indicate that the odds of women using the *glottal_oral* pronunciation in contrast to the *glottal_nasal* are higher. The odds ratio of 10.719 indicates that gender has a large effect on pronunciation. More specifically, the odds are 10 times greater that females will use the *glottal_oral* over the *glottal_nasal* when compared to males.

Percent of time spent living in Utah and age are also significant, but they are continuous variables and are interpreted a bit differently. The odds ratio of 1.057 tells us that the odds of using the *glottal_oral* over the *glottal_nasal* is increased by a factor of 1.057 when the time that someone has lived in Utah increases by 1%. Another way of saying this is that the chances of using the *glottal_oral* over the *glottal_nasal* goes up 5.7% for every year lived in Utah. This is calculated by subtracting the odds ratio from one ($1 - 1.057 = -.057$, interpret this as a 5.7%

increase since the odds ratio is larger than one). On the other hand, the odds ratio for age is smaller than one (and the coefficient is negative). This indicates that as age goes up, the use of the *glottal_oral* pronunciation goes down. When the odds ratio is subtracted from one it is more easily interpreted than the odds ratio itself (1 − .901 = .099 = 9.9% decrease, since the odds ratio is smaller than one). So, there is about a 10% decrease in the use of the *glottal_oral* versus the *glottal_nasal* when age goes up a year.

So far we've been comparing the *glottal_oral* and *glottal_nasal* outcomes, but ignoring the *non-glottal* outcome. In order to compare it to the reference value of *glottal_nasal*, we need to choose *non-glottal* from the *Multinomial* drop-down menu, which yields Table 9-15. I'll leave the interpretation of those data up to you.

Table 9-15. *Fixed Coefficients* window table style for *non-glottal* with options at the bottom of the screen included.

Fixed Coefficients

Target:Pronunciation
Reference Category:glottal_nasal

Model Term	Coefficient ▼	Std.Error	t	Sig.	Exp(Coefficient)	95% Confidence Interval for Exp (Coefficient)	
						Lower	Upper
Intercept	-2.305	0.811	-2.841	.005	0.100	0.020	0.490
Gender=f	-0.526	0.467	-1.127	.260	0.591	0.237	1.476
Gender=m	0ª						
Percent_in_UT	0.021	0.008	2.581	.010	1.021	1.005	1.038
Word_order	0.010	0.025	0.408	.683	1.010	0.962	1.061
Age	-0.032	0.013	-2.475	.013	0.969	0.945	0.993

Probability distribution:Multinomial
Link function:Generalized logit

Style: Table ▼   Multinomial non-glottal ▼   Exponential

9.4.1 Using SPSS to carry out a multinomial logistic regression

The steps for a multinomial logistic regression are almost identical to those for a binomial. The assumptions are the same as well. The only difference between a binomial and a multinomial has to do with filling out the dialog box in Figure 9-5. The *Target* in this case is the dependent variable, *Pronunciation,* which has all three values of the outcome. The *Reference value* needs to be specified as *glottal_nasal,* and *Multinomial logistic regression*, rather than *Binary logistic regression, should be checked.* If you already have the syntax for the previous binomial regression, it is a simple matter of modifying it so it looks like this:

```
GENLINMIXED
/DATA_STRUCTURE SUBJECTS=Participant*Word
/FIELDS TARGET=Pronunciation TRIALS=NONE OFFSET=NONE
/TARGET_OPTIONS REFERENCE='glottal_nasal'
   DISTRIBUTION=MULTINOMIAL LINK=LOGIT                       ·
/FIXED EFFECTS=Gender Percent_in_UT Word_order Age USE_INTERCEPT=TRUE
/RANDOM USE_INTERCEPT=TRUE SUBJECTS=Participant COVARIANCE_TYPE=VARIANCE_COMPONENTS
/RANDOM USE_INTERCEPT=TRUE SUBJECTS=Word COVARIANCE_TYPE=VARIANCE_COMPONENTS
/BUILD_OPTIONS      TARGET_CATEGORY_ORDER=ASCENDING      INPUTS_CATEGORY_ORDER=ASCENDING
   MAX_ITERATIONS=100
   CONFIDENCE_LEVEL=95 DF_METHOD=RESIDUAL COVB=MODEL
/EMMEANS_OPTIONS SCALE=ORIGINAL PADJUST=LSD.
```

The differences in the syntax are highlighted in boldface. Remember to change the second random effect so that it is *Word* not *Participant*Word.*

9.5 Other Ways of Accounting for Repeated Measures

So far, the examples we've seen take care of the repeated effects by including a random intercept for *Participant* and another one for *Word.* However, in some studies, participants are measured at different points in time, or under different experimental conditions, or they respond to multiple trials of the same test items. In these cases, it is wise to allow each participant a random slope over time, condition, or trial. It may also be possible to add a repeated effect to the random slope to further account for the repeated measures by specifying the structure of the residuals.

An example of a study of this nature is one I carried out with a colleague (Taylor & Eddington 2009). It had to do with how /t/ is pronounced word-finally. In American English the /t/ in *right,* when followed by a word beginning with a vowel, such as *ankle,* can be pronounced [t], [ɾ], or [ʔ] (*righ[t] ankle, righ[ɾ] ankle, or righ[ʔ] ankle*). The question we asked was whether gender, age, and region (Western United States versus non-Western United States) affect which

---

pronunciation is used. The participants in the study heard 19 sentences such as *The jet engines were loud* and *She twisted her right ankle.* Their job was to repeat each sentence they heard three times immediately after hearing them. However, the test sentences were modified so that the /t/ in question was replaced with a beep to hide the actual pronunciation of /t/, so that it wouldn't influence how the participants would say it (e.g., *The je*{beep} *engines were loud*). The dependent variable was whether they pronounced the /t/ as [t], [ɾ], or [ʔ] in each sentence. Repeated measures exist because each participant was measured repeating all 19 test sentences, and they repeated each test sentence three times.

Let's consider two ways of accounting for these repeated measures. The first is by allowing each participant to have a random slope over each of the 19 test items. This is only possible because they repeated each test item three times. In addition to the random slope, we'll add a repeated effect to see whether accounting for the residuals is helpful as well. The second method is to deal with the repeated effects using a marginal model. We'll see that later.

9.5.1 Using a random slope and repeated effect to account for repeated measures in a binomial logistic regression

In this model, the binomial dependent variable is glottal stop pronunciation of /t/ versus the other two pronunciations (i.e., [t] and [ɾ]) combined. The data appear in *Taylor&Eddington.sav.* The independent variables are *Gender, Age,* and *Region.* Each participant was allowed a random slope over the 19 test items, and information about the resulting residuals was given in a repeated effect. The repeated effect is specified on the *Data Structure* tab as in Figure 9-13. (I won't repeat the step-by-step instructions for doing a logistic regression; I'll just highlight how they are different for the present analysis.) The participants gave repeated measures because they responded to 19 test items. You may wonder why, if this is the case, *Repetition* needs to be figured into the equation. The truth is that if you just include *Participant* as the subject of the repeated effect, and *Item* as the repeated measure, you will get an error message, because SPSS needs to know that each item was responded to more than once, so the repeated effect needs to be *Participant* over *Test Item* by *Repetition.* In order to choose a covariance structure for the repeated effect, you need to click on *More* at the bottom of the window, which expands the window so that you can see the *Repeated covariance type* drop-down menu.[7] Setting up the random slope of *Participant* over *Item* is done by filling out the random effects windows as shown in Figure 9-14. Click on *Add Block* to open the *Random Effect Block* window.

Figure 9-13. Setting up a repeated effect in the *Data Structure* tab.

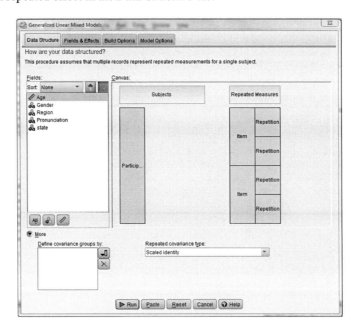

---

[7] I tried other covariance structures and only the model with Scaled Identity would run without errors.

Figure 9-14. Creating a random slope for *Participant* over *Item.*

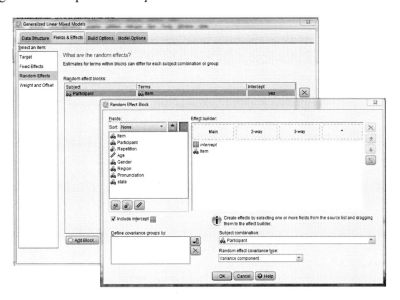

The syntax for this model is

```
GENLINMIXED
/DATA_STRUCTURE SUBJECTS=Participant REPEATED_MEASURES=Item*Repetition
    COVARIANCE_TYPE=IDENTITY
/FIELDS TARGET=BinaryPron TRIALS=NONE OFFSET=NONE
/TARGET_OPTIONS REFERENCE='Other' DISTRIBUTION=BINOMIAL LINK=LOGIT
/FIXED EFFECTS=Age Gender Region USE_INTERCEPT=TRUE
/RANDOM EFFECTS = Item USE_INTERCEPT=TRUE SUBJECTS=Participant  COVARIANCE_TYPE=
    VARIANCE_COMPONENTS
 /BUILD_OPTIONS TARGET_CATEGORY_ORDER=ASCENDING INPUTS_CATEGORY_ORDER=ASCENDING
    MAX_ITERATIONS=100  CONFIDENCE_LEVEL=95 DF_METHOD=RESIDUAL COVB=MODEL
/EMMEANS TABLES=Gender CONTRAST=NONE
/EMMEANS TABLES=Region CONTRAST=NONE
/EMMEANS_OPTIONS SCALE=ORIGINAL PADJUST=LSD.
```

Table 9-16. *Covariance Parameters* table with Wald statistic for the repeated effect.

Covariance Parameters

Target:BinaryPron

Covariance Parameters	Residual Effect	1
	Random Effects	2
Design Matrix Columns	Fixed Effects	6
	Random Effects	21 [a]
Common Subjects		58

Common subjects are based on the subject specifications for the residual and random effects and are used to chunk the data for better performance.

[a]This is the number of columns per common subject.

Residual Effect	Estimate	Std.Error	Z	Sig.	95% Confidence Interval	
					Lower	Upper
Variance	0.104	0.003	38.345	.000	0.099	0.109

Covariance Structure:Scaled Identity
Subject Specification:Participant

Effect Residual ▼

What we would like to know is whether there is enough variability in the random slope and repeated effect that they need to be included in the model. It's unfortunate that we can't trust the $-2LL$ statistic to help us test the fit, but we can check the Wald statistic to see if the random or repeated effects are significant. You'll find this at the bottom of the window (Table 9-16). When *Residual* is chosen from the *Effect* drop-down menu at the bottom of the window, the significance of the repeated effect is given. (Remember that repeated effects have to do with the residuals.) In this case it is significant. When *Block 1* is chosen rather than *Residual,* the Wald statistic for the random slope is shown in the

Var(Item) row (Table 9-17). It is also significant, so both should be left in the model to account for the repeated measures.

Table 9-17. *Covariance Parameters* table with Wald statistic for the random slope.

Random Effect	Estimate	Std.Error	Z	Sig.	95% Confidence Interval	
					Lower	Upper
Var(Intercept)	2.646	0.772	3.426	.001	1.494	4.689
Var(Item)	11.880	0.727	16.332	.000	10.537	13.395

Covariance Structure:Variance components
Subject Specification:Participant

Effect: [Block 1 ▼]

Now that we've accounted for the repeated effects we can look at the results of the analysis in Table 9-18. The reference category is *Other*, so the statistics in the table refer to the use of the glottal stop pronunciation as it contrasts with the other pronunciations. Only *Age* and *Gender* are significant. The negative coefficient for age, and the odds ratio (exponentiated coefficient) that is smaller than one indicate a negative relationship between age and the use of glottal stops. As age goes down, the use of glottal stops increases. To put it another way, older participants are less likely to use the glottal stop. The odds ratio of 4.059 for females tells us that the odds of pronouncing the test words with a glottal stop are four times greater for females than for males when the effect of the other variables is held constant.

Table 9-18. Results of the /t/ pronunciation experiment.

Fixed Coefficients

Target:BinaryPron
Reference Category:Other

Model Term	Coefficient ▼	Std.Error	t	Sig.	Exp(Coefficient)	95% Confidence Interval for Exp (Coefficient)	
						Lower	Upper
Intercept	-3.641	1.144	-3.183	.001	0.026	0.003	0.247
Age	-0.087	0.029	-3.004	.003	0.917	0.866	0.970
Gender=F	1.401	0.542	2.586	.010	4.059	1.403	11.739
Gender=M	0[a]						
Region=West	0.887	0.618	1.435	.151	2.428	0.722	8.161
Region=ZNonWes	0[a]						

Probability distribution:Binomial
Link function:Logit

9.5.2 Using a marginal model to account for repeated measures in a binomial logistic regression

The results of mixed effects and marginal models are very comparable when the dependent variable is numeric, however, in logistic regression mixed effects and marginal models may give quite different results. Mixed effects logistic regression models are not accurate when the dataset is highly unbalanced (Pacheco, Hattendorf, Colford, Musezahl, and Smith (2009) or small (Moineddin, Matheson, and Glazier 2007). Under these circumstances marginal models give results that are more generalizable to the general population and ought to be used instead of a mixed effects logistic regression (Roy 2013). Data sets that contain fewer than 30-50 tokens per speaker, and have fewer than 30-50 speakers are better analyzed with marginal logistic regression rather than mixed effects logistic regression. Marginal models are also called for when, in spite of your best efforts, a mixed-effects model gives you nothing but Hessian errors and non-convergence messages.

Remember that a marginal model is one that contains a repeated effect without any random effects. For the present data, running a marginal model would entail setting up the repeated effect in Figure 9.13, without including the random slope depicted in Figure 9.14. The syntax for a marginal model would be identical to the syntax for the mixed-effects model described above except that it would exclude the command for the random slope:

/RANDOM EFFECTS = Item USE_INTERCEPT=TRUE SUBJECTS=Participant   COVARIANCE_TYPE= VARIANCE_COMPONENTS

Another thing to keep in mind is that the covariance structure of the repeated effect that works in a mixed-effects model is not necessarily the best structure for the repeated effect in a marginal model, so you need to experiment with that parameter. For these data, Compound Symmetry worked in the marginal model.

9.6 Speeding Up Processing Time

Mixed models were not applied very often in the past due to their computational intensity, but this has changed recently as fast computers have become widely available. In spite of this, your computer may chug along for hours on certain data sets. There are a number of things you can do to speed up processing time and to avoid errors and nonconvergence issues.

- Avoid using Unstructured covariance structures.
- Use fewer independent variables or random effects.
- When subjects are clustered, renumber them. For example, if there are 80 subjects in three classrooms, rather than numbering the subjects 1–80, number them according to class: Class A, 1–22, Class B, 1–28, Class C, 1–30.
- Use a marginal model to account for repeated measures rather than random effects.
- Center the continuous variables (see Chapter 7).
- Transform variables so that they have more similar ranges. Smaller numbers are easier to work with. Sometimes slowdowns occur because one continuous variable has a narrow range of values (e.g. 0–1) and another has a wide range (3500–10,000).

9.7 Recipe for Carrying Out a Mixed-Effects Logistic Regression

1. Try a model that includes all possible independent variables, their interactions, and all relevant random and repeated effects.
2. Remove all insignificant random or repeated effects and rerun the analysis.
3. Eliminate any insignificant independent variables one at a time (if you want to eliminate insignificant variables) and rerun the analysis.
4. Test the assumptions. If they are not met, deal with any issues that arise with transformations, eliminating variables, and so on. Calculate the by-chance accuracy rate and compare it with the actual accuracy rate.
5. Rerun the analysis and report the final model. Use the coefficients and odds ratios to interpret the numeric results of the analysis.

9.8 Hands-On Exercises for Mixed-Effects Logistic Regression

Answers are available at http://linguistics.byu.edu/faculty/eddingtond/Data_Sets/answers.pdf

9.8.1 Negative imperatives in Argentine Spanish

In Argentine Spanish, the negative imperative varies as far as stress is concerned. Negative imperatives based on the verbal forms associated with the second-person singular pronoun *tú* have penultimate stress (e.g., *no véngas, no cómas* "don't come, don't eat"). On the other hand, negative imperatives that are related to verbal forms that correspond to the pronoun *vos* have final stress (e.g., *no vengás, no comás*). Johnson and Grinstead (2011) studied the variation between the *tú* and *vos* forms. They did this by giving participants 20 situations (10 urgent and 10 nonurgent), all of which would require a negative imperative response. The participants could respond with either the *tú* or *vos* variety. The researchers tested how gender, age, education, location (Buenos Aires, Buenos Aires Province, outside Buenos Aires), and the urgency of the situation influenced the choice of imperative. Their data are found in the SPSS file *Johnson & Grinstead.sav*.

1. Use *answer* as the dependent variable, and *sex, age, education, location,* and *urgency* as independent variables. Each independent variable has a value that begins with Z (e.g., *Zmale, Zveryyoung*). Use those as the reference values. Use *T* (*tú*) as the reference value of *answer*. Set the sorting orders as *Descending*, and choose *Pairwise* for contrast types. Model 1: Try a random intercept for *item* and *speaker*.
   ```
   /RANDOM USE_INTERCEPT=TRUE SUBJECTS=speaker  COVARIANCE_TYPE= VARIANCE_COMPONENTS
   /RANDOM USE_INTERCEPT=TRUE SUBJECTS=item  COVARIANCE_TYPE= VARIANCE_COMPONENTS
   ```

2. Which of these random effects shows a significant enough amount of variation so that it needs to be included in the model?
3. Model 2: Try a random intercept for *item* and a random slope for *speaker* over *urgency*. Use only Variance Components for the random slope. Unstructured takes too long. This covariance structure accounts for the possibility that speakers may vary their responses depending on the urgency of the context.

```
/RANDOM USE_INTERCEPT=TRUE SUBJECTS=item  COVARIANCE_TYPE= VARIANCE_COMPONENTS
/RANDOM EFFECTS=urgency USE_INTERCEPT=TRUE SUBJECTS=speaker
   COVARIANCE_TYPE=VARIANCE_COMPONENTS
```

4. Which of these random effects does not significantly add to the fit of the model (and should not be included)?
5. Using the random effects in Model 1, run a series of analyses in which you remove all the independent variables that are not significant one by one, starting with the least significant one. Which variables remain? Use the coefficients and odds ratios to interpret the numeric results of the analysis. Also use the results of the pairwise comparison to interpret the results. How do the variables favor or disfavor the use of the *vos* negative imperative?
6. Calculate the by-chance accuracy rate of the final model and compare it with actual accuracy rate. How much better or worse is the accuracy rate from the by-chance accuracy rate?

9.8.2 /r/ deletion in Indian English

Chand (2010) investigated /r/ deletion in Indian English by examining when speakers retained or deleted /r/. Among other things, she considered the following independent variables: the gender of the speaker, whether /r/ appeared in a stressed or stressless syllable, whether the social situation was formal or informal, and the phonetic position that /r/ occurred in (i.e. preconsonantally preceded by any kind of vowel (e.g., *fourth, bird*), word-finally preceded by a nonschwa vowel (e.g., *beer*), syllable-finally preceded by a nonschwa vowel (e.g., *surprise*), word- and syllable-finally preceded by schwa (e.g., *murder, butter*)).[8]

The determination of whether /r/ was deleted or retained was done impressionistically by a number of different coders. This means that there is a relationship that we need to take into consideration by nesting speaker by coder. This is done in the *Data Structure* tab (see Figure 9-5) or in the syntax:

```
/DATA_STRUCTURE SUBJECTS=Coder*Speaker
```

A number of random slopes need to be considered as well. Speakers may vary their pronunciations over *Position, Stress*, or *Formality*. To account for this, three random slopes can be input using the menu (Figure 9-14) or adding the following line to the syntax:

```
/RANDOM EFFECTS=Position Stress Formality USE_INTERCEPT=TRUE
   SUBJECTS=Speaker*Coder
   COVARIANCE_TYPE=VARIANCE_COMPONENTS
```

Notice that *Speakers* are nested by *Coder* in the random slope command.

Open the file *Chand2010.sav*. Run a binomial mixed-effects logistic regression with *RPronunciation* as the dependent variable. Set the reference value to *ZRetained*. The independent variables are *Gender, Formality, Stress,* and *Position*. Each independent variable has a value that begins with Z. Use these as the reference values. Nest *Speakers* by *Coder,* and include random slopes for *Speaker* over *Position, Stress*, and *Formality*. Ask for pairwise comparisons between the values of each variable.

1. Determine which of the three random slopes are not significant and remove any insignificant random slopes from the analysis. Which are significant?
2. Rerun the analysis with the significant random slopes and calculate the by-chance accuracy rate. How does it compare to the actual accuracy rate?
3. Which independent variables are significant? Use the coefficients, odds ratios, and pairwise comparisons to interpret how each variable affects deletion of /r/ in Indian English.

---

[8] I don't quite understand this coding scheme myself.

BIBLIOGRAPHY

Allison, Paul. 2012. "When Can You Safely Ignore Multicollinearity?" *Statistical Horizons*. Last modified September 10, 2012. www.statisticalhorizons.com/multicollinearity.

Anderson, Robert. 2007. *Modern Methods for Robust Regression*. Thousand Oaks: Sage.

Baayen, R. H. 2008. *Analyzing Linguistic Data: A Practical Introduction to Statistics Using R*. Cambridge: Cambridge University Press.

Baayen, R. H., D. J. Davidson, and D. M. Bates. 2007. "Mixed Effects Modeling with Crossed Random Effects for Subjects and Items." *Journal of Memory and Language* 59: 390–412.

Balota, David A., Melvin J. Yap, Michael J. Cortese, Keith A. Hutchison, Brett Kessler, Bjorn Loftis, James H. Neely, Douglas L. Nelson, Greg B. Simpson, and Rebecca Treiman. 2007. "The English Lexicon Project." *Behavior Research Methods* 39: 445–459.

Barr, Dale J., Roger Levy, Christoph Scheepers, and Harry J. Tily. 2013. "Random Effects Structure in Mixed Effects Models: Keep It Maximal." *Journal of Memory and Language* 68: 255–278.

Bayaga, Anass. 2010. "Multinomial Logistic Regression: Usage and Application in Risk Management." *Journal of Applied Quantitative Methods* 5: 288–297.

Bickel, Robert. 2007. *Multilevel Analysis for Applied Research*. New York: Guilford Press.

Bradley, Travis G., and Ann M. Delforge. 2006. "Phonological Retention and Innovation in the Judeo-Spanish of Istanbul." In *Selected Proceedings of the 8th Hispanic Linguistics Symposium*, edited by Timothy L. Face and Carol A. Klee, 73–88. Somerville: Cascadilla Proceedings Project.

Butler, Christopher S. 1985. *Statistics in Linguistics*. Oxford: Blackwell.

Cantos Gómez, Pascual. 2013. *Statistical Methods in Language and Linguistic Research*. Sheffield: Equinox Publishing.

Carifio, James, and Rocco J. Perla. 2007. "Ten Common Misunderstandings, Misconceptions, Persistent Myths and Urban Legends about Likert Scales and Likert Response Formats and Their Antidotes." *Journal of Social Sciences* 3: 106–116.

Chand, Vineeta. 2010. "*Postvocalic (r) in Urban Indian English.*" *English World-Wide* 31: 1–39.

Clark, Herbert H. 1973. "The Language-as-Fixed-Effect Fallacy: A Critique of Language Statistics in Psychological Research." *Journal of Verbal Learning and Verbal Behavior* 12: 335–359.

Cohen, Jacob. 1983. "The Cost of Dichotomization." *Applied Psychological Measurement* 7: 249–254.

—. 1994. "The Earth Is Round ($p < .05$)." *American Psychologist* 49: 997–1003.

—. 1988. *Statistical Power Analysis for the Behavioural Sciences*. 2nd ed. Hillsdale: Lawrence Erlbaum.

Costea, Adrian. 2006. "Economic Performance Competitor Benchmarking Using Data-Mining Techniques." *Economy Informatics* 1 (4): 64–69.

Dąbrowska, Ewa. 2010. "Naive vs. Expert Intuitions: An Empirical Study of Acceptability Judgments." *The Linguistic Review* 27: 1–23.

Dalal, Dev K., and Michael J. Zickar. 2012. "Centering Predictor Variables in Moderated Multiple Regression and Polynomial Regression." *Organizational Research Methods* 15: 339–362.

Derwing, Bruce L. 1976. "Morpheme Recognition and the Learning of Rules for Derivational Morphology." *The Canadian Journal of Linguistics* 21: 38–66.

Dewaele, Jean-Marc. 2007. "Multilinguals' Language Choice for Mental Calculation." *Intercultural Pragmatics* 4: 343–376.

Dewey, Dan P., Jennifer Bown, Wendy Baker, Rob A. Martinsen, Carrie Gold, and Dennis Eggett. 2014. "Language Use in Six Study Abroad Programs: An Exploratory Analysis of Possible Predictors." *Language Learning* 64: 36–71.

Durán Pacheco, G., Hattendorf, J., Colford, J. M., Musezahl, D., and Smith, T. 2009. "Performance of Analytical Methods for Overdispersed Counts in Cluster Randomized Trials: Sample Size, Degree of Clustering and Imbalance. *Statistics in Medicine* 28: 2989-3011.

Eddington, David. 2001. "Surface Analogy and Spelling Rules in English Vowel Alternations." *Southwest Journal of Linguistics* 20: 85–105.

—. 2011. "What Are the Contextual Phonetic Variants of /β, ð, γ/ in Colloquial Spanish?" *Probus* 23: 1–19.

Eddington, David, and Matthew Savage. 2012. "Where Are the Mou[ʔə]ns in Utah." *American Speech* 87: 336–349.

Eddington, David, and Michael Taylor. 2009. "T-Glottalization in American English." *American Speech* 81: 298–314.

Edgell, Stephen E., and Sheila M. Noon. 1984. "Effect of Violation of Normality on the T Test of the Correlation Coefficient." *Psychological Bulletin* 95: 576–583.

Faber, Judith G., and Evelyn R. Klein. 1999. "Classroom-Based Assessment of a Collaborative Intervention Program with Kindergarten and First-Grade Students." *Language, Speech, and Hearing Services in Schools* 30: 83–91.

Fears, Thomas R., Jacques Benichou, and Mitchell H. Gail. 1996. "A Reminder of the Fallibility of the Wald Statistic." *The American Statistician* 50: 226–227.

Field, Andy. 2013. *Discovering Statistics Using IBM SPSS*. 4th ed. Los Angeles: Sage.

Gelman, Andrew, and Jennifer Hill. 2007. *Data Analysis Using Regression and Multilevel Hierarchical Models*. Cambridge: Cambridge University Press.

George, Darren, and Paul Mallery. 2011. *SPSS for Windows Step by Step*. 11th ed. Boston: Allyn & Bacon.

Gries, Stefan Th. 2013.*Statistics for Linguistics with R: A Practical Introduction*. 2nd ed. Berlin: Mouton de Gruyter.

Harrell, Frank E. 2001. *Regression Modeling Strategies: With Applications to Linear Models, Logistic Regression, and Survival Analysis*. New York: Springer-Verlag.

Hatch, Evelyn, and Hossein Farhady. 1982. *Research Design and Statistics for Applied Linguistics*. Cambridge: Newbury House.

Hilpert, Martin. 2008. "The English Comparative—Language Structure and Language Use." *English Language and Linguistics* 12: 395–417.

Hoekstra, Rink, Henk A. L Kiers, and Addie Johnson. 2012. "Are Assumptions of Well-Known Statistical Techniques Checked, and Why (Not)?" *Frontiers in Psychology* 3: 1–9.

Hox, Joop J. 2010. *Multilevel Analysis: Techniques and Applications*. 2nd ed. New York: Routledge.

Huberty, Carl J. 1989. "Problems with Stepwise Methods—Better Alternatives." *Advances in Social Science Methodology* 1: 43–70.

Hurvich, Clifford M., and Chih-Ling Tsai. 1990. "The Impact of Model Selection on Inference in Linear Regression. *American Statistician* 44: 214–217.

Johnson, Daniel E. "Getting off the GoldVarb Standard: Introducing Rbrul for Mixed Effects Variable Rule Analysis." *Language and Linguistics Compass* 3 (2009): 359–383.

Johnson, Keith. *Quantitative Methods in Linguistics*. Malden: Blackwell, 2008.

Johnson, Mary, and John Grinstead. 2011. "Variation in the *Voseo* and *Tuteo* Negative Imperatives in Argentine Spanish." *University of Pennsylvania Working Papers in Linguistics* 17: 99–104.

Keller, Frank, and Mirella Lapata. 2003. "Using the Web to Obtain Frequencies for Unseen Bigrams." *Computational Linguistics* 29: 459–484.

Kline, Rex B. 2004. *Beyond Significance Testing: Reforming Data Analysis Methods in Behavioral Research*. Washington, DC: American Psychological Association.

Lance, Charles E. 1988. "Residual Centering, Exploratory and Confirmatory Moderator Analysis, and Decomposition of Effects in Path Models Containing Interactions." *Applied Psychological Measurement* 12: 163–175.

Larson-Hall, Jenifer. 2010. *A Guide to Doing Statistics in Second Language Research Using SPSS*. New York: Routledge.

Meehl, Paul E. 1978. "Theoretical Risks and Tabular Asterisks: Sir Karl, Sir Ronald, and the Slow Progress of Soft Psychology." *Journal of Consulting and Clinical Psychology* 46: 806–834.

Miller, J. F., and R. S. Chapman. 1981. "The Relations between Age and Mean Length of Utterance." *Journal of Speech and Hearing Research* 24: 154–161.

Moineddin, Rahim, Flora I. Mathson, and Richard H. Glazier. 2007. "A Simulation Study of Sample Size for Multilevel Logistic Regression Models. *BMC Medical Research Methodology* 7. www.biomedcentral.com/1471-2288/7/34

Moore, David S., and George P. MacCabe. 2006. *Introduction to the Practice of Statistics*. 5th ed. New York: W.H. Freeman and Company.

Naderi, Habibollah, Rohani Abdullah, H. Tengku Aizan, Jamaluddin Sharir, and V. Kumar. 2009. "Self Esteem, Gender, and Academic Achievement of Undergraduate Students." *American Journal of Scientific Research* 3: 26–37.

Nemati, Azadeh. 2012. "On the Dimensions of Test Anxiety and Foreign Language Learners." *International Journal of English and Literature* 3: 97–102.

Nickerson, Raymond S. 2000. "Null Hypothesis Significance Testing: A Review of an Old and Continuing Controversy." *Psychological Methods* 5: 241–301.

Osborne, Jason. "Notes on the Use of Data Transformations." *Practical Assessment, Research & Evaluation* 8 (6): AREonline.net/getvn.asp?v=8&n=6.

Parker, Steve. 2008. "Sound Level Protrusions as Physical Correlates of Sonority." *Journal of Phonetics* 36: 55–90.

Pedhazur, Elazar J. 1997. *Multiple Regression in Behavioral Research*. Fort Worth: Harcourt Brace.

Plonsky, Luke, and Fredrick L. Oswald. 2014. "How Big Is Big? Interpreting Effect Sizes in L2 Research." *Language Learning* (forthcoming).

Pryce, Gwilym. 2002. "Heteroscedasticity: Testing and Correcting in SPSS." Manuscript. Glasgow University.

R Development Core Team. 2011. R: A Language and environment for statistical computing. Vienna: R Foundation for Statistical Computing.

Rasinger, Sebastian M. 2008. *Quantitative Research in Linguistics*. London: Continuum.

Razali, Nornadiah M., and Yap B. Wah. 2011. "Power Comparisons of Shapiro-Wilk, Kolmogorov-Smirnov, Lilliefors and Anderson-Darling Tests." *Journal of Statistical Modeling and Analytics* 2: 21–33.

Rea, Louis M., and Richard A. Parker. 1992. *Designing and Conducting Survey Research*. San Francisco: Jossey-Bass.

Roy, Joseph. 2013. "Sociolinguistic Statistics: The Intersection between Statistical Models, Empirical Data and Sociolinguistic Theory." In *Proceedings of Methods XIV: Papers from the 14th International Conference on Methods in Dialectology,* Edited by Alena Barysevich, Alexandra D'Arcy, and David Heap, 261-275. Frankfurt am Main: Peter Lang

Rozeboom, William W. 1997. "Good Science Is Abductive, Not Hypothetico-Deductive. In *What If There Were No Significance Tests?*, edited by L. L. Harlow, S. A. Mulaik, and J. H. Steiger, 335–392. Mahwah: Lawrence Erlbaum.

Sankoff, Gillian, and Héléne Blondeau. 2007. "Language Change across the Lifespan: /r/ in Montreal French." *Language* 83: 560–588.

Serlin, Ronald C., and Joel R. Levin. 1985. "Teaching How to Derive Directly Interpretable Coding Schemes for Multiple Regression Analysis." *Journal of Educational Statistics* 10: 223–238.

Sheskin, David J. 2003. *Handbook of Parametric and Non-parametric Statistical Procedures.* 3rd ed. Boca Raton: Chapman and Hall.

Smyth, Gordon K. 2002. "An Efficient Algorithm for REML in Heteroscedastic Regression." *Journal of Graphical and Computational Statistics* 11: 836–847.

Taylor, Michael, and David Eddington. 2009. "T-Glottalization in American English." *American Speech* 81: 298–314.

Tight, Daniel G. 2012. "The First Noun Principle and Ambitransitive Verbs. *Hispania* 95: 103–115.

UCLA Statistical Consulting Group. "Analyzing Correlated (Clustered) Data." Institute for Digital Research and Education. www.ats.ucla.edu/stat/stata/library/cpsu.htm.

Ulrich, Rolf, and Jeff Miller. 1994. "Effects of Truncation on Reaction Time Analysis." *Journal of Experimental Psychology* 123: 34–80.

Velleman, Paul F., and David C. Hoaglin. 1981. *Applications, Basics, and Computing of Exploratory Data Analysis.* Boston: Suxbury Press.

Wendorf, Craig A. 2004. "Primer on Multiple Regression Coding: Common Forms and the Additional Case of Repeated Contrasts." *Understanding Statistics* 3: 47–57.

West, Stephen G., Leona S. Aiken, and Jennifer L. Krull. 1996. "Experimental Personality Designs: Analyzing Categorical by Continuous Variable Interactions." *Journal of Personality* 64: 1–48.

Winter, Bodo, and Benjamin Bergen. 2012. "Language Comprehenders Represent Object Distance Both Visually and Auditorily." *Language and Cognition* 4: 1–16.

Winter, Bodo, and Sven Grawunder. 2012. The Phonetic Profile of Korean Formal and Informal Speech Registers." *Journal of Phonetics* 40: 808–815.

Wurm, Lee H., and Sebastiano A. Fisicaro. 2014. "What Residualizing Predictors in Regression Analyses Does (And What It Does Not Do)." *Journal of Memory and Language* 72: 37–48.

INDEX